THRIFTS
UNDER SIEGE

THRIFTS
UNDER SIEGE

Restoring Order to American Banking

R. Dan Brumbaugh, Jr.

Library of Congress Cataloging-in-Publication Data

Brumbaugh, R. Dan.
    Thrifts under siege : restoring order to American banking / R. Dan Brumbaugh, Jr.
        p. cm.
    Originally published: Cambridge, Mass. : Ballinger Pub. Co., c1988. in series: The
Institutional investor series in finance.
    Includes bibliographical references and index.
    ISBN 1-893122-39-5
    1. Thrift institutions--United States. 2. Savings and loan association failures--United
States. I. Title

HG1922.B78 1999
332.3'2'0973--dc21

                    99-049359

Printed in the United States of America

CONTENTS

LIST OF FIGURES

LIST OF TABLES

PREFACE

The title of this book took shape at the beginning of 1985. Whether the word *siege* suggested a greater problem than really existed was worrisome. After all, industry profits for that year were being reported at levels rivaling calmer times, and by year-end 1985 the marked-to-market value of the mortgages held by thrifts was positive for the first time in the 1980s. I questioned whether these developments signaled an end to the crisis of the 1980s and whether words suggesting transition or evolution would be more appropriate.

The survival of the original title reflects the conviction that rapidly changing economic forces still threaten the viability of many, if not most, thrift institutions, despite the improved overall profitability through 1986. In the metaphor of siege, the fall in interest rates that generated the profits of 1985 represents the retreat of one of several assault waves against a heavily damaged rampart. As this book shows, the effect of the relatively modest increases in interest rates in 1987 reveals the industry's vulnerability to another assault wave.

This book analyzes the economic forces battering depository institutions by focusing on those hit hardest at the moment—the thrift institutions—and shows how their distress suggests the need for dramatic reform of thrift and commercial bank regulation. Savings and loan associations constitute the major group of thrift institutions, and the book does not address specific issues involving the other two groups of thrift institutions, mutual savings banks and credit unions. The book refers interchangeably to thrift institutions and savings and loan associations.

Chapter 1, which reviews the origin and growth of thrifts and other financial firms, reveals that the battle for survival is not being waged on the interest-rate front alone. Not a day passes without news of a financial innovation or a technological or regulatory change that erodes the functional distinctions that in the past have separated thrifts from commercial banks and other less regulated financial institutions. Each news item about greater homogenization of the provision of financial services heralds a competitive threat to thrifts. The economic forces driving homogenization are rapidly eroding the distinctions imposed by legislation and regulation on thrifts, commercial banks, and other financial institutions. As the book demonstrates, attempts to maintain the separations designed in the 1930s between thrifts, commercial banks, and other financial institutions squander economic resources and are probably futile.

Chapters 2 and 3 describe how thrifts suffered two crises between 1980 and 1987, showing how some of the regulatory responses to the first crisis created the second. The first crisis began with the soaring interest rates following monetary policy changes in 1979. The second crisis developed during a period of deflation as hundreds of open, insolvent thrifts gambled for resurrection more gravely wounding themselves and harming other institutions. Understanding the evolution of these two crises is fundamental to discovering the means to end the continuing siege and to restore order to American depository-institutions' regulation.

The remainder of the book deals with the short-term and longer-term measures necessary to achieve these goals. Chapter 4 emphasizes that the first step must be the closing of insolvent thrifts and describes how the thrifts can be closed in a way that minimizes the cost. Chapter 5 describes why the required minimum net worth or capital for the remaining institutions must rise and goes on to propose that the best defense against future crises lies in better monitoring, primarily through greater reliance on market-value accounting, accompanied by a rule requiring the closing of depository institutions approaching market-value insolvency.

An implication of Chapters 4 and 5 is that reform of deposit insurance is not necessary to resolve the current crisis. It is widely believed that the replacement of the flat-rate deposit-insurance premium with one that varies with the risks taken by thrifts and banks is an important component of a program to resolve the current crisis. Support for risk-based capital requirements is also widespread. Because the current crisis involves open insolvent institutions, however, the role for deposit-insurance reform in its cure is negligible at best. Following resolution of the crisis, more reliance on market-value net worth and the power to close institutions before their market-value net worth is zero replaces deposit-insurance reform entailing risk-based pricing.

Chapters 4 and 5 make recommendations for resolving the current crisis and avoiding another one based on a continuation of the current depository-institution regulatory framework. The thrift-industry crisis, however, points out the need to redesign the fundamental structure of depository-institution regulation. Chapter 6's historical review of the legislation that created the current regulatory structure, along with the previous chapters' analysis of the thrift-industry crisis, shows that balance-sheet compartmentalization, primarily between thrifts and banks, is rapidly eroding. As a result, the elimination of separate regulation for thrifts and banks seems inevitable.

Chapter 7 makes the case for regulatory consolidation of thrift and bank regulation. The rationalization of thrift and bank regulation is an intermediate step toward further deregulation of depository intermediaries and the rollback of deposit insurance. Chapter 7 shows how relatively recent economic forces that appear to be permanent have made thrifts and banks inherently weaker and more unstable. This chapter also indicates why balance-sheet regulation and deposit insurance tend to exacerbate the new instability and to confront the American taxpayer with a large and growing contingent liability. Finally, the chapter discusses what can replace the current system and can achieve the efficiency and stability sought by balance-sheet regulation and deposit insurance.

Although the book provides many tables and much data, it is written so that the narrative provides a full picture requiring little or no additional reference to the tables to understand the thrift crisis. The tables and data, however, provide substantial detail about the issues discussed in the narrative and help corroborate the conclusions reached.

A reader who wants immediate information concerning the modern thrift-industry crisis can go directly to Chapters 2 and 3 and then to Chapters 4 and 5 for the recommended solutions. The more fundamental reforms presented in Chapter 7 also follow directly from Chapter 5. Approached this way, Chapters 1 and 6 can serve as subsequent background against which the modern thrift crisis and the proposed reforms can be viewed.

ACKNOWLEDGMENTS

I owe a debt of gratitude to many individuals who interacted with me in preparing this book. James Barth, Donald Bisenius, Andrew Carron, Eric Hemel, Daniel Sauerhaft, and George Wang coauthored papers with me and in the process stimulated my thoughts. The collaboration with James Barth on many papers was particularly rewarding. Dan Sauerhaft demonstrated remarkable prowess and judgment in collecting, organizing, and evaluating complicated data.

Though many references indicate the manifold contributions of other economists to the subjects in this book, I have particularly benefited from the work of and discussions with Frederick Balderston, George Benston, Michael Bradley, Charlotte Chamberlin, Jack Corgel, Robert Eisenbeis, Mark Flannery, Joseph Grundfest, Stuart Greenbaum, Jack Guttentag, Alan Hess, Paul Horvitz, Dwight Jaffe, Edward Kane, John Kareken, George Kaufman, Robert Litan, G. S. Maddala, William Poole, Ronald Rogers, Martin Regalia, Kenneth Rosen, Myron Scholes, Kenneth Scott, P. A. V. B. Swamy, James Wilcox, and Susan Woodward.

I am also grateful for the assistance of Andrea Mills and Tracie McKenzie in preparing the manuscript and Connie Young in processing data. Dhayalini Ranganathan helped bring everything together at the very end. Sarah St. Onge's editing was superb. I especially thank Carolyn Casagrande for the unexpected invitation to do the book and for patiently waiting for it.

San Francisco, California   **R. Dan Brumbaugh, Jr.**
December, 1987

1 THRIFT INSTITUTIONS IN THE U.S. ECONOMY
Evolution Leading to Revolution

The United States is now experiencing sweeping market-driven changes, which have put the thrift industry under siege and portend a revolution in American banking. As with previous periods of change, the current period follows a crisis. It began in 1980 when soaring interest rates drove many thrifts to insolvency and has continued despite falling interest rates, as deflation has taken hold and hopelessly insolvent institutions have been gambling for resurrection with deposits protected by federal deposit insurance.

To many people, the change in the services provided by thrift institutions and commercial banks and the large number of failures among these institutions since 1980 seem like new phenomena. We are now undergoing contractions in the number of thrifts and banks, shifts in the composition of assets and liabilities on the balance sheets of financial and nonfinancial firms, and changes in the geographic scope of firms' activities. However, similar changes have been experienced at various times since the creation of thrifts and banks in this country, and then, as now, the changes were influenced by government regulation, with pressure from trade associations and the industries themselves significantly affecting government regulation.

HOW TO DISTINGUISH CONTEMPORARY THRIFT INSTITUTIONS AND COMMERCIAL BANKS FROM OTHER FINANCIAL AND NONFINANCIAL FIRMS

Thrift institutions are distinguished from other financial and nonfinancial firms primarily by their balance sheets, the types of assets and liabilities that generate the firms' profits. A nonfinancial firm's tangible assets consist largely of plant and equipment, and the firm's liabilities consist predominantly of debt and equity. A financial firm's tangible assets, on the other hand, consist mainly of pieces of paper—for example, loans—and the firm's liabilities consist primarily of deposits, other debt, and equity. Financial firms whose liabilities consist largely of deposits, such as thrifts and banks, are called depository financial firms, whereas those without deposits, such as insurance companies and pension funds, are called nondepository financial firms.

The tangible assets of nonfinancial firms typically comprise more "real" assets, whereas the tangible assets of financial firms are "financial" assets, generally backed or collateralized by real assets. Both the liabilities and assets of commercial banks tend to be shorter in term to maturity than those of thrift institutions. When bank and thrift assets and liabilities become similar in nature and term to maturity, economic distinctions between them begin to blur. Moreover, to the extent that financial firms engage directly in investment in real assets, they become more like nonfinancial firms. Thus, distinctions begin to fade when basically financial firms like insurance companies and pension funds invest in real assets, thrift and bank holding companies have nonfinancial-institution affiliates, or thrifts invest in real assets, as some of them have recently been allowed to do.

Making these balance-sheet distinctions among firms helps clarify that nonfinancial firms' investment in plant and equipment and selected financial firms' investment in real assets can directly generate economic growth. Further, all financial firms indirectly provide for growth by channeling funds from savers to investors, the traditional role of depository financial firms. Through such intermediation, depository financial firms also channel funds from savers to dissavers wanting to smooth consumption around irregular income streams.

Contemporary government regulations have been formulated and applied to maintain balance-sheet distinctions among firms by barring them from certain kinds of activities. Thus, the government, as well as the market, contributes to the shaping of business firms' balance sheets in this country. As a result of government regulation, depository financial firms are currently identified by their preponderance of deposits and financial assets, nondepository financial firms by their preponderance of nondeposit liabilities and mix of real and financial assets, and nonfinancial firms by their preponderance of nondeposit liabilities and real assets. Regulatory battles usually arise with the growing similarities among these kinds of firms. The major issue is how similar the balance sheets of all these firms should be, and, if there are to be differences, how the market and the government should determine what they are.

ORIGIN AND SPECIALIZATION OF AMERICAN THRIFT INSTITUTIONS

The first American thrift institution, the Oxford Provident Building Association, was organized in Frankford, Pennsylvania, on January 3, 1831. Its purpose was to enable its shareholders, most of whom were wage earners in the textile trade, to obtain funds to build residential homes. Participants were called shareholders, not depositors, because their contributions to the association represented equity in the assets rather than a debt obligation backed by the assets. Every shareholder could borrow funds, with the association liquidating after the last member was accommodated. New shareholders were elected by ballot, and no loans could be made for homes located more than five miles from Frankford.[1] Associations like Oxford were originally called building societies because they bought land and built houses for their members. When these institutions began making loans to people who planned to build houses on their own land, as well as financing the acquisition of existing homes, the associations came to be called building and loan societies.

The associations' liabilities consisted entirely of shareholders' equity. These shares, moreover, were meant to be invested over the life of the association and thus represented savings. Members wishing to withdraw their shares were required to give a month's notice and charged a penalty for early withdrawal. The associations held almost entirely financial assets, in the form of residential mortgage loans. The first thrift institution, therefore, encouraged thrift via savings and residential home acquisition through mortgage loans. In other words, the original balance sheets of thrift institutions in this country consisted mainly of residential mortgage loans on the asset side and savings shares on the liability side.

The emergence of specialized housing-finance lenders raises the question of why other financial firms did not provide these services earlier. Commercial banks existed even before 1789, and mutual savings banks since 1816. Credit unions did not appear until 1909. Commercial banks, however, made primarily commercial loans, accepted mostly demand deposits, and were relatively uninterested in residential mortgage loans or savings deposits, especially in the small amounts available from wage earners. Even by 1900, time or savings deposits represented only a small proportion of the total deposits of commercial banks.

Mutual savings banks, although also entirely dependent upon savings deposits, held more diversified assets than thrifts, extending consumer loans as well as mortgage loans. Furthermore, the savings accounts at mutual savings banks were more flexible in their denominations, term to maturity, and the ease and frequency of withdrawal. Unlike the other two types of depository financial firms, mutual savings banks emphasized serving lower-income groups, which meant less emphasis on mortgage loans and longer-term savings deposits.

The three kinds of financial depository firms in existence, then, specialized in various activities that were reflected in the composition of their balance sheets. Like today, separation of activities was a function of business decisions and, as discussed shortly, government limitations of balance-sheet activities. Unlike today, there were no financial "supermarkets" offering an almost full range of financial services, nor were there structures that allowed the same firms to provide both financial and non financial services.

Following the organization of the first thrift institution, the phenomenon spread throughout the United States. Figure 1–1 shows when each state's first thrift institution began operations. The movement spread from Philadelphia to New York in 1836, then to South Carolina in 1843, and finally to Oklahoma in 1890. As thrifts extended throughout the country, innovations occurred. National thrifts, which drew deposits and made mortgage loans nationwide

Figure 1-1. Year of the First Savings and Loan Activity in Each State.

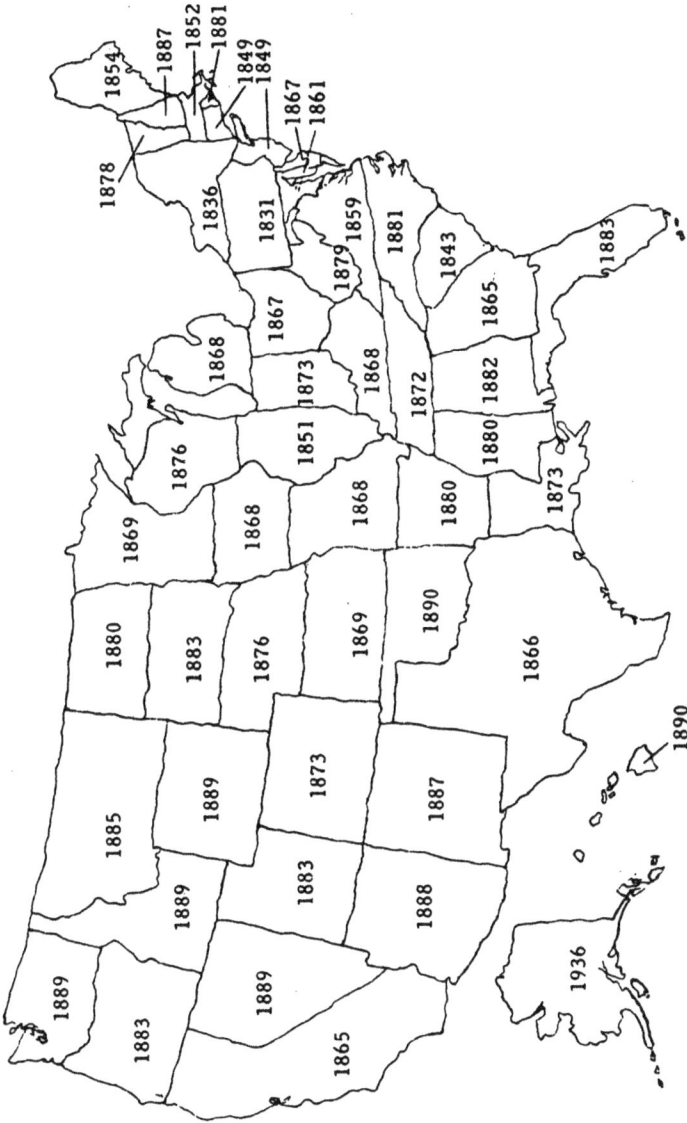

Source: Dates are from Josephine Hedges Ewalt, *A Business Reborn: The Savings and Loan Story, 1930–1960* (Chicago: American Savings and Loan Institute Press, 1962).

through branch offices and the mail, were organized in the late 1880s; until then thrifts had been entirely local, making mortgage loans only in the areas where they operated. Self-liquidating thrifts were replaced by self-perpetuating thrifts that were no longer operated with relatively near-term extinction dates. In the original thrifts, shareholders were also savers who were obliged to take out a mortgage loan; eventually, however, shareholders who did not desire mortgage loans were selected. The pool of funds available for mortgage loans thus grew.

State and eventually federal regulations accompanied the growth of the thrift industry. State supervision of thrift institutions evolved in the late 1800s and early 1900s from reports to state officials to voluntary state examinations and then to required examination by state officials. In addition to supervision, states showed "their disapproval of loans for purposes not strictly within the building and loan field, which is the financing of single-family residences. . . ."[2] Also, "a rather common power given to the state official in charge of the supervision of building and loan associations is that of refusing to grant charters where there does not seem to be a necessity for another building and loan association."[3] As the thrift industry grew, the degree of state supervision and regulation thus expanded to include limitation of activities on institutions' balance sheets.

With one major exception, the federal government did not enter the field of thrift regulation until the Great Depression. The exception was a tax exemption for thrifts provided by the U.S. Congress in 1894, which was later included in the Revenue Act of 1913 that established a federal income tax.

Accurate data on the number and assets of thrift institutions are not available before 1893. In that year, these institutions numbered 5,598. As a result of the recession in 1893, as Table 1–1 shows, this number declined to 5,356 in 1900. Thrifts numbered 3,246 in 1985. Between those years, the number grew to over 12,000 in the 1920s and shrank tremendously in the 1930s. The number of commercial banks and mutual savings banks also grew substantially around 1920 and then shrank. Despite this shrinkage in number, nominal assets continued to grow for all three types of institutions.

Table 1-1. Number and Assets of Major Depository Financial Institutions (1800-1985).

	Savings and Loan Associations		Commercial Banks		Mutual Savings Banks	
Year	Number	Assets[a]	Number	Assets[a]	Number	Assets[a]
1800	0	0	n/a	n/a	0	0
1810	0	0	88	n/a	0	0
1820	0	0	297	30	10	1[b]
1830	0	0	293	34	36	7[b]
1850	n/a	n/a	716	489	108	43[b]
1860	n/a	n/a	1,284	851	278	149[b]
1870	n/a	n/a	1,420	1,231	517	550[b]
1880	n/a	n/a	2,726	2,517	629	882
1890	n/a	n/a	7,280	4,612	921	1,743
1900	5,356	571	12,427	9,059	626	2,328
1905	5,264	629	18,152	14,542	615	2,969
1910	5,869	932	24,514	19,324	637	3,598
1915	6,806	1,484	27,390	24,106	627	4,257
1920	8,633	2,520	30,291	47,509	618	5,586
1925	12,403	5,509	28,442	54,401	610	7,831
1930	11,777	8,829	23,679	64,125	594	10,164
1935	10,266	5,875	15,488	48,905	559	11,046
1940	7,521	5,733	14,534	67,804	542	11,925
1945	6,149	8,747	14,126	146,245	534	15,924
1950	5,992	16,893	14,146	156,914	530	22,252
1955	6,071	37,656	13,780	199,244	528	30,383
1960	5,320	71,476	13,503	243,274	516	39,598
1965	6,185	129,580	13,805	356,110	505	56,383
1970	5,669	176,183	13,690	534,932	497	76,373
1975[c]	4,931	338,200	14,657	974,700	476	121,100
1980	4,613	629,800	14,870	1,543,500	460	166,600
1985	3,246	1,069,547	15,282	2,731,000	403	157,400

a. Assets are in millions of dollars.
b. Deposits rather than assets.
c. Data before 1975 are for June 30; after 1970, the data are for December 31.
Source: Based upon data from U.S. Department of Commerce, Bureau of the Census, Historical Statistics of the United States: Colonial Times to 1970 (Washington, D.C.), Part 2; and Federal Reserve Bulletin, various issues.

EARLY FINANCIAL CRISES AND
THRIFT INSTITUTIONS

In only two periods during their first one hundred and fifty years did thrift institutions seriously suffer failures. The first period occurred during the early 1890s during a severe economic depression. One of the major consequences of this crisis was the disappearance of national thrifts. When the troubles of the early 1890s eventually took their toll, however, "locals" suffered as well.

Competition between nationals and locals and the severe economic troubles of the early 1890s resulted in the establishment in 1892 of the United States League of Local Building and Loan Associations, which later became the United States League of Savings Institutions, today the largest and most powerful thrift trade association. The clash between the two types of organizations and their economic problems also eventually led to " . . . the enactment in several states of restrictive legislation which curbed the activities of the 'nationals' and finally drove them out of business."[4]

The second period of acute economic strain was the Great Depression of the 1930s. Although thrifts did not accept demand deposits, they nonetheless suffered withdrawals, as their members drew down their savings to maintain consumption. Thrifts, however, were hard-pressed to meet substantial withdrawals because their assets were almost entirely illiquid mortgages. In fact, "as a matter of tradition and in order to maintain high earnings, associations sought and boasted of a low cash position."[5] Furthermore, reserves for losses were relatively low, since "many state laws rather discouraged the accumulation of reserves and some supervisory authorities practically forced the distribution of all earnings."[6] As the depression deepened, thrifts' assets shrank as withdrawals mounted, and many failed.[7]

From 1930 to 1933, as Table 1–2 reflects, the size of the thrift industry shrank by about 15 percent. During that period, more than 500 thrifts failed, and another 1,200 or so failed from 1933 to 1939. As Table 1–1 also shows, the attrition rate of nearly 30 percent from 1980 through 1985 swamps the rate during the depths of the Great Depression, despite a substantial federal regulatory apparatus assuring that depository institutions adhered to "safe and sound" practices. In addition, more than 600 commercial banks failed in 1930, and between 1930 and 1933 approximately 9,000 banks failed—nearly half the number existing in 1930. As banks failed in the 1930–1933 period, depositors were converting deposits into currency, thus increasing the demand for liquidity on the part of solvent banks. The Federal Reserve, as lender of last resort, did not provide sufficient liquidity, and a large number of banks were forced to liquidate their assets simultaneously in a depressed market.[8] Severe losses and more bank failures resulted.

The end came when President Roosevelt declared a bank holiday—closing all banks two days after his inauguration in 1933. Shortly thereafter, the Congress passed the Banking Act of 1933, which created the Federal Deposit Insurance Corporation (FDIC) and required all federally chartered banks to become members. A year earlier, the Federal Home Loan Bank Act had created the Federal Home Loan Bank Board and twelve district Federal Home Loan Banks to provide liquidity to savings and loan associations. The Home Owners' Loan Act of 1933 gave the Bank Board power to charter and to regulate savings and loans. Although the federal government had begun chartering commercial banks during the Civil War, it was not until the Great Depression that federal charters were extended to thrift institutions. Finally, in 1934 Congress enacted the National Housing Act, which created the Federal Savings and Loan Insurance Corporation (FSLIC). By 1933 roughly comparable federal regulatory systems existed for banks and thrifts, and, through deposit insurance, the federal government assumed substantial direct risk for the deposits at these financial depository institutions.

One purpose of the Federal Home Loan Bank act was to authorize "the Federal Home Loan Bank Board, following certain principles as to need and effect on existing institutions, to charter Federal Savings and Loan Associations following the best principles of existing local mutual organizations."[9] The original act specified that most loans at federal associations had to be mortgage loans secured by houses within fifty miles of the association's home office. All federal associations also had to be mutual-type thrifts. A fund was provided for organizing new institutions—both state and federal—in areas without any.[10]

Funds loaned through the Federal Home Loan Bank System to savings and loan associations were intended to be lent ultimately to home borrowers. In short, the main stated purpose of the Federal Home Loan Bank system was to strengthen savings and loan associ-

Table 1-2. Savings and Loan Association Failures and Losses (1920–1939 and 1980–1986).[a]

Year	Total Number	Total Assets (in millions of dollars)	Number of Failures	Percentage of Failed Institutions to Total Institutions	Losses (in millions of dollars)	Percentage of Losses to Total Assets
1920	8,663	2,520	2	0.0	c	0.0
1921	9,255	2,891	6	0.1	c	0.0
1922	10,009	3,343	4	0.0	c	0.0
1923	10,744	3,943	9	0.1	c	0.0
1924	11,844	4,766	18	0.2	c	0.0
1925	12,403	5,509	26	0.2	1	0.0
1926	12,626	6,334	12	0.1	c	0.0
1927	12,804	7,179	21	0.2	1	0.0
1928	12,666	8,016	23	0.2	1	0.0
1929	12,343	8,695	159	1.3	2	0.0
1930	11,777	8,829	190	1.6	25	0.3
1931	11,442	8,417	126	1.1	22	0.3
1932	10,997	7,750	122	1.1	20	0.3
1933	10,727	6,978	88	0.8	44	0.6
1934	10,919	6,450	68	0.6	10	0.2
1935	10,266	5,875	239	2.3	16	0.3
1936	10,042	5,772	144	1.4	9	0.2
1937	9,225	5,682	269	2.9	16	0.3
1938	8,762	5,632	277	3.2	11	0.2
1939	8,006	5,597	183	2.3	27	0.5

1980	4,002	618,466	35	0.9	167	0.0
1981	3,779	651,068	81	2.0	1,018	0.2
1982	3,343	692,663	252	7.5	1,213	0.2
1983	3,040	819,168	102	3.3	993	0.1
1984	3,167	978,514	41	1.4	850	0.1
1985	3,246	1,069,547	45[b]	1.4	946	0.1
1986	3,220	1,165,320	54[b]	1.7	3,239	0.3

a. The pre-1980 data concentrate on failed non-FSLIC institutions, whereas the post-1980 data refer exclusively to failed FSLIC institutions.

b. No loss data are available for an additional twenty-five institutions that were placed into the newly created Management Consignment Program in 1985 and another twenty-nine institutions in 1986.

c. Less than $500,000.

Source: Based upon data from James R. Barth, R. Dan Brumbaugh, Jr., and Daniel Sauerhaft, "Failure Costs of Government-Regulated Financial Firms: The Case of Thrift Institutions" (research working paper no. 123, Federal Home Loan Bank Board, Office of Policy and Economic Research, Washington, D.C., October 1986); Luther Harr and Carlton Harris, Banking Theory and Practice (New York: McGraw-Hill Book Co., 1936); and Leon Kendall, The Savings and Loan Business (Englewood Cliffs, N.J.: Prentice-Hall Publishers, 1962).

ations financially in order to promote home ownership. The institutions initially eligible for membership were savings and loan associations, insurance companies, and savings banks. The latter two generally did not join the system. As two contemporary observers noted, however, "the Federal Home Loan Bank Board System is not intended to 'bail out' embarrassed financial institutions. It is, rather, a permanent system which must inspire confidence if it is to market its bonds, hence, the dealings of the banks must be confined to institutions that are solvent and reasonably safe credit risks."[11]

The National Housing Act of 1934 made membership in the FSLIC compulsory for federal thrifts and optional for state-chartered thrifts, although today almost all states require FSLIC insurance as a condition of granting a charter. The insurance amount was initially $5,000 per account and is currently $100,000. By one account, "deposit insurance plans have developed as a means of combating a universal lack of confidence in financial institutions which has adversely affected the sound banks otherwise able to survive the acute financial crisis."[12] As a result, "insurance of commercial bank deposits and of savings and loan accounts does not meet all assumptions of insurance theory, for it admittedly deals with expectancies that have no actual history or measurement because of the unpredictable and incalculable changes that accompany the business cycle."[13]

Some potential problems of deposit insurance were noted early: "Insurance may tend to eliminate differences among associations. It may reduce the incentive for good management because, on the one hand, some institution's may become dependent upon insurance, and because, on the other hand, sound and efficiently staffed institution's may be penalized for the careless policy and poorly trained personnel of others. Furthermore, the public may become indiscriminate in selecting the association with which it wishes to deal."[14]

In addition, economist Irving Fisher's March 30, 1932, testimony on the bill to provide federal insurance for depositors in commercial banks stated that the bill should be changed to allow that "the comptroller—or some other authority—may add to said premium 25 percent, 50 percent, or 100 percent in individual cases which are regarded by him as extrahazardous or may refuse to insure altogether."[15] In other words, a risk-sensitive insurance premium was advocated two years before the creation of the FSLIC and one year before the creation of the FDIC in 1933.

POST-DEPRESSION GROWTH, RISING INTEREST RATES, AND THE BEGINNING OF THE MODERN THRIFT-INSTITUTION CRISIS

From the Great Depression to the 1980s, savings and loan associations experienced tremendous asset growth. As Table 1-1 shows, thrifts surpassed mutual savings banks in total assets for the first time in 1954 and grew to nearly half the size of the commercial-banking industry in 1980. This dramatic expansion was spread throughout the industry and included both large and small institutions. The magnitude of these changes are illustrated in Table 1-3, which shows the role of savings and loans relative to other financial service firms in the United States economy since 1900.

In 1900 total private financial assets totaled $15 billion. Of this, savings and loan associations held a meager 3 percent, compared to 66 percent for commercial banks. By 1985, however, savings and loan associations had increased their share of the total to 16 percent,

Table 1-3. Percentage of Total U.S. Financial Assets Held by Major Financial Intermediaries (*1900-1985*).

	1900	*1929*	*1933*	*1945*	*1955*	*1965*	*1975*	*1985*
Commercial banks	66	60	51	65	44	36	37	30
Savings and loan associations	3	7	7	3	9	14	16	16
Mutual savings banks	16	9	12	7	8	6	6	3
Credit unions	—	—	—	1	1	1	2	2
Life insurance companies	12	16	23	18	21	17	13	12
Other[a]	3	8	7	6	17	26	26	33
Total ($ billions)	15	110	90	247	424	921	2,136	6,603

a. The "other" category includes such financial intermediaries as private pension funds, state and local government retirement funds, finance companies, other insurance companies, and money-market funds.

Source: Based on data from Raymond A. Goldsmith, *Financial Intermediaries In the American Economy since 1990* (Princeton, N.J.: Princeton University Press, 1958; and Board of Governors of the Federal Reserve System, "Flow of Funds Accounts" (various years).

while the share for commercial banks had dropped to 30 percent. Mutual savings banks also lost considerable ground during this period, and life insurance companies initially expanded and then contracted. Overall, although the share of total private financial assets accounted for by all depository financial service firms declined from 85 to 51 percent, the share of savings and loan institutions quintupled. Nondepository financial service firms, "other" in Table 1–3, have therefore grown at the expense of the share of total financial assets held by the nonthrift depository financial service firms. This increased competition has resulted from inflation, improved techniques for managing cash, innovation in financial instruments, and the deregulation of financial markets.

Dramatic changes also occurred in the balance sheets of savings and loans and banks. In the late 1960s half of the deposits in commercial banks were noninterest-bearing demand deposits; in 1985, however, demand deposits made up only one-fifth of commercial bank deposits. In the late 1960s, passbook savings accounts supplied three-fourths of all deposits in savings and loans. In 1985 these small accounts provided less than one-twelfth of the deposits at these institutions.

During the 1960s and into the early 1980s, moreover, rates of interest rose along with inflation. Laws and regulations, however, generally prohibited banks from paying interest on checking accounts and set ceilings on the rates payable by thrifts and banks on various other types of deposits. Although separate regulations were applied to thrifts and banks, with the ceilings set slightly higher for thrifts, the regulations were generally known as Regulation Q, which specifically refers to the interest-rate regulations of the Federal Reserve. As market rates of interest rose above the ceilings that thrifts and banks could pay, customers began looking for financial instruments that paid the higher market rates of interest. This movement of funds away from depository institutions increased the popularity of existing market-sensitive instruments and spurred the introduction and development of new ones.

In response to the unattractiveness of commercial-bank demand deposits paying no interest during a period of high and rising market rates of interest, some financial depository institutions created interest-bearing checking accounts, such as share drafts at credit unions and negotiable orders of withdrawal (NOW) accounts at commercial banks and mutual savings banks, to substitute for demand deposits.

This new type of account was first introduced by a mutual savings bank in Massachusetts in 1972. In addition, by the late 1970s money-market funds, also first introduced in 1972, had become a serious competitive threat to depository financial institutions.

The firms offering these new money-market funds were not subject to interest-rate regulations. They attracted customers by offering higher rates of interest than financial depository service firms could pay on a mutual fund investment with limited check-writing privileges. The higher market rates threatened the prospect of disintermediation—flight of depositors from banks and thrifts to the new money-market funds. The first regulatory reaction came in June 1978, when regulators authorized banks and thrifts to offer six-month money-market certificates (MMCs) in $10,000 denominations priced slightly above six-month U.S. Treasury bill rates. Within one year, 20 percent of all savings and loan deposits were in the form of MMCs.

The rising rates not only spawned potentially disastrous disintermediation but also imposed operating losses on thrifts because, due to regulation, thrifts' deposits were shorter in duration (time to re-pricing) than the predominance of mortgage assets. Rising interest rates therefore increased deposit costs faster than returns from mortgages. In October 1979 the Federal Reserve made a decision with ruinous results for the thrift industry. The Federal Reserve changed from a policy of stabilizing interest rates to a policy of slowing money growth to combat inflation. This contributed to a spike in interest rates that led to an unprecedented increase in thrifts' cost of funds, which rose from under 9 percent in 1980 to more than 11 percent at the end of 1981, with almost no corresponding increase in revenues due to the preponderance of fixed-rate mortgages being held.

This was the beginning of the modern thrift crisis. As with previous crises, the Congress responded by passing historic legislation that modified the allowable liabilities and assets in thrift and bank portfolios and removed interest-rate ceilings on deposits. In March 1980 Congress passed the Depository Institutions Deregulation and Monetary Control Act, which authorized interest-bearing checking accounts for individuals and nonprofit customers of thrifts. It also phased out deposit-rate ceilings by March of 1986. In October 1982 Congress enacted the Garn-St Germain Depository Institutions Act authorizing demand-deposit accounts for business customers at thrifts and a new money-market account to compete with money-market funds. It also authorized thrifts to offer commercial real estate loans, provided additional consumer loan authorization, and increased authority for investment in commercial paper and corporate debt securities.

This resulted in shifts on the asset side of the balance sheet for saving and loan associations. As Table 1-4 shows, savings and loans have always been more heavily concentrated in mortgages than other financial depository intermediaries. Yet savings and loan associations had decreased the share of their assets represented by mortgages to just under 62 percent in 1985, with ten percentage points accounted for by mortgage-backed securities. Consumer and commercial loans, as well as direct investments in real estate and corporate stock, have grown more than proportionately to reflect the greater asset diversification permitted.

Savings and loan associations have become very similar to mutual savings banks and differ now from commercial banks and credit unions more in degree than in kind in comparison to the original balance sheets displayed by these financial depository institutions. As Table 1-4 also shows, the liability-side of the balance sheets of thrifts and commercial banks have become more similar as banks have moved more heavily into time and savings accounts and thrifts into transactions accounts. Savings and loans can now accept demand deposits and make commercial loans, the activities that legally define a bank under the One-Bank Holding Company Act of 1970.

ORGANIZATIONAL FORM IN THE
THRIFT INDUSTRY

Most savings and loan associations have been mutual- rather than stock-type organizations. When the original holding-company legislation for savings and loan institutions, the Spence Act, was enacted in 1959, there were only 480 stock associations out of 6,223 savings and loans, accounting for 13 percent of all assets. A reason for mutual-institution dominance is that the Congress and the Bank Board had imposed a moratorium from 1955 to 1974 on the conversion of federal associations from the mutual to stock organizations. Although some state mutual associations did convert, relatively little information about the number and the amount of funds raised from

Table 1-4. Selected Balance Sheet Items for Major Depository Financial Institutions (1900–1985).

Type of Financial Institution	Percentage of Total Assets									
	1900	1920	1940	1960	1980	1981	1982	1983	1984	1985
Commercial Banks										
Mortgages	5.3	6.8	6.5	12.8[b]	20.4	20.4	20.0	20.2	20.7	21.2
Mortgage-backed securities	0	0	0	0	n/a	n/a	n/a	n/a	n/a	n/a
Transaction accounts	48.0	45.4	49.4	55.0	25.9	25.1	24.7	23.7	22.7	23.1
Savings and time accounts	12.0	23.4	23.0	27.5	37.4	37.6	41.6	46.3	45.4	45.0
Mutual Savings Banks										
Mortgages	36.9	41.0	40.5	65.8	58.2	56.9	53.8	50.3	50.5	51.0
Mortgage-backed securities	0	0	0	0	8.1	7.9	8.0	9.4	9.4	9.0
Transactions accounts	0	0	0	0	n/a	n/a	1.6	1.8	1.9	2.3
Savings and time accounts	91.5	92.3	89.0	89.6	88.5	87.1	87.0	86.1	85.1	81.7
Savings and Loan Associations										
Mortgages	82.9	91.8[a]	72.0	84.0	79.7	77.8	68.9	64.5	62.3	61.7
Mortgage-backed securities	0	0	0	0	4.3	5.0	8.5	10.8	11.0	10.2
Transaction accounts	0	0	0	0	n/a	0.1	0.1	0.2	2.8	3.3
Savings and time accounts	86.1	86.7[a]	75.4	86.9	80.6	78.2	76.5	77.4	73.6	72.1

a. These figures are for 1922.
b. Data from 1960 for commercial banks are from flow of funds from the Federal Reserve and reported as a percentage of financial assets. In 1985 the ratio of financial assets to total assets was .92. Also, time and savings is net of large certificates of deposit.

Source: Based on data from U.S. Department of Commerce, Bureau of the Census, *Historical Statistics of the United States: Colonial Times to 1970* (Washington, D.C.), Part 2; and the Board of Governors of the Federal Reserve System, *Federal Reserve Bulletin* (various issues).

these conversions is available. Before 1980 fewer than twenty states allowed stock savings and loans to operate.

The rapidly deteriorating net-worth position of the savings and loan industry during the early 1980s clearly demonstrated the need for associations to have as much access as possible to the capital markets. Mutual associations, however, could only increase their net worth through retained earnings or through the sale of subordinated debt. They could not raise external equity capital.

Although the Bank Board authorized conversions on an experimental basis from 1974 to 1976, and on a more regular basis since then, only 142 conversions had been consummated from 1976 to 1982, raising $600 million. The Garn-St Germain Act in 1982, however, greatly facilitated conversions. As a result, 255 conversions, raising $4.8 billion, occurred from 1983 to 1985. Table 1–5 shows that 62 percent of all thrift assets were in stock institutions in December 1986, an increase from 27 percent in 1980. In addition, Appendix A presents a state-by-state breakdown for 1986, as well as a state-by-state breakdown of federally and state-chartered savings and loans. In 1986, 64 percent of thrift assets were in federal institutions. (For information on the concentration of assets within the industry, see Appendix B.)

The first savings and loan holding company, Great Western Financial Corporation in California, was organized in 1955 by Lehman Brothers in New York. Beginning with one savings and loan association, it obtained six more within four years. Eventually, Great Western also controlled at least twenty non-savings and loan subsidiaries, including an insurance agency, two land-development companies, and fifteen escrow companies. In an attempt to slow the growth in multiassociation holding companies, the Congress enacted the Spence Act to limit holding companies of FSLIC-insured institutions to no more than one insured association.

Under the more comprehensive Savings and Loan Holding Company Act of 1968, a savings and loan holding company is defined as any company controlling an insured savings and loan institution or another savings and loan holding company. Current law makes it unlawful to become a savings and loan holding company or for an existing holding company to acquire another insured or uninsured association without the FSLIC's prior approval. Subject to the exceptions in the emergency provisions of the Garn-St German Act, no applications can be approved that result in a multiple savings and

Table 1-5. Organizational Form of Savings and Loan Associations (1980-1986).

Year	Number of Stock Associations	Percentage of All Insured	Assets of Stock Associations (in billions of dollars)	Percentage of All Insured Assets	Number of Savings and Loan Holding Companies		
					Multiple	Unitary	Total
1980	789	19.7	168.0	27.2	n/a	n/a	n/a
1981	791	20.9	188.4	28.9	9	146	155
1982	755	22.6	206.9	30.0	8	166	176
1983	738	24.3	298.2	39.5	18	211	229
1984	934	29.5	511.1	52.2	24	264	288
1985	1,087	33.5	601.6	56.2	29	313	342
1986	1,189	36.9	722.3	62.0	29	358	387

Note: The number of unitary holding companies includes both diversified and nondiversified, with a diversified company being one whose savings-and-loan-related activities represent less than 50 percent of consolidated net worth and net income. Of the 358 unitary holding companies at year-end 1986, 69 were diversified.

Source: Author's calculations based on data from the Federal Home Loan Bank Board.

loan holding company controlling FSLIC-insured associations in more than one state. Unitary savings and loan holding companies that meet a "thriftness test" (primarily a specified percentage of assets in mortgages and selected securities) of the Internal Revenue Code may engage, through non-FSLIC subsidiaries, in any activity, without restriction under the Savings and Loan Holding Company Act. This explains how Sears, Roebuck, and Company can operate a retailing business, insurance company, securities firm, and a single savings and loan institution, all through a holding company, and yet not violate the Savings and Loan Holding Company Act.

Multiple savings and loan holding companies (and unitary companies failing to meet the "thriftness test") may only engage in those activities determined to be permissible by the FSLIC. The FSLIC has thus far permitted savings and loan companies, or subsidiaries thereof that are neither insured institutions nor service corporations of insured institutions, to engage in such activities as operating an insurance agency, operating an escrow business, processing data, developing unimproved real estate, and preparing federal and state tax returns. Table 1–5 presents data on the number and type of thrift holding companies.

Besides holding companies, it is important to mention service corporations, which are corporations organized under the law of the state in which the savings and loan association has its home office and whose stock is available for purchase only by state or federal associations also having a home office in that state. Federal associations are currently authorized by law to invest up to 3 percent of their assets in the stock of service corporations. Utilizing these corporations, federal associations may engage in stock brokerage and insurance brokerage and agency activities, among other activities, as well as join together in different states to carry out mutually advantageous ventures on a nationwide scale. At the end of 1986, 4,327 service corporations existed.

TRADE ASSOCIATIONS AND THRIFT-INDUSTRY INFLUENCE ON REGULATORY POLICY

The thrift industry and its trade associations have exercised significant influence over congressional and regulatory policies since thrifts faced their first major crises in 1892, when the newly formed U.S. League of Local Building and Loan Associations—note the word "local" in the name—lobbied for legislation restricting the activities of national associations. It should surprise no one that firms would attempt to influence the regulation of their industry, since regulation alters the allocation of resources and therefore affects who gains and who loses due to regulatory decisions. As this chapter has shown, thrift and banking regulators have determined prices, entry and exit, allowable products and product quantity, allowable geographic location, organizational form, and disclosure of information. In fact, in no other industry in the United States can regulatory control be as complete as with thrift institutions and banking. The extent of regulatory control is indicated in Table 1-6, which shows which regulator regulates which function for all U.S. depository institutions.

Contemporary economic analysis of the incentives and behavior of regulated firms has developed from the pioneering work of Nobel laureate economist George Stigler under the general title of the capture theory of regulation. Regulated firms have an economic interest in "capturing" and using the regulator to the extent possible for their own benefit. In effect, there is a demand for regulation—firms attempt to gain the "potential uses of public resources and power to improve their economic status."[16] There is also a supply of regulation in "the characteristics of the political process which allow relatively small groups to obtain regulation."[17]

In 1971 Stigler even cited some examples of bank and thrift regulation that corresponded to his ideas about why some regulations develop. If the government will not forbid entry into an industry, for example, existing competitors have an interest in limiting the growth rate of new firms. Stigler concluded that the power to insure banks "had been used by the FDIC to reduce the rate of entry into commercial banking by 60 percent."[18] He also noted that "no new savings and loan company may pay a dividend rate higher than that prevailing in the community in its endeavors to attract deposits," which limited competition for capital.[19] He went on to observe that the Bank Board also controlled the amount of advertising and areas of competition other than price controls.

Neither Stigler nor any other economist would postulate that all regulatory actions are motivated by the self-interest of the regulated firms or that each regulation that is so motivated is necessarily motivated for that reason alone by all relevant parties. What most economists would say is that if the regulation has the effect of providing a subsidy, setting a price, limiting entry of new firms, or affecting the

22   THRIFTS UNDER SIEGE

Table 1-6. Structure of Depository Institution Regulation.

Savings and Loan Associations

Function	Federally Chartered FSLIC Insured	State Chartered FSLIC Insured	State Chartered Non-FSLIC Insured
Chartering	FHLBB	State	State
Regulation	FHLBB	FHLBB, State	State
Examination	FHLBB	FHLBB, State	State
Supervision	FHLBB	FHLBB, State	State
Insurance	FHLBB	FHLBB	State
Liquidity	FHLBS, FRS[a]	FHLBS, FRS[a]	FRS[a], FHLBS[b]

Commercial Banks

Function	National Bank FRS Member	State Bank FRS Member	State Bank Non-FRS Member
Chartering	OCC	State	State
Regulation	OCC (FRB, FDIC)	FRB, State (FDIC)	State (FDIC)[c]
Examination	OCC (FDIC, FRB)	FRB, State (FDIC)	FDIC[c], State
Supervision	OCC (FRB, FDIC)	FRB, State (FDIC)	FDIC[c], State
Insurance	FDIC	FDIC	FDIC, State
Liquidity	FRS	FRS	FRS[a]

Mutual Savings Banks

Function	Federally Chartered FSLIC Insured	Federally Chartered FDIC Insured	State Chartered FDIC Insured	State Chartered Non-FDIC Insured
Chartering	FHLBB	FHLBB	State	State
Regulation	FHLBB	FHLBB, FDIC	State	State
Examination	FHLBB	FHLBB, FDIC	State, FDIC	State
Supervision	FHLBB	FHLBB, FDIC	FDIC (State)	State
Insurance	FHLBB	FDIC	FDIC[c]	State
Liquidity	FHLBS, FRS[a]	FHLBS, FRS[a]	FRS[a], FHLBS[b]	FRS[a], FHLBS[b]

Credit Unions

| | Federally Chartered | State Chartered | |
	NCUA Insured	NCUA Insured	Non-NCUA Insured
Chartered	NCUA	State	State
Regulation	NCUA	State (NCUA)	State
Examination	NCUA	State (NCUA)	State
Supervision	NCUA	State (NCUA)	State
Insurance	NCUA	NCUA	State/none
Liquidity	CLF[b], FRS[a]	CLF[b], FRS[a]	CLF[b], FRS[a]

Note: Agencies in parentheses have the authority but do not normally exercise it.

CLF   = Central Liquidity Facility
FDIC = Federal Deposit Insurance Corporation
FHLBB = Federal Home Loan Bank Board
FHLBS = Federal Home Loan Bank System
FRB   = Federal Reserve Board
FRS   = Federal Reserve Systems
NCUA = National Credit Union Administration
OCC   = Office of the Comptroller of the Currency

a. For institutions offering transactions accounts, as provided by the Depository Institutions Deregulation and Monetary Control Act of 1980.

b. If member.

c. If insured by the FDIC.

d. Mutual savings banks that convert to federal charter may retain FDIC insurance.

e. Insurance of accounts over $100,000 at FDIC-insured Massachusetts mutual savings banks provided by state.

Source: Federal Home Loan Bank Board, Agenda for Reform, A Report to the Congress (Washington, D.C.: Federal Home Loan Bank Board, March 1983), pp. 138–139.

provision of substitute or complementary goods or services, the self-interest of some existing firms is being served, and whether consumers or society are also being served ought to be examined closely.

There are many such cases in the thrift industry, most dramatically illustrated by the activities since 1893 of the major trade association for savings and loans, currently named the United States League of Savings Institutions.[20] One of the first actions of the association was to collect data on savings and loan associations, with annual reports filed beginning in 1897. Each year thereafter, as more states passed laws requiring their associations to file reports with a state official, these data were compiled for the league's annual report on savings and loan association statistics. In 1927, for the first time, complete statistics for the previous year were listed for all states and the District of Columbia, although five states had to be estimated.[21] In addition, until the Great Depression, "the United States League and the several state leagues were primarily responsible for the supervision and public inspection or visitation of savings and loan associations."[22]

The United States League has always taken a particular interest in the laws and regulations that separate thrifts from other institutions, an interest based on the stated belief that "the savings and loan business desires uniformity along sound lines" and "that every institution gains if the public finds that it can expect the same type of operation and same service from savings and loan associations whether they are across the street from each other, in different cities, or in different regions."[23] The opposition to national savings and loan associations in the late 1880s and 1900s reflected this view, as did the federal government's chartering of savings and loan associations, beginning in the 1930s. Under the terms of the charter, the associations were restricted to making only residential mortgage loans and then only within a fifty-mile radius. The federal associations, moreover, had to operate as mutual thrifts. Each of these developments, supported by league positions, is consistent with limiting competition, despite the stated motivations.

The United States League was also instrumental in keeping thrifts exempt from federal taxes until 1951, and it played a crucial role in establishing the Federal Home Loan Bank System and the Federal Savings and Loan Insurance Corporation. During the Great Depression, one of the first members of the Federal Home Loan Bank Board said that "practically every plan or general proposal of the league was adopted by the Government in full or in modified form and thrown into the breach to stabilize the situation and prevent a sweeping collapse."[24] League leaders participated in the actual drafting of the Federal Home Loan Bank Act, and "President Hoover appointed the President of the United States League and the Executive Manager to represent the building and loan program on the original Board."[25] Regarding federal deposit insurance, the "proposal of the United States League was included as Title IV of the National Housing Act."[26] The U.S. League was thus involved in creating and staffing the Bank Board and in determining the shape of the legislation concerning federal insurance of accounts at savings and loan associations. The league also managed to change the original draft of the Securities Act of 1933 to exempt savings and loans from its reporting requirements. In addition, it opposed the original version of the Banking Act of 1935, which "would have removed practically all restrictions from commercial banking institutions with regard to making mortgage loans and the facilities of the Federal Reserve System were even made available for loans and discounts on long-term mortgage paper."[27]

More generally, it is reported that "traditionally, the Federal Home Loan Bank Board has been strongly influenced by the industry and its present activity is the product of some special factors, which are not likely to continue forever."[28] Actually, in "the old days . . . the United States Savings and Loan League wrote many FHLBB regulations."[29] The extent to which the United States League influences the Bank Board is particularly important because the Bank Board not only oversees federal savings and loan associations, but all state-chartered savings and loans that are members of the Federal Home Loan Bank System, as well as the Federal Savings and Loan Insurance Corporation and the Federal Home Loan Mortgage Corporation.

The Federal Home Loan Bank System was created in 1933 primarily to provide liquidity to the thrift industry. In general, the Banks have provided liquidity by issuing debt and distributing the resulting funds in borrowings (called "advances") to the thrift institutions that are members of the system. The debt is backed by the Banks' assets, which consist mainly of loans to thrifts and U.S. Treasury securities. The debt is priced at only a small spread over Treasury issues of similar maturities, first, because the advances are collateralized by mortgages whose value generally exceeds 100 percent of the advances and, second, because the system has attained "agency" status. That is, although the Banks are private institutions, their close affiliation with the government has led the market to infer that the government would cover defaults the Banks did not cover. Thus, the market to some extent treats the Banks as if they were government agencies.

The contemporary role of the Banks, however, goes far beyond providing liquidity. The officers and directors of the Banks advise the Bank Board, both formally and informally. Monthly Bank president's meetings, for example, are regularly attended by Bank Board members and senior staff. Staffs of economists, lawyers, and other professionals provide analysis and support for the Banks' positions on issues facing the thrift industry. The staffs of the Banks are also frequently used by the Bank Board for projects relating to Bank Board policy. Most recently, from 1985 to the fall of 1987, senior Bank System staff members were made directors of the FSLIC and the Office of Policy and Economic Research, two of the most important offices at the Bank Board. Moreoever, the Bank's presidents are the thrift industry's Primary Supervisory Agents (PSAs), with overall control of the supervision of thrifts insured by the FSLIC. The federal examiners are also employees of the Banks.

The Banks, then, have significant influence over many aspects of thrift-institution regulation, supervision, and examination. In the context of the capture theory of regulation, it is important, therefore, to examine the control of the Banks, which means looking first at their boards of directors. Each Bank is governed by at least fourteen directors, two of whom are designated yearly by the Bank Board as chair and vice-chair. The chair of the Bank must be an "appointed" member; the vice-chair must be an "elected" member. The number of elected members cannot exceed thirteen, and they must outnumber appointed members by a four-to-three ratio. All elected directors are from the savings and loan industry and serve three-year terms, while appointed directors serve four-year terms. Elected members are almost exclusively the presidents and chairs of the boards of individual associations. Appointed directors do not come directly from the thrift industry but instead from independent private businesses, usually universities, law firms, and businesses related to real estate. The composition of appointed directors varies between districts, although directors are frequently involved in businesses closely related to the thrift industry. In 1985, for example, most of California's appointed directors came from construction firms or from law firms representing thrift institutions. In addition to controlling the Banks' general policies, directors specifically elect a president, who must be approved by the Bank Board and serves a term of one year.

In contrast, industry representation is more diluted for the twelve Federal Reserve Banks, which provide services for commercial banks similar to those provided by the Federal Home Loan Banks for the thrift industry. The Federal Reserve Banks act as the intermediaries between the Board of Governors and the individual banks and provide liquidity for the banks. Nine outside directors, three of whom are Class A directors elected from member banks as their representatives, guide each Reserve Bank. Class B directors consist of three individuals, who are also elected by the member banks but are not from banks. Finally, three Class C directors are appointed by the board of governors of the Federal Reserve System. Each Class B and Class C director is prohibited from being an officer, director, or employee of a bank while in office; Class C directors are further prohibited from owning stock in a bank. Only Class C directors are appointed chair and deputy chair.

It is difficult not to conclude that, by a combination of direct and indirect avenues, primarily through the Federal Home Loan Banks and trade associations, the thrift industry has heavily influenced regulatory policy since the 1930s. Without doubt, the degree of this influence has exceeded what is necessary to assure that relevant industry expertise finds its way into regulatory deliberations. To those steeped in the capture theory of regulation, however, it is not surprising to find that what appears to be the most regulated industry also appears to have the greatest influence over its regulators. The result in the 1980s has been the selection of regulatory approaches that have favored the short-term interests of existing thrift institutions at the expense of consumers of financial services, society in general, and even the long-term interests of stockholders and employees of those thrift institutions that will ultimately survive.

SUMMARY AND CONCLUSIONS

Savings and loan associations developed in the nineteenth century to satisfy a demand for housing finance. Other financial institutions with different balance sheets also developed as a result of market forces. With the development and evolution of financial institutions came laws and government regulations that influenced the composition of their balance sheets. Although specialization apparently developed initially based upon comparative advantage in the supplying of credit in a world of imperfect and costly information, market forces have since changed, and the distinctions among the various types of firms have blurred, especially among the financial depository firms.[30]

In addition, particularly since the Great Depression, the federal government has not only kept depository institutions and commerce separate but has also kept financial industries somewhat compartmentalized. The frequently stated reason for this balance-sheet compartmentalization is the protection of the safety and soundness of the financial system. An analysis of the modern thrift-industry crisis sheds considerable light on whether the financial system would be less safe and sound without such government intervention and whether efficiency is excessively sacrificed for presumed safety and soundness.[31]

NOTES

1. These practices were presumably intended to minimize the losses on loans that inevitably occur in a world of imperfect and costly information.
2. John Lintner, *Mutual Savings Banks in the Savings and Mortgage Markets* (Andover, Mass.: Andover Press, 1948), p. 130.
3. Morton Bodfish, "The Depression Experience of Savings and Loan Associations in the United States," Address delivered in Salzburg, Austria, 1935, p. 129.
4. Morton Bodfish and A. D. Theobald, *Savings and Loan Principles* (New York: Prentice-Hall, 1940), p. 54.
5. Bodfish, "The Depression Experience of Savings and Loan Associations," p. 7.
6. *Ibid.*, p. 7.
7. Interestingly enough, Bodfish points out that "many state legislatures passed moratorium bills temporarily suspending the rights of mortgagees in repossessing properties." As a result, he states, this "... led a great number of people, who had capacity to pay, to refrain from carrying out their obligations." It should also be noted that withdrawals were subject to notice and in many cases distributed on a pro-rata basis. *Ibid.*, p. 13.
8. For an analysis of the Federal Reserve's failure to act, see Milton Friedman and Anna J. Schwartz, *A Monetary History of the United States, 1867–1960* (Princeton, N.J.: Princeton University Press, 1963).
9. Bodfish, "The Depression Experienced of Savings and Loan Associations," p. 22.

10. According to Bodfish, ". . . one-half of the counties in the United States, as a result of the depression, now had no mortgage-loan institutions or facilities" (*ibid.*).

11. Bodfish and Theobald, *Savings and Loan Principles*, p. 301.

12. *Ibid.*, p. 482.

13. *Ibid.*, pp. 480–481.

14. *Ibid.*, p. 502.

15. Hearings on a Guarantee Fund for Depositors in Banks, U.S. House of Representatives, 1932, p. 153.

16. George J. Stigler, "The Theory of Economic Regulation," *Bell Journal of Economics and Management Science* (Spring 1971): 3. For a review of competing theories, see also Richard Posner, "Theories of Economic Regulation," *Bell Journal of Management Science* (Autumn 1974): 336. Another interesting example is Sam Peltzman, "Entry into Commercial Banking," *Journal of Law and Economics* (October 1966): 11–50.

17. Stigler, "The Theory of Economic Regulation," p. 5.

18. *Ibid.*

19. *Ibid.*

20. The earliest form of trade association in the savings and loan industry was the state league, with one formed in Pennsylvania in 1877. See Bodfish and Theobald, *Savings and Loan Principles*, p. 591.

21. Morton Bodfish, *History of Building and Loans in the United States* (Chicago: U.S. Building and Loan League, 1931), pp. 152–153.

22. Bodfish, "The Depression Experience of Savings and Loan Associations," p. 9.

23. Bodfish and Theobald, *Savings and Loan Principles*, p. 616.

24. Bodfish, "The Depression Experience of Savings and Loan Associations," p. 17.

25. *Ibid.*, p. 9.

26. *Ibid.*, p. 24.

27. *Ibid.*, p. 27.

28. Thomas Marvell, *The Federal Home Loan Bank Board* (New York: Praeger Publishers, 1969), p. 225.

29. *Ibid.*, p. 255.

30. For a closely related discussion of the issues examined in this chapter, see James R. Barth and Martin A. Regalia, "The Evolving Role of Regulation in the Savings and Loan Industry," in *The Financial Services Revolution: Policy Directions for the Future*, ed. Catherine England and Thomas F. Hertas (Norwell, Massachusetts: Kluiver Academic Publishers, 1988), pp. 113–161. This paper in part draws upon earlier work done by Barth and Brumbaugh.

31. For a recent treatment of these issues, primarily in the context of commercial banks, see Robert Litan, *What Should Banks Do?* (Washington, D.C.: Brookings Institution, 1987).

2 THE MODERN THRIFT CRISIS (PART ONE)
A Precipitous Increase in Failures Accompanies Sharply Rising Interest Rates

WEAKNESSES IN THE REGULATORY SYSTEM MAKE IT VULNERABLE TO THE UNEXPECTED INCREASE IN INTEREST RATES IN 1980

With the establishment of federal deposit insurance after the Great Depression, depository institutions in the United States entered a lengthy period of stability. This ended abruptly in the early 1980s, however, when thrift institutions and commercial banks began experiencing financial distress that led to record failures. From the founding of the FSLIC in 1934 through 1986, 75 percent of the 890 failures of FSLIC-insured thrifts occurred in the last seven years. Forty-three percent of the 994 failures of FDIC-insured commercial banks occurred over the same short period. This chapter explains what caused the sudden end to stability in 1980 and precipitated part one of a two-part thrift-industry crisis.[1]

The overall description of the damage-control mechanism of the U.S. regulatory system for depository financial institutions can be synthesized into one sentence. The federal deposit-insurance corporations, the FDIC and the FSLIC, and the Federal Reserve were established to prevent runs, and these and other federal agencies were given various regulatory powers to reduce further the likelihood of runs by helping to ensure safe and sound practices by the insured

31

institutions. A further distinction between the deposit insurers' and the Federal Reserve's roles regarding insolvent and solvent institutions is important. The FDIC and the FSLIC are supposed to generate such confidence on the part of depositors in the safety of their deposits that the prospect of widespread runs is virtually eliminated. This is done by closing insolvent institutions promptly—through liquidation or merger—and thereby guaranteeing depositors the value of their insured deposits. In the event that the two insurance funds do not accomplish their objective, the Federal Reserve is supposed to lend to solvent institutions experiencing runs due to the inability of depositors to determine which institutions are insolvent.

Depositor confidence in the system derives more from faith, however, than reliance on explicit U.S. government guarantees and specific legal requirements that the FDIC, FSLIC, and the Federal Reserve act as they have been designed to act. Although many Americans may not realize it, there is no explicit legal requirement, for example, that the U.S. government must stand behind the FDIC's and FSLIC's guarantees to pay depositors up to $100,000 per account that have been in effect since 1980. In 1982 the Congress did pass a nonbinding resolution, pledging the full faith and credit of the U.S. government behind the FDIC and FSLIC; however, the nonbinding resolution did not explicitly commit the U.S. government to make funds available in an emergency and has expired. A similar sense of the Congress's commitment was made in banking legislation passed in August 1987.

Depositors' faith has been built to some extent on misinformation. In an article in the spring of 1987, a nationally syndicated columnist wrote that the "FSLIC is bankrupt, so technically it is no longer guaranteeing anything."[2] The columnist then observed that "the U.S. Treasury stands behind the insurance fund" and "you may not lose money as a depositor, because Congress stands behind FSLIC." Technically, the FSLIC may borrow up to $750 million from the U.S. Treasury under specified circumstances, but, as stated above, not even a sense of congressional resolution existed when the column appeared. Ultimately, informed depositors' faith rests on the perception that Congress realizes that no insured depositor could lose so much as a mill without dangerously raising the probability of destabilizing runs. Because of this potential danger, one can conclude with great confidence that Congress will not allow federally insured depositors to lose money. After all, Ohio and Maryland assumed the obligations of private insurance funds in their states when these collapsed in 1985.

Beginning in 1985 the Bank Board began to acknowledge publicly that the FSLIC fund's existing reserves of approximately $4.6 billion were more than $10 billion short of the amount estimated to be needed at that time to close all thrift institutions that the Bank Board considered insolvent.[3] The Bank Board and independent analysts have since concluded that the cost to close all insolvent institutions has grown since 1985, while the FSLIC's reserves have declined. Thus, for the first time since the insurance funds were established in the 1930s, one—the FSLIC—does not have the financial resources to close all insolvent thrift institutions and, hence, to act as Congress had designed it by closing insolvent institutions promptly.

Furthermore, the precarious health of the thrift industry does not guarantee that adequate premium income will be forthcoming to close the gap between the reserves and the closure costs. The law does not authorize the insurance corporations to raise insurance premia to cover large losses. The FSLIC, for example, may charge an annual premium of 1/12 of 1 percent of industry deposits and impose an additional annual premium of 1/8 of 1 percent, as it has done since 1985. The expected premium income for 1987 is approximately $1.9 billion. The FSLIC has not imposed an additional one-time assessment of 1 percent of liabilities, although it is authorized to do so. Such an assessment at year-end 1986 would have eliminated more than one-fourth of the thrift industry's GAAP net worth. In an effort to overcome these limitations, the Congress has authorized a borrowing plan to augment FSLIC reserves over time. The plan is analyzed in Chapter 3.

Depositor confidence, therefore, must lie in the belief that Congress will ultimately support the FSLIC, especially after the U.S. General Accounting Office's early 1987 declaration that the FSLIC was insolvent as of year-end 1986. Yet the absence of explicit guarantees combined with the lack of other explicit requirements to deal with large numbers of seriously troubled institutions makes the financial system potentially unstable. As discussed in Chapter 1, although the Federal Reserve is supposed to loan funds to solvent institutions, in the Great Depression it did not provide enough liquidity to prevent widespread runs. And although the federal deposit-insurance corporations were designed to close insolvent institutions, they are not explicitly required to do so by law. Hence, the FSLIC has not closed all insolvent thrifts, not even those deemed to be insolvent according to standard accounting methods.

It is important to emphasize why the U.S. government has been so concerned about bank and thrift-institution runs and why the regulatory system's vulnerabilities are disquieting. The Federal Reserve, the FDIC, and the FSLIC were not created to prevent runs *per se*. Were they intended to prevent each and every bank run, they would merely protect individual depository institutions against failure. There is no more justification for protecting individual banks and thrifts from failure than there is for protecting any other retailer of goods and services. Instead, the Federal Reserve, FDIC, and FSLIC were created to protect against the potential externalities, or larger social costs, caused by widespread runs.

Social costs from widespread, as distinct from individual, bank runs result from a breakdown in the intermediation function and (what has traditionally been viewed as more important) a disruption of the payments system. The costs can arise in the following chain reaction. Depositors withdraw funds from both solvent and insolvent institutions. Withdrawals force solvent institutions to liquidate assets precipitously in order to satisfy depositors. The hasty sale of assets can result in prices below those that orderly sales can produce, thus driving solvent banks into insolvency. If the chain reaction continues long enough the intermediation process and payments mechanism can falter.[4]

In addition to the establishment of the FDIC and the FSLIC, the Great Depression experience led to regulations restricting the asset and liability powers of commercial banks and thrift institutions. These limited the rates of interest that could be paid on certain liabilities and restricted competition not only among thrifts but also among the different types of financial institutions. Hence, while government-provided deposit insurance was intended to reduce the likelihood and consequences of widespread depository-institution failures through runs, government regulations limiting institutions' activities and deposit rates were intended to reduce the likelihood of depository-institution insolvencies and failures due to excessive risk-taking and competition.

Government regulation was also designed to limit social costs by reducing the adverse incentives created by deposit insurance. Providing government insurance at a flat or nonrisk-adjusted rate, as the government has done since 1934, creates a problem referred to as "moral hazard." Financial institutions have an incentive to seek higher-risk portfolios than they would if the price of insurance were positively related to portfolio risk.[5] At the same time, insured depositors have no incentive to monitor institutions' activities because their deposits are insured. The government, then, uses deposit insurance to reduce the potential social costs caused by runs—but at the cost of increased portfolio risk due to moral hazard and, thus, at the cost of a greater likelihood of failure. Portfolio restrictions and other regulatory requirements have been justified as a way to contain this moral hazard.

Until the 1980s the financial system generally functioned as its designers intended. Commercial banks made commercial loans and provided demand deposits or, more generally, transaction accounts without significant bank failures. For their part, thrift institutions provided savings deposits and funds for housing, also without significant failures. Pressure on the financial system began to build in the 1970s, when technological change and financial-service innovation developed with unprecedented speed and rapidly eroded the differences among firms hitherto providing distinct financial services. For example, in the early 1970s, some thrift institutions began offering checkable deposits, and several states granted state-chartered institutions expanded asset powers. The result was increased competition between commercial banks and thrift institutions.

At the same time, commercial banks and thrift institutions began competing more with other types of financial firms providing interest-earning deposits and checkable-type accounts.[6] Furthermore, the first "nonbank bank" was established in California in 1980, resulting in de facto if not de jure interstate banking. A 1970 amendment to the Bank Holding Company Act of 1956 defines a bank as an institution that both accepts demand deposits and makes commercial loans. A nonbank bank performs only one of these services and therefore was initially viewed by some as a legal way to avoid the geographical restrictions of the Bank Holding Company Act.

Thus, by 1980 the stage was set for act one of part one of the modern thrift crisis. The fissures in the regulatory apparatus existed but drew little attention because the apparatus had experienced little pressure in nearly fifty years. The insurance funds had always been adequate to pay for losses incurred when institutions failed, so the question of emergency funding went largely unexamined. The need for explicit closure rules was not addressed because, with relatively stable interest rates, interest-rate controls, and well-defined balance sheets, there were few insolvencies, and those few were fairly obvious and promptly handled. With interest-rate controls, narrowly defined allowable assets and liabilities, and examination staffs in sufficient numbers for placid times, the moral hazard embedded in flat-rate insurance premia also appeared to be contained. Then, in an effort to combat inflation in October 1979, the Federal Reserve began to pay more attention to money aggregates than to interest rates. Interest rates rose sharply and—like the single first shot that signals full-fledged battle—set off the modern thrift crisis whose outcome is still unknown.

MONETARY POLICY CHANGES IN OCTOBER 1979, INTEREST RATES SOAR, AND FAILURES MOUNT

As Figure 2–1 indicates, the average cost of funds for all federally insured thrifts in 1980 was rising faster than the returns on their primary assets—mortgages—and this trend continued until 1982. As Table 1-4 shows, mortgages and mortgage-backed securities constituted 84 percent of thrift institutions' total assets in 1980 and 77 percent in 1982. Although interest rates had been rising since 1965, they escalated sharply in the late 1970s. The average cost of funds for thrifts rose from 7 percent in 1978 to just over 11 percent in 1982, while the average return on mortgages rose from over 8 percent in 1978 to just under 11 percent in 1982. In 1981 and 1982, as Figure 2–1 shows, the average cost of funds exceeded the average return on mortgages.

As Table 2–1 shows, the effect on the thrift industry's profitability was immediate and profound.[7] Net income fell from an anemic but positive level in 1980 to negative numbers in 1981 and 1982. The 1980 net income represented 0.14 percent of industry assets, well below the 0.67 percent average of the previous ten years. The nearly $9 billion in negative net income in 1981 and 1982 eroded 14 percent of industry regulatory net worth in 1981 and 15 percent in 1982.

Regulatory net worth is based on regulatory accounting principles (RAP) and is most frequently referred to as RAP net worth. Regulatory accounting principles applied to the thrift industry are determined by the Bank Board and now differ significantly from the most

Figure 2-1. Thrift Spreads, Money-Market Yields, and the Number of Failures and Insolvencies for All FSLIC-Insured Thrift Institutions (1980–1986).

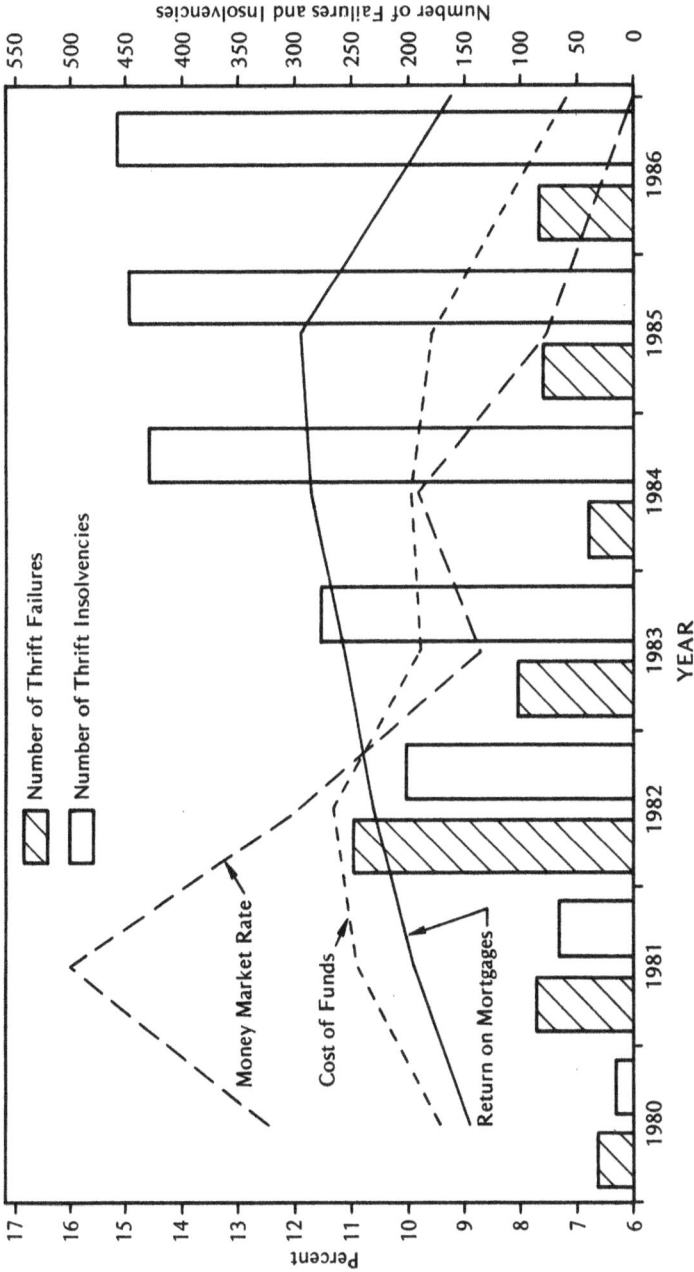

Note: The term "failure" refers to all FSLIC-assisted cases as well as institutions merged or liquidated under the supervision of the Federal Home Loan Bank Board. Insolvent Institutions are those with GAAP net worth less than or equal to zero.

Source: Data are from James R. Barth, Donald J. Bisenius, R. Dan Brumbaugh, Jr., and Daniel Sauerhaft, "The Thrift Industry's Rough Road Ahead," *Challenge: The Magazine of Economic Affairs* (September/October 1986): 38–43. Reprinted in *Current Readings on Money, Banking, and Financial Markets*, James A. Wilcox, ed. (Boston: Little Brown & Company, March 1987), pp. 150–155.

Table 2-1. Profitability of FSLIC-Insured Thrift Institutions (1980-1986) (in millions of dollars).

Year	Net Income[a]	Net Operating Income[b]	Net Nonoperating Income[c]	Income Taxes	Regulatory Net Worth	Net Income as Percent of Previous Year's Regulatory Net Worth
1980	$ 781	$ 790	$ 398	$ 407	$32,436	2.5
1981	-4,631	-7,114	964	-1,519	27,572	-14.3
1982	-4,142	-8,761	3,041	-1,578	25,386	-15.0
1983	1,945	- 46	2,567	576	32,980	7.7
1984	1,165	1,044	911	788	37,927	3.5
1985	3,839	3,685	2,266	2,112	46,839	5.5
1986	1,240	4,725	-339	3,146	53,114	2.6

Note: In both 1985 and 1986 there were sizable negative adjustments to prior period income. These adjustments were made as a result of the determination by the FHLBB that previously reported income figures were too high. After these adjustments are made, net income declines to $2,806 million and a negative $356 million in 1985 and 1986, respectively.

a. Net income is net operating income plus net nonoperating income less income taxes. Due to rounding, the components may not add up exactly to net income.

b. Net operating income is operating income less operating expenses and interest charges on liabilities.

c. Net nonoperating income is nonoperating income less nonoperating expenses where nonoperating income comes primarily from profits on the sale of assets and nonoperating expenses comes primarily from losses from the sale of assets.

Source: Author's calculations based on data from the Federal Home Loan Bank Board.

widely used principles, called generally accepted accounting principles (GAAP). Generally accepted accounting principles are mainly
determined by the Financial Accounting Standards Board (FASB),
although the Securities and Exchange Commission (SEC) has legal
authority over accounting practices in publicly traded firms. The
FASB and SEC generally negotiate when they disagree over accounting practices. The differences between RAP and GAAP play a central
role in the thrift-industry crisis.

With the erosion of net worth, it is not surprising that the number
of both insolvent and failed thrift institutions began to rise. Table
2-2 presents the extraordinary number of thrift-institution failures
from 1980 through 1986. Before 1980, the largest number of FSLIC-
insured thrifts to fail in a single year was thirteen, in 1941. The 664
failures from 1980 through 1986 accounted for nearly 50 percent of
the attrition among FSLIC-insured thrift institutions during that
time. The total decline (including all mergers) was 1,452 institutions—from 4,002 in 1980 to 3,220 in 1986. The number of failures
peaked in 1982 when 7.5 percent of all institutions failed—a total of
252 FSLIC-insured institutions.

As if direct losses due to the maturity mismatch of thrift assets
and liabilities were not problem enough, a potential for massive disintermediation began to arise in 1979. Ironically, the source of this
problem was the regulation of interest rates imposed on banks during
the Great Depression and thrifts in 1966 that limited the rates these
institutions could pay on their deposits. As long as thrifts competed
primarily with banks for deposits, this arrangement provided mo-
nopoly-like pricing and profitability for both thrifts and banks in
garnering deposits, with thrifts given a guaranteed 25-basis-point
spread above bank rates to attract savings deposits (one percentage
point equals 100 basis points).

Regulated interest rates also conveyed what has been called the
greatest benefit of a monopoly—a quiet life for the monopolists.
Alas, however, the rapid rise of market interest rates that began in
1980 prompted vigorous growth in the mutual money-market funds
that had first appeared in 1972. As Figure 2-1 shows, money-market
mutual fund rates that had been just under 7 percent in 1978 rose to
16 percent in 1982. In 1981 and 1982 deposit withdrawals at thrifts
exceeded new deposits by $32 billion. Most of these funds fled to
mutual money-market accounts that were at times paying approximately 500 basis points above the average rate paid by thrift insti-

Table 2-2.   FSLIC-Insured Failures (1980–1986).

Year	Number of Failures	Number of Insured Institutions	Number of Insured Accounts of Failed Institutions	Number of Insured Accounts for all Institutions (thousands)
1980	35	4,002	161,702	92,189
1981	81	3,779	1,860,233	98,748
1982	252	3,343	2,817,742	98,986
1983	102	3,040	1,995,031	103,214
1984	41	3,167	1,439,712	108,738
1985	70	3,246	n/a	113,489
1986	83	3,220	n/a	109,464

Note: Failure is defined as a case requiring supervisory action or FSLIC assistance.
Insured-accounts data encompass only the failed institutions that received FSLIC assistance.
Source: Author's calculations based on data from the Federal Home Loan Bank Board.

tutions. Due to interest credited to accounts that remained in thrifts, however, deposits at thrift institutions increased by $51 billion in 1981 and 1982. Nonetheless, the potential for full-blown, staggering disintermediation existed.

REGULATORY AND CONGRESSIONAL RESPONSES TO THE CRISIS

In light of this potential disruption, the federal regulators of depository institutions began to relax interest-rate restrictions in 1978 by allowing institutions to offer money-market certificate accounts with a term of six months and a minimum denomination of $10,000 at market-related interest rates. By the following year, these money-market accounts represented 20 percent of total deposits at thrift institutions. While this reduced the threat of disintermediation by allowing the cost of thrift funds to rise above levels that would have otherwise prevailed, it also reduced thrifts' earnings.

The decision by the regulators to reduce the danger of disintermediation at the cost of higher thrift interest expenses was the first

Table 2-2. continued

Assets of Failed Institutions (in millions of dollars)	Assets of All Institutions (in millions of dollars)	Percentage of Failed Institutions	Percentage of Insured Accounts Held by Failed Institutions	Percentage of Assets Held by Failed Institutions
$ 2,948	$ 618,466	0.87	8.18	8.48
15,057	651,068	2.14	1.88	2.31
46,837	692,663	7.54	2.85	6.76
16,602	819,168	3.32	1.93	1.95
5,774	978,514	1.33	1.32	0.98
6,530	1,069,547	2.16	n/a	0.61
13,812	1,165,320	2.58	n/a	1.19

of many significant regulatory responses, which are summarized in Table 2–3. The initial decision to deregulate interest rates was based on the perception that the disintermediation threat would portend an even greater profit loss than would increased costs if deposit withdrawals forced widespread asset sales. Since most of thrift assets were in mortgages whose values were declining precipitously with rising interest rates, widespread asset sales could have been disastrous.

In an effort to reduce the adverse effects of the unexpected increases in interest rates, Congress passed the Depository Institutions Deregulation and Monetary Control Act in March 1980. This act established a committee to phase out interest-rate ceilings on deposits by March 1986. To reduce the variability in thrifts' income, the act also gave thrift institutions various asset-diversification powers. In addition, in April 1981, the Bank Board authorized federally chartered thrifts to make, purchase, or participate in adjustable-rate mortgages in an attempt to permit thrifts to adjust to rising and volatile interest rates without having to diversify away from home mortgages.

Thrift institutions nonetheless continued to suffer from deteriorating net worth. Liabilities were repricing at market rates, but income from long-term assets could not rise fast enough to offset the higher

Table 2-3. Significant Regulatory Changes Affecting Thrift Institutions (*1980-1986*).

1980   Federal associations may establish branch offices and mobile facilities statewide (was within the home state and 100 miles of the home office).

Depository Institutions Deregulation and Monetary Control Act.

FSLIC insurance coverage is $100,000 (was $40,000) per owner for insured accounts at insured institutions.

FSLIC members may now borrow up to 50 percent of assets (was 50 percent of savings), although only 25 percent of assets may be pledged to secure outside borrowings; may accept more liabilities maturing within a three-month period; may otherwise borrow under more liberal rules than formerly.

Florida Savings Association Act (July 1, 1980) expands state-chartered thrift investment powers as was done previously in Maine (1975) and Texas (1972).

FSLIC members may make real estate loans without regard to the geographic location of the security property; may make loans in excess of 90 percent of value on one- to four-family properties.

Statutory reserve requirement reduced from 5 percent of insured accounts to 4 percent. Minimum net worth set at 4 percent of liabilities.

1981   Introduction of nationwide NOW accounts.

Institutions permitted to defer losses from the sale of assets with below-market yields.

Federal Home Loan Bank Board liberalizes its regulations regarding the conversion of federally chartered institutions from mutual to stock-type of organization.

Adjustable-rate mortgages authorized.

Federal association service corporations may now engage in a greatly enlarged list of activities without prior approval; may deal with a broader range of customers; and may borrow subject to fewer restrictions than formerly.

FHLB members may now borrow from their district Bank up to the lesser of (a) their legal maximum borrowing limit or (b) 50 percent of assets.

Qualifying mutual capital certificates included as RAP net worth.

Income capital certificates introduced.

1982   Joint Concurrent Resolution passes, placing the full faith and credit of the U.S. government behind the insurance funds' liabilities.

FSLIC members may exclude from liabilities in computing net worth certain contra-asset accounts, including loans in process, unearned discounts, and deferred fees and credits.

Table 2-3. continued

1982   Garn-St Germain Depository Institutions Act.

Federal institutions may elect to be chartered as associations or savings banks; state savings banks may obtain federal mutual or stock charters while keeping FDIC insurance.

Money Market Deposit Account established.

Net-worth certificates, qualifying subordinated debentures, and appraised equity capital included as RAP net worth.

Net-worth requirement reduced to 3 percent of liabilities; statutory reserve requirement reduced to 3 percent of insured accounts.

1983   California legislature passes the Nolan Bill (January 1, 1983), allowing state-chartered thrifts to broaden their investment activities.

Super NOW accounts introduced.

FHLBs may make FSLIC-insured advances to institutions without customary credit evaluations.

State savings banks that convert to federal savings institution charters may continue to exercise the powers they had under the state charter.

FHLBs may make advances for terms of up to twenty (was ten) years.

Minimum capital requirements raised, other restrictions imposed on institutions seeking FSLIC insurance.

1984   Secondary Mortgage Market Enhancement Act.

Federal associations may establish finance subsidiaries to issue securities for the parent institution.

Insured institutions must establish policies for the management of interest-rate risk in the institutions operations.

1985   Regulation raising minimum net-worth requirements.

Regulation limiting direct investments by state-chartered insured thrifts.

1986   Deposit Account Ceilings lifted.

Interest-rate ceilings removed.

---

costs. Furthermore, since the sale of assets whose market value was less than book value would force thrifts to realize an immediate loss, most thrifts were hesitant to restructure their portfolios even to improve their expected long-run viability. To encourage thrifts to restructure, the Bank Board passed a resolution in October 1981 altering regulatory accounting principles by allowing thrifts to amortize the losses on any assets sold over the remaining contractual life of the assets. Thus, thrifts were no longer forced to record an immediate capital loss at the time of sale but instead could spread the loss over a number of years.

This action on loss deferrals created a major divergence between RAP and GAAP measures of net worth. Just how big the difference has become is apparent in Table 2-4, which presents the components of the RAP-GAAP net-worth differential. The deferral of loan losses grew to over $6 billion in 1984. In 1981 qualifying mutual and income-capital certificates, essentially promissory notes from the FSLIC, were allowed to count as net worth. In 1982 appraised equity capital, an adjustment allowing institutions to book as net worth the excess of appraised value of their owned branches over book value, was provided by the Bank Board. At the same time, qualifying subordinated debentures were allowed to count as net worth. The total difference between RAP and GAAP net worth reached $9 billion by 1984.

By raising RAP net worth above what it would have been otherwise, the accounting changes lowered the number of thrift institutions that were technically insolvent and could be closed—liquidated or merged—by the Bank Board. The effect that the different accounting practices have on determining the number of financially weak thrifts are shown in Tables 2-5 and 2-6. As the tables show, only 251 institutions were insolvent according to RAP at the end of 1986, whereas 468 institutions were insolvent according to GAAP. Hence, the accounting change in 1981 substantially reduced the number of institutions considered to be insolvent for regulatory purposes and, therefore, candidates for closure by the FSLIC.

In addition to altering RAP accounting for income and net worth, the Bank Board also reduced the minimum net-worth requirement from 5 to 4 percent in 1980, and then to 3 percent in 1982. When an institution's net worth falls below the minimum net-worth requirement, the Bank Board has substantially increased authority over the institution's operation. Tables 2-5 and 2-6 show that forbearance in the form of reducing the net-worth requirement and relaxing the definition of RAP net worth did not halt the financial deterioration taking place in the industry. In 1984, based on RAP accounting, 877 institutions—representing about 31 percent of insured institutions' assets—were at or below the minimum net-worth requirement of 3 percent. Had the minimum net-worth requirement been 5 percent and based on GAAP accounting, 2,090 institutions—representing

Table 2-4. Historical Comparison for All FSLIC-Insured Institutions of Net Worth Defined by Regulatory Accounting Principles (RAP) and Generally Accepted Accounting Principles (GAAP) (in thousands of dollars).

Year	Items Included in RAP but not in GAAP Net Worth				Items Deducted (Added) when Computing GAAP but not RAP Net Worth	Total of All Previous Columns	Amount by Which RAP Net Worth Exceeds GAAP Net Worth
	Qualifying Mutual Capital Certificates	Income Capital and Net Worth Certificates[a]	Qualifying Subordinated Debentures	Appraised Equity Capital	Deferred Losses (Gains) on Assets Sold		Total Differential As Percentage of Total Assets
1980	0	0	0	0	5,784	5,784	0.001
1981	39,560	0	0	0	752,509	792,069	0.122
1982	59,626	472,260	225,624	674,515	3,637,990	5,070,023	0.739
1983	20,252	1,005,628	333,419	1,236,808	4,556,874	7,152,981	0.878
1984	109,794	191,997	1,046,798	1,472,701	6,375,050	9,196,340	0.941
1985	3,106	2,858,769	2,047,877	1,720,384	6,360,928	12,991,064	1.214
1986	5,533	2,236,729	3,398,003	2,197,732	5,548,512	13,386,509	1.149

a. In 1984, accounting procedures were changed to include income capital certificates in GAAP net worth, where previously they had been included in net worth only under RAP accounting. Hence, the 1984 figure for this category only reflects net-worth certificates.

Source: Author's calculations based on data from the Federal Home Loan Bank Board.

Table 2-5. Net Worth of Weakest Federally Insured Thrift Institutions Based on Regulatory Accounting Principles (RAP) (1980–1986).

Year	Number of Institutions NWTL ≤ 0	Assets of Institutions NWTL ≤ 0 (in thousands of dollars)	Percentage of Total Assets	Number of Institutions 0 < NWTL ≤ .03	Assets of Institutions 0 < NWTL ≤ .03 (in thousands of dollars)	Percentage of Total Assets
1980	17	127,001	0.02	280	35,123,008	5.82
1981	41	7,190,973	1.12	636	129,372,410	20.22
1982	80	13,056,846	1.90	791	190,865,575	27.81
1983	54	12,613,895	1.55	770	201,451,226	24.76
1984	71	12,048,402	1.23	806	294,541,283	30.11
1985	130	25,649,843	2.39	536	217,252,727	20.31
1986	251	66,699,700	5.73	346	144,348,369	12.39

Note: NWTL is the ratio of net worth (total assets minus total liabilities) to total liabilities. RAP net worth includes preferred stock; permanent, reserve, or guaranty stock; paid-in surplus; qualifying mutual capital certificates; income-capital/net-worth certificates; undivided profits (retained earnings); and net undistributed income; and, after December 1982, qualifying subordinated debentures, appraised equity capital and reserves.

Source: Author's calculations based on data from the Federal Home Loan Bank Board.

79 percent of insured institutions' assets—would have been at or below the requirement.

Due to two other regulatory provisions, the minimum RAP net-worth requirement may be even lower than 3 percent of total liabilities for some institutions. Until March 1985, when the Bank Board began phasing out the provisions, institutions could use techniques known as "five-year averaging" and "twenty-year phase-in" to lower their regulatory net-worth requirement. With five-year averaging, an institution could average its past fiscal year's liabilities with the preceding four fiscal years and thus reduce the denominator in calculating the ratio of its net worth to total liabilities. With twenty-year phase-in, institutions that had not reached their twentieth anniversary of insurance were permitted to calculate a lower minimum net-worth requirement by multiplying 3 percent of liabilities by a fraction, the numerator of which was the number of consecutive years of insurance, and the denominator of which was twenty. For example, an institution insured for only five years had a minimum net-worth requirement of only three-fourths of one percent [$(.03) \times (5/20) = 0.0075$].

Deterioration of the thrift industry's financial condition is reflected not only by the weakest thrift institutions, but also by the industry as a whole. As Table 2–7 shows, both RAP and GAAP net worth for the industry were 5.26 percent of assets in 1980 but declined to 3.80 and 2.86 percent, respectively, by 1984. Tangible net worth shows an even larger decline, to 0.41 percent in 1984 from 5.23 percent in 1980. Tangible net worth subtracts the value of such intangible assets as goodwill from GAAP net worth. Market-value net worth, however, improved significantly—due to declining interest rates beginning in late 1982—and continued to improve into 1985, as interest rates have continued to fall. The market-value calculation adjusts tangible net worth by marking to market the mortgage portfolio of the industry. Although the recent decline in interest rates represents a significant improvement over the early 1980s, the thrift industry still has negative market-value net worth.

Despite the deregulatory provisions of the Depository Institutions Deregulation and Monetary Control Act and the new Bank Board asset-loss amortization regulation, the financial position of the thrift industry continued to worsen. In response, Congress passed the Garn-St Germain Depository Institutions Act in October 1982. This act relaxed the quantitative restrictions on commercial real-estate

48   THRIFTS UNDER SIEGE

Table 2-6. Estimated Net Worth of Weakest Federally Insured Thrift Institutions Based on Generally Accepted Accounting Principles (GAAP) (*1980-1986*).

Year	Number of Institutions NWTL ≤0	Assets of Institutions NWTL ≤0 (in thousands of dollars)	Percentage of Total Assets	Number of Institutions 0 < NWTL ≤.03
1980	17	127,001	0.02	280
1981	65	17,303,469	2.70	653
1982	201	48,716,430	7.10	842
1983	287	78,906,404	9.70	883
1984	434	107,319,626	10.39	856
1985	466	129,767,978	12.13	673
1986	468	126,241,537	10.83	515

Note: NWTL is the ratio of net worth (total assets minus total liabilities) to total liabilities. GAAP assets include: preferred stock; permanent, reserve, or guaranty stock; paid-in surplus, reserves; undivided profits (retained earnings); and net undistributed income. Liabilities include: deferred net losses (gains) on loans sold (estimated for periods prior to March 1984); deferred net losses (gains) on other assets sold. The data were not collected by the Board until March 1984 and do not include all data needed to calculate GAAP net worth.

Source: Author's calculations based on data from the Federal Home Loan Bank Board.

lending and on the combined holdings of consumer loans, commercial paper, and debt securities from the 20 percent of assets required under the 1980 act to 40 percent. In addition, thrifts could make commercial loans up to a 10-percent limit. Finally, the 1982 act allowed thrifts to invest in the time and savings deposits of other thrifts and to offer a money-market deposit account.

Simultaneously, some state regulators granted state-chartered, federally insured institutions powers far greater than those of federally chartered institutions. Most notably, in 1983 California substantially removed asset restrictions for state-chartered institutions. This action was preceded by similar actions in Florida and Texas that expanded state-chartered thrifts' investment powers in 1980 and 1972, respectively. By the end of 1984 more than one-third of the states had granted state-chartered thrifts investment powers beyond those of federally chartered institutions. These expanded powers enabled

Table 2-6. continued

Assets of Institutions $0 < NWTL \leq .03$ (in thousands of dollars)	Percentage of Total Assets	Number of Institutions $0 < NWTL \leq .05$	Assets of Institutions $0 < NWTL \leq .05$ (in thousands of dollars)	Percentage of Total Assets
35,123,008	5.82	1,357	241,083,868	39.9
126,666,356	19.80	1,834	379,804,220	59.4
204,252,098	29.77	1,824	504,221,332	73.5
242,667,975	29.82	1,770	555,963,440	68.3
350,360,796	34.54	1,656	675,539,320	69.1
270,100,000	25.24	n/a	n/a	n/a
255,100,000	21.90	n/a	n/a	n/a

thrifts to invest in assets heretofore severely restricted or prohibited, such as direct investment in commercial real estate.

THE INUNDATION OF THE FSLIC

Despite declining interest rates, greater diversification powers, the phasing-out of deposit-rate ceilings, adjustable-rate mortgages, and accounting modifications, the FSLIC confronted a record number of financially distressed thrifts in 1982. In the thrift industry, the decision about when to close a distressed institution is regulatory rather than determined solely by market forces. This fact is reflected in Figure 2-1 by the widening gap between the number of closed and insolvent thrifts. Four factors explain this phenomenon: 1) the FSLIC's closure rule; 2) the procedures and limited reserves of the FSLIC; 3) the limited number of employees available to handle the distressed institutions; and 4) the declining economic incentive for financial institutions to acquire distressed thrifts.

If thrifts could be closed at the exact moment their market-value net worth became zero, the FSLIC would incur only administrative costs. Such timing is difficult, however, because examinations occur

Table 2-7. Total Net Worth of Federally Insured Thrift Institutions
(*1936-1986*).

Year	RAP Net Worth as a Percentage of Total Assets	GAAP Net Worth as a Percentage of Total Assets[a]	Tangible Net Worth as a Percentage of Total Assets	Market-Value Net Worth as a Percentage of Total Assets
1936	6.09	—	n/a	n/a
1940	6.56	—	n/a	n/a
1950	7.19	—	n/a	n/a
1960	7.02	—	n/a	n/a
1970	6.98	—	n/a	n/a
1980	5.26	5.26	5.23	-12.47
1981	4.27	4.15	3.91	-17.32
1982	3.69	2.95	0.54	-12.03
1983	4.02	3.14	0.47	- 5.64
1984	3.80	2.86	0.41	- 2.74
1985	4.36	3.15	0.81	n/a
1986	4.56	3.41	1.33	n/a

Note: Tangible net worth is equal to GAAP net worth less goodwill and other intangible assets. The market value is based on yearly averages of estimated portfolio yields and market interest rates. Market-value net worth in this table adjusts tangible net worth by marking to market value the mortgage loan portfolio of the institutions. The present-value calculation for a given asset is:

$$PV = \sum_{j=1}^{m} \frac{\frac{A\,(i/12)}{1 - (1 + i/12)^{-n}}}{(1 + r/12)^{j}} + A\,\frac{1 - (1 + i/12)^{m-n}}{\frac{1 - (1 + i/12)^{-n}}{(1 + r/12)^{-m}}}$$

where A = the book value of the mortgages,
i = coupon rate on the mortgages,
r = current market rate for mortgages,
n = months to maturity by contract,
m = months to prepayment, and
PV = market value of the mortgages.

The first term on the right side of the equation is the present discounted value of the monthly cash flow of scheduled payments. The second term is the present value of the lump-sum prepayment of outstanding principal at the end of m months.

In this calculation, the number of months to prepayment is assumed to be 12 years, based on historical rates of prepayment. The calculation does not include an adjustment for credit risk or "charter value," which became increasingly important in 1985 and 1986.

The author thanks Don Edwards of the FHLBB for his help in making the market-value calculations based on a revision of a method developed by Edward Kane.

a. Through 1980 RAP and GAAP net worth were virtually identical.

Source: Author's calculations based on data from the Federal Home Loan Bank Board.

at uneven intervals, sometimes exceeding a year, and financial reports are filed only quarterly and primarily report the book value, not market value of assets. Changes in economic events, or non-economic events like fraud, can undermine an institution's financial position between examinations or reports. Furthermore, even examination and analysis of reports may fail to uncover problems, especially when the reported accounting measures of net worth are permitted to vary widely from market measures. Because book-value accounting can be designed, as RAP accounting is today, to cover up problems, financial reports can even provide forbearance for troubled institutions.

When the Bank Board does close an institution, the FSLIC often bears a cost, resulting from either the need to cover insured desposits exceeding the liquidation value of a failed institution's assets or the need to provide financial assistance in the case of a supervisory-arranged merger with another institution. Until recently, the FSLIC's reserves were increasing despite occasional thrift failures. But the accumulation of failures has changed this situation. In 1984, for the first time in recent years, the fund actually declined.

As Table 2–8 shows, the FSLIC's reserves fell from nearly $6.5 billion in 1980 to $4.6 billion in 1985—about $1.9 billion in all. Since total industry assets were rising during this period, the ratio of the FSLIC's reserves to the size of the industry fell even farther, reaching 0.57 percent of total assets in 1984. Despite additional quarterly assessments in 1985 of 1/32 of 1 percent of deposits that generated approximately $1 billion, the fund continued to decline in 1985. Furthermore, due to the ongoing increase in assets of insured institutions, the ratio of funds to these assets dropped further to 0.43 percent in 1985. In early 1987, when the General Accounting Office (GAO) declared the FSLIC insolvent, the fund had a negative reserve balance of just over $6 billion. These figures underscore just how few financial resources have been directly available to the FSLIC to deal with financially troubled thrifts.

The FSLIC estimated the cost to dispose of the assets of the 462 institutions that were GAAP-insolvent in 1985 at $16.4 billion, an increase from the $15.8 billion in 1984.[8] The FSLIC's estimates for 1985 excluded the twenty-five institutions with $17.7 billion in assets that constituted the Management Consignment Program (MCP) caseload. (These are institutions over which the Bank Board has taken control, delegating management to new managers and boards

Table 2-8. Profile of the Thrift Industry and Its Insurer (1980-1986).

Year	Number of Insured Institutions	Assets of Insured Institutions (in billions of dollars)	FSLIC Primary and Secondary Reserves (in millions of dollars)	FSLIC Reserves as a Percentage of Total Assets	RAP Net Worth as a Percentage of Total Assets	GAAP Net Worth as a Percentage of Total Assets
1980	4,002	618	6,462	1.04	5.26	5.26
1981	3,779	651	6,302	0.97	4.27	4.15
1982	3,343	693	6,331	0.91	3.69	2.95
1983	3,040	819	6,425	0.78	4.02	3.14
1984	3,167	979	5,606	0.57	3.80	2.86
1985	3,246	1,070	4,557	0.43	4.36	3.15
1986	3,220	1,165	-6,333	-0.54	4.56	3.41

Note: Using generally accepted accounting principles, the U.S. General Accounting Office (GAO), which is specified by the law as the FSLIC's auditors, found the FSLIC to be insolvent as of December 31, 1986. This opinion, issued in May 1987, resulted in the Secondary Reserve being extinguished. Since the Secondary Reserve is carried on the books of thrift institutions as an asset, the effect was a decline in the industry's net worth by approximately $800 million.

Source: Author's calculations based on data from the Federal Home Loan Bank Board.

of directors.) If these institutions had been included, the FSLIC's cost estimates would likely have risen. Given estimated costs of $25 billion or more at the end of 1986, it is no surprise that the FSLIC moved slowly in closing insolvent institutions and that the Bank Board was proposing legislation to recapitalize the FSLIC.

The limited financial resources of the FSLIC are only a partial explanation for the widening gap between the number of failed and insolvent thrift institutions. There is also a limited staff available to deal with the unprecedented number of troubled institutions. In 1980 there were 34 FSLIC employees to handle 297 troubled institutions. By 1985, the FSLIC staff had grown to 159 (over half of whom had only two years of experience), but the number of troubled institutions had risen to 655. Over the same period, the number of field examiners declined. In 1980 there were 700 examiners to handle 297 troubled institutions. By 1985, the number of examiners had decreased to 679, while the number of troubled institutions had increased to 791. Thus, even if the FSLIC's reserves had been adequate, the limited number of personnel and their relative inexperience would have made it difficult to address the growing problem of insolvent institutions in a timely manner.[9]

Finally, the FSLIC must choose the least costly way to resolve an insolvent thrift institution. In most cases, a merger results. Since the establishment of the FSLIC in 1934 through 1986, there have been fewer than sixty liquidations. Arranging a merger in recent years has become more difficult, however, due to the advent of nonbank banks that may expand geographically without mergers. To the extent that geographical expansion is more accessible without mergers, the FSLIC must devote more time to arrange a merger. This can lengthen the time between an institution's insolvency and its closure, which potentially results in a higher cost to the FSLIC.

As Table 2-9 shows, in the 1980s the cost to the FSLIC of liquidating problem institutions was significantly greater than that of arranging an alternative solution, such as a merger. Despite this, there were seventeen liquidations from 1980 through 1984. Regardless of the method chosen for dealing with problem institutions, the resolution cost as a percent of assets of the failed institutions rose sharply in 1984 and jumped again in 1986.

Furthermore, Table 2-10 shows that FSLIC's vulnerability to sudden movements in uninsured funds has increased since 1980. The $20 billion in uninsured deposits in 1980 represented 3.2 percent of

Table 2-9. Thrift-Institution Failure Costs (*1980–1986*).

Year	Cost if Liquidated (in millions of dollars)[a]	Actual Cost of Resolution (in millions of dollars)[a]	Ratio of Actual Resolution to Liquidation Cost	Actual Resolution Cost as a Percentage of Total Assets of Failures Involving FSLIC Assistance
1980	277	166	0.60	11.4
1981	3,721	1,018	0.27	7.3
1982	6,983	1,213	0.17	4.2
1983	3,522	993	0.28	6.0
1984	1,527	850	0.56	14.7
1985	1,508	946	0.63	14.5
1986	n/a	3,239	n/a	23.5

a. The liquidation cost and actual resolution cost are present-value estimates that are calculated by the FSLIC to determine how to resolve each case. In the case of mergers, the costs represent an agreed-upon figure between the FSLIC and the institution acquiring the failed thrift, and thus to this degree represents a market-determined figure. In cases where liquidation is less expensive than an alternative solution, the liquidation cost appears in the second column as well as the first column. With exception of the Management Consignment Program cases that are excluded due to unavailability of data, these cost figures correspond to the failures involving FSLIC assistance reported in Table 2-2.

Source: Author's calculations based on data from the Federal Home Loan Bank Board.

total industry assets. By 1984, that figure had grown to $61 billion, representing 6.2 percent of total assets. Uninsured deposits are a portion of large certificates of deposit referred to as Jumbo CDs, which also currently have an insured portion of $100,000. When depositors withdraw uninsured deposits, they also tend to withdraw the insured portion of the Jumbo CDs. As Table 2-10 shows, in 1986 Jumbo CDs in the thrift industry exceeded $116 billion, or 10 percent of the industry's total assets (TA). A significant withdrawal of Jumbo CDs could cause an industrywide drain on liquidity.

Table 2-10 also indicates that a substantial portion of industry deposits are in broker-originated deposits. Broker-originated deposits tend to be garnered in insured denominations but are usually more mobile than other insured deposits because they are made primarily by institutional investors who constantly evaluate their positions. The level of broker-originated funds was about $44 billion in 1986, or 3.8 percent of total industry assets. For the industry, the combined percentage of assets represented by Jumbo CDs and

Table 2-10. Magnitude of Uninsured Deposits, Broker-Originated Deposits (BOD), and Jumbo CDs (JCD) in FSLIC-Insured Institutions (1980–1986).

Year	Uninsured Deposits in Insured Institutions (in millions of dollars)	Ratio of Uninsured to Total Deposits	BOD (in thousands of dollars)	BOD/TA (percentage)	JCD (in thousands of dollars)	JCD/TA (percentage)	BOD + JCD (in thousands of dollars)	(BOD + JCD)/TA (percentage)
1980	20,126	3.2	3,860,867	0.6	39,667,320	6.6	43,528,187	7.2
1981	21,837	3.3	3,251,658	0.5	47,483,749	7.4	50,735,407	7.9
1982	26,342	3.8	8,134,000	1.2	55,501,790	8.1	63,635,790	9.3
1983	44,961	5.5	29,711,673	3.7	80,051,685	9.8	109,763,358	13.5
1984	61,208	6.2	42,987,890	4.4	113,480,890	11.6	156,468,780	16.1
1985	64,142	6.0	40,987,204	3.8	108,520,519	10.1	149,507,723	13.9
1986	66,770	5.7	44,101,885	3.8	116,619,710	10.0	160,721,595	13.8

Note: Maximum insurance coverage was as follows for the indicated dates: 1934–49, $5,000; 1950–65, $10,000; 1966–68, $15,000; 1969–73, $20,000; 1974–79, $100,000 for government accounts, $40,000 for all other accounts; 1980–86, $100,000.

Source: Author's calculations based on data from the Federal Home Loan Bank Board.

broker-originated funds is 13.8 percent. In the Eleventh Federal Home Loan Bank District, which includes California, Jumbo CDs and broker-originated deposits represent nearly one-third of total assets.

TRANSITION TO PART TWO OF THE MODERN THRIFT CRISIS

Part one of the modern thrift crisis began in 1980 with an unexpected increase in interest rates. It began to abate with an equally sudden decline in interest rates in 1982, as demonstrated in Figure 2–1 by the decrease in thrifts cost of funds. By late 1982 the average return on mortgages exceeded thrifts' average cost of funds. Almost simultaneously, the rates paid by money-market mutual funds dropped, and by 1982 thrifts were paying depositors rates exceeding money-market funds.

Although these events were a godsend for most thrift institutions, the regulatory damage-control mechanism was thoroughly strained. The FSLIC fund was inundated by record failures and was performing triage on a record number of insolvent but open institutions. Inadequate numbers of FSLIC staff, many of whom lacked experience, were overwhelmed, further burdened with monitoring institutions enabled to use new asset and liability powers to cope with lower earnings and greater competition. Growing amounts of "hot money"—brokered deposits and growing jumbo deposits—complicated events. Finally, by 1982 misgivings began to develop about the regulatory forbearance embodied in reduced net-worth requirements, accounting techniques used to maximize short-run income and regulatory net worth, and failure to close GAAP-insolvent institutions. Would this forbearance, some asked, lead to new problems? The answer, as Chapter 3 develops, is "yes."

NOTES

1. For other discussions of many of these same issues, see James R. Barth, R. Dan Brumbaugh, Jr., Daniel Sauerhaft, and George H. K. Wang, "Insolvency and Risk-Taking in the Thrift Industry: Implications for the Future," *Contemporary Policy Issues* (Fall 1985): 1–32; *Idem.*, "Thrift Institution Failures: Causes and Policy Issues" (proceedings of a confer-

ence on bank structure and competition, Federal Reserve Bank of Chicago, 1985), pp. 184–216; James R. Barth, Donald J. Bisenius, R. Dan Brumbaugh, Jr., and Daniel Sauerhaft, "The Thrift Industry's Rough Road Ahead," *Challenge* (September/October 1986): 38–43; Edward J. Kane, *The Gathering Crisis in Federal Deposit Insurance* (Cambridge, Mass.: MIT Press, 1985); Frederick E. Balderston, *Thrifts in Crisis: Structural Transformation of the Federal Savings and Loan Industry* (Cambridge, Mass.: Ballinger Publishing, 1985); John J. Merrick, Jr. and Anthony Saunders, "Bank Regulation and Monetary Policy," *Journal of Money, Credit, and Banking* part 2 (November 1985): 691–717; Paul M. Horvitz, "The Case against Risk-Related Deposit Insurance Premiums," *Housing Finance Review* (July 1983): 253–64; and *Idem.*, "Deposit Insurance after Deregulation: A Residual Role for Regulation" (paper presented at the Ninth Annual Conference of the Federal Home Loan Bank of San Francisco, December 1983); Stuart I. Greenbaum, "Reform of the Thrift Industry" (Banking Research Center working paper no. 123, March 1985); Andrew S. Carron, *The Plight of the Thrift Institutions* (Washington, D.C.: Brookings Institution, 1982); and *Idem.*, *The Rescue of the Thrift Industry* (Washington, D.C.: Brookings Institution, 1983).

2. Jane Bryant Quinn, "Staying Ahead: Keeping a Close Eye on Your Savings and Loan," *San Francisco Chronicle*, April 17, 1987, p. 38.

3. For the first published estimate of the cost of $15.8 billion, see Barth, Brumbaugh, Sauerhaft, and Wang, "Insolvency and Risk-Taking in the Thrift Industry."

4. For studies of the implications of deposit insurance and contemporary bank and thrift failures—primarily of large institutions—see George G. Kaufman, "Implications of Large Bank Problems and Insolvencies for the Banking System and Economic Policy," *Issues in Bank Regulation* (Winter 1985): 35–42; and *Idem.*, "The Truth About Bank Runs," in *The Financial Services Revolution: Policy Directions for the Future*, ed. Catherine England and Thomas F. Huertas (Norwell, Massachusetts: Klurver Academic Publishers, 1988), pp. 9–40. For a more general discussion of the role of the lender of last resort in dealing with financial crises, see James R. Barth and Robert E. Keleher, "Financial Crises and the Role of the Lender of Last Resort," *Economic Review* (Federal Reserve Bank of Atlanta) (January 1984): 58–67.

5. More detailed descriptions of this phenomenon, especially in the context of current difficulties faced by thrift institutions, appear in R. Dan Brumbaugh, Jr. and Eric I. Hemel, "Federal Deposit Insurance as a Call Option: Implications for Depository Institution and Insurer Behavior" (research working paper no. 116, Federal Home Loan Bank Board, Office of Policy and Economic Research, Washington, D.C., October 1984). Also see John H. Kareken, "Deposit Insurance Reform or Deregulation is the Cart, Not

the Horse," *Quarterly Review* (Federal Reserve Bank of Minneapolis) (Spring 1983): 1–9; *Idem.*, "The First Step in Bank Deregulation: What about the FDIC?" *American Economic Review* (May 1983): 198–203; Stephen A. Buser, Andrew H. Chen, and Edward J. Kane, "Federal Deposit Insurance, Regulatory Policy, and Optimal Bank Capital," *Journal of Finance* (March 1981): 51–60; Eugenie D. Short and Gerald P. O'Driscoll, "Deregulation and Deposit Insurance," *Economic Review* (Federal Reserve Bank of Dallas) (September 1983): 11–22; Robert T. Clair, "Deposit Insurance, Moral Hazard, and Credit Unions," *Economic Review* (Federal Reserve Bank of Dallas) (July 1984): 1–12; George J. Benston, "Financial Disclosure and Bank Failure," *Economic Review* (Federal Reserve Bank of Atlanta) (March 1984): 5–12; Larry D. Wall, "The Future of Deposit Insurance: An Analysis of the Insuring Agencies' Proposals," *Economic Review* (Federal Reserve Bank of Atlanta) (March 1984): 26–39; William R. Keeton, "Deposit Insurance and the Deregulation of Deposit Rates," *Economic Review* (Federal Reserve Bank of Kansas City) (April 1984): 28–46; and Mark J. Flannery and Aris A. Protopapadakis, "Risk-Sensitive Deposit Insurance Premia: Some Practical Issues," *Business Review* (Federal Reserve Bank of Philadelphia) (September/October 1984): 3–10.

6. For a discussion of the increasing competition in the financial-services industry, see Harvey Rosenblum, Diane Siegal, and Christine Pavel, "Banks and Nonbanks: A Run for the Money," *Economic Perspectives* (Federal Reserve Banks of Chicago) (May/June 1983): 3–12.

7. More detailed historical data beginning in 1934 on thrift institution failures, the FSLIC's condition and losses, and selected commercial bank data are provided in Barth, Brumbaugh, Sauerhaft, and Wang, "Insolvency and Risk-Taking in the Thrift Industry."

8. See Barth, Brumbaugh, Sauerhaft, and Wang, "Insolvency and Risk-Taking in the Thrift Industry."

9. Lack of sufficient staff may also have affected enforcement actions, as the following table shows:

| | | Enforcement Actions | | | Number of Investigations Completed by Office of Enforcement | |
Calendar Year	Cease and Desist Orders	Number of Individuals Removed or Prohibited	Supervisory Agreements	Consent Merger Resolutions	Formal	Informal
1980	3	1	1	6	6	10
1981	8	2	0	33	8	6
1982	13	6	5	49	10	10
1983	17	21	39	22	17	15
1984	13	22	116	38	24	20
1985	28	22	233	65	30	22

Source: Based on data from the Federal Home Loan Bank Board.

3 THE MODERN THRIFT CRISIS (PART TWO)
Gambling for Resurrection

NOT ALL INSOLVENT THRIFTS ARE CLOSED

Macroeconomic factors leading to unexpectedly high interest rates were responsible for the initial financial distress of thrift institutions in the early 1980s. This part of the modern thrift crisis is well understood because of the traditional danger in the thrift industry of borrowing short at flexible rates and lending long at fixed rates without adequate hedging. Less well understood is that the continuing distress in the industry despite a sharp decline in interest rates after 1982 is due to increased risk-taking, primarily by insolvent institutions. Mainly because of the depleted resources of the FSLIC, several hundred insolvent institutions remain open. These institutions, paying a flat-rate insurance premium regardless of the risks they take and garnering funds largely from insured depositors who have no incentive to monitor the risks, have been gambling for resurrection.[1] Sometimes this gambling includes fraud.[2] For most of the insolvent institutions, the gambling is not paying off.

In December 1987 Bank Board officials announced that the number of thrifts with RAP net worth less than or equal to zero rose to 340, up 36.0 percent from the year-end 1986 level of 251 reported in Table 2-5. These institutions had approximately $90 billion in assets compared to $67 billion in assets in RAP-insolvent institutions in 1986. They had a negative $15 billion in RAP net worth. The number of GAAP-insolvent thrifts rose to approximately 500, up 7.0 percent from 468 in 1986. The significant relative growth of RAP-insolvent thrifts in 1987 indicates an escalating decline in the performance of thrifts in the worst condition, a trend that Table 3–1 shows has existed for several years.

Table 3–1 provides data on the institutions in the worst condition, for whom the incentive to gamble for resurrection is the greatest. As the table shows, at year-end 1986, out of a total of 468 GAAP-insolvent institutions, 341 were earning negative net income. As Table 2–1 demonstrates, net income for all thrifts was positive from 1982 through 1986. However, the positive 1986 net income for the industry as a whole was achieved despite the GAAP-insolvent institutions' negative net income of $3.0 billion in that year.

In December 1987 Bank Board officials also announced that for the first nine months of the year thrifts had negative income of $3.0 billion. In the third quarter of 1987, the thrifts negative income was $1.6 billion, $1.3 billion of which was due to losses in thirty-nine thrifts in Texas. In total, 2,244 thrifts earned $1.5 billion and 934 thrifts lost $3.1 billion. The 1987 income report and Table 3–1 income data suggest that a dichotomy exists in the thrift industry, with one relatively large class of solvent institutions earning profits and another class of insolvent institutions suffering substantial losses. Forty-eight percent of the losses accounted for by 4.2 percent of the firms reporting negative income in the third quarter of 1987 also suggests that losses may be highly concentrated in a few thrifts.

Table 3–1 also indicates that the condition of insolvent institutions with negative income has been deteriorating. In each quarter from the first quarter of 1984 through 1986, the negative net income of these institutions has declined, falling from negative $147 million to negative $3.0 billion in fourth quarter 1986. The rate of decline escalated dramatically between fourth quarter 1985 and second quarter 1986, when the negative net income of GAAP-insolvent institutions nearly doubled. It then nearly doubled again from the third to fourth quarter of 1986. Reflecting this decline, the institutions' GAAP net worth has also fallen from negative $1.9 billion in first quarter 1984 to negative $10.1 billion in fourth quarter 1986.

The drop in income occurred during the precipitous fall in interest rates through 1986, which was accompanied by an overall increase in income for the thrift industry from the greater value of its mortgage portfolio. This suggests that the 341 GAAP-insolvent institu-

Table 3-1. Data on FSLIC-Insured Thrift Institutions with GAAP Net Worth Less than Zero and Net Income Less than Zero.

	1984		1985				1986			
	I	III	I	II	III	IV	I	II	III	IV
Number of institutions	223	225	268	210	235	245	261	275	301	341
Assets (billions of dollars)	50	56	62	51	55	67	61	67	73	93
Total RAP net worth (millions of dollars)	564	441	147	-46	-496	-465	-1,430	-3,009	-4,362	-6,978
Total GAAP net worth (millions of dollars)	-1,853	-1,967	-2,336	-1,736	-2,390	-3,804	-4,627	-6,179	-7,146	-10,068
Net income (millions of dollars)	-147	-212	-231	-413	-494	-859	-699	-1,527	-1,541	-3,016

Source: Author's calculations based on data from the Federal Home Loan Bank Board.

tions with negative net incomes absorbed losses in the value of their nonmortgage assets. The decline reflects failed risk-taking interacting with unexpected regional deflation in real-estate values and national resources, primarily oil and timber. The deflation worsened an already bad situation.

The decline in profitability from 1984 to 1986 narrowed the difference between RAP and GAAP net worth. Based on the data in Table 3–1, RAP net worth exceeded GAAP net worth by 130 percent at the GAAP-insolvent institutions earning negative net income at the beginning of 1984. By the third quarter of 1986, the gap had narrowed by 91 percent. Apparently, the RAP accounting changes broadly designed to diminish the effect of the declining value of mortgage assets on thrift balance sheets did not minimize the effect of losses from nonmortgage sources as thoroughly.

The remaining large difference between RAP and GAAP net worth at these institutions represents one of the ironies of the thrift-industry crisis. As Table 2–4 indicates, the major component differentiating RAP from GAAP net worth is the deferral of losses on assets sold, which was adopted in 1981 to encourage institutions to sell assets, primarily mortgages, whose market values had fallen due to the increased interest rates. The underlying principle was that, if institutions concluded that it made good economic sense to sell underwater assets, they should not be discouraged from doing so by accounting rules. By 1985 the industrywide RAP and GAAP net-worth levels were $46.9 billion and $36.3 billion, respectively; RAP net worth now exceeded GAAP net worth by approximately 30 percent. For the institutions in Table 3–1, the difference at year-end 1985 was approximately 80 percent, despite the narrowing of the two measures. This implies that the GAAP-insolvent institutions exercised the deferral option more frequently than did the industry as a whole. With the fall in interest rates that began in 1982, these institutions would have been better off going into 1986 had they not taken advantage of the deferred-loss provision. Hindsight reveals that the very accounting tolerance that was intended to boost the economic position of thrifts in fact encouraged behavior that damaged them further.

The number of insolvencies would be even greater if assets and liabilities were based upon market rather than book values. Some may argue that the large number of GAAP-insolvent institutions does not actually pose a threat to the FSLIC fund, since some of these institutions might be solvent in market-value terms. For this argument to hold, however, the market value of a GAAP-insolvent institution's assets would have to exceed their book value by at least the absolute value of the institution's GAAP net worth. The current performance of these institutions, however, suggests that they are market-value insolvent. In 1986 net income for all 460 GAAP-insolvent institutions was negative $2.6 billion; in contrast, the net income for all institutions was approximately $1.2 billion. Moreover, it is unlikely that the GAAP-insolvent institutions have been immune to the asset-quality problems faced by the institutions that constitute the FSLIC caseload.

Regardless of why institutions are insolvent, their opportunities to gamble have grown with deregulation. Deregulation of interest rates and other regulatory and legislative changes were generally viewed as necessary to avoid industrywide insolvencies caused by disintermediation and to allow solvent thrift institutions to adjust to the high and volatile interest rates of the early 1980s through greater portfolio diversification. Without the deregulation of interest rates, much more of the thrift industry would have perished in the early 1980s, and the losses to the FSLIC would have been far greater than those experienced then and anticipated now. Without opportunities for portfolio diversification, moreover, thrifts would have been hampered in reducing their interest-rate risk exposure, although variable-rate mortgages and hedging practices were introduced as other ways to reduce risk. By 1982, however, the number of insolvent institutions was growing, and the wider powers provided by deregulation created numerous opportunities for increased risk-taking by the insolvent institutions.

The existence of insolvent thrift institutions open and operating under the direction of the owners and managers who were in charge at the time of insolvency has greatly complicated the issue of the appropriate level of regulation. Deregulated interest rates allowed insolvent institutions to bid for deposits to fund high-risk assets in the hope of earning their way back to solvency. These wider portfolio options also encouraged insolvent thrifts to take high risks in areas more difficult for examiners to monitor and control than more traditional lending activities. Opportunities for misconduct and fraud also proliferated.

It is reasonable to conclude that any institution with negative GAAP net worth in 1986 that was also earning negative net income had little or no hope of regaining even book-value solvency. For the remaining GAAP-insolvent institutions, the hope is greater but still negligible, considering that from 1982 to 1987 such institutions had been operating with increasingly favorable interest rates. Furthermore, as Table 2-6 shows, there were at least 515 more institutions operating close to GAAP insolvency at year-end 1986. That the number of insolvencies has grown while the number of failures has decreased is one of several pieces of information indicating that the Bank Board and the FSLIC are overwhelmed and unable or unwilling to close all insolvent institutions. This and other indications of the Bank Board's inability or unwillingness to monitor and supervise insolvent institutions have created strong incentives to take excessive risks.

THE PERVERSE INCENTIVES CREATED BY INSOLVENCY AND AUGMENTED BY AN OVERWHELMED INSURER

To understand the second part of the modern thrift crisis, it is helpful to refer back to Figure 2-1. As that figure shows, the peak failure year since 1980 was 1982, when 252 thrifts failed. Since then, the number of failures has sharply declined. One cannot be too sanguine about this decline because, as Figure 2-1 also shows, there has been a large and growing number of operating insolvent institutions since 1982. From 287 such institutions in 1982, the number has grown fairly steadily to 468 in December 1986 and approximately 500 in December 1987, a year in which only 48 thrifts were closed.

The behavior of interest rates after 1982 cannot explain the deterioration of the condition of these institutions because, as Figure 2-1 demonstrates, money-market yields fell below the average cost of funds for thrifts. At the same time, the return on mortgages rose above thrifts' cost of funds. Thus, on average, thrifts no longer faced the problem of disintermediation and could earn profits on their mortgage portfolios. Why then did the troubles of the thrift industry continue?

The situation can be explained by the risk-taking incentives for the large number of insolvent and nearly insolvent institutions that were open and operating after 1982. In Figure 2-1, we see that even though 252 institutions were closed in 1982, another 201 were left open. In 1982 another 842 institutions had net worth greater than zero but less than or equal to 3 percent. Many of these institutions were on the brink of insolvency.

The growing level of insolvency among FSLIC-insured institutions promoted greater risk-taking. Financial gains accrue primarily to owners and managers if an insolvent institution takes a significant risk that succeeds, while the deposit insurer bears most of the cost if the risk fails. Deposit insurance thus fosters a "heads, I win; tails, the FSLIC loses" attitude in insolvent institutions that are allowed to continue operating. These perverse effects of deposit insurance also apply to depository institutions that are likely to become insolvent. Increased risk-taking offers possible improvement and resurrection in a relatively short period of time for the owners and managers of such institutions.

Since 1980 the incentive for insolvent and nearly insolvent institutions to take greater risks likely increased because FSLIC-insured institutions realized that only a few of the more conspicuous outliers among insolvent institutions would be closed by the Bank Board, given the FSLIC's available reserves and the inadequate supervision and monitoring rules in place to close institutions in a timely, and thereby relatively low-cost, manner. This situation was almost certainly unavoidable as early as 1981, when the FSLIC failed to respond to the abrupt and staggeringly large increase in insolvent and nearly insolvent institutions with any corresponding supplement to the FSLIC fund or change in the supervision and monitoring rules.

Between 1980 and 1981, the assets of institutions with GAAP net worth less than or equal to 3 percent rose by $109 billion, and the FSLIC fund fell slightly from $6.46 billion to $6.30 billion. The ratio of FSLIC reserves to the assets of FSLIC-insured institutions with GAAP net worth less than or equal to 3 percent dropped steadily from 18.3 percent in 1980 to 1.3 percent in 1984 and rose only slightly in 1985, to 1.6 percent. If even a small fraction of insolvent institutions had been closed between 1981 and 1985, the FSLIC would itself have been declared insolvent earlier than year-end 1986. For insolvent and nearly insolvent institutions that were aware of this, the incentive to take additional risks may have been enormous.

The impression that the Bank Board could close only the weakest institutions has been strengthened by data on the FSLIC's reserves and outlays and the costs that it was willing to incur from 1980 through 1985. The FSLIC's reserves were almost constant from 1980 through 1983; however, FSLIC reserves as a percent of assets in GAAP insolvent institutions declined from 5,088 percent in 1980 to 4 percent in 1985. The relatively constant reserve fund and coverage ratios were maintained by substantially reducing the present-value cost of new FSLIC cases after 1982 and until 1986, even though the number of insolvent institutions was growing.

The estimated present-value cost of new assistance cases that is charged against the FSLIC is the best measure of the burden the FSLIC takes on in a year. These assistance cases stretch out over five to ten years, so the present-value costs are FSLIC estimates. Unexpected changes in interest rates and in the disposal value of assets can significantly affect the actual cost. It took $167 million to resolve eleven problem cases in 1980. These costs increased sharply the following year, when the FSLIC committed itself to an estimated $1 billion to resolve twenty-eight problem cases. The second most costly year thus far in the FSLIC's history was 1982, when resolving seventy-seven problem cases cost an estimated $1.2 billion in present-value terms. The cost of new FSLIC-assisted cases declined to just under $1 billion in 1983, remained relatively stable through 1985, and then ballooned to $3.2 billion in 1986. As these numbers became public, the rapidly growing number of insolvent and nearly insolvent institutions may have inferred that the FSLIC's policy had been to manage costs in order to keep the FSLIC reserve fund relatively constant. By 1984, when both the reserve fund and the coverage ratio dropped sharply, it became apparent that the FSLIC could no longer maintain the level of reserves or coverage even by closing fewer institutions that year.

Moreover, as discussed in Chapter 2, RAP net worth began to deviate from GAAP net worth in 1981. Due to the accounting redefinition, the difference between the number of institutions insolvent by RAP accounting and the number of those insolvent by GAAP accounting grew steadily from 24 in 1981 to 363 in 1984. The altered RAP net-worth calculation was another strong indication that the Bank Board and the FSLIC were pursuing a closure rule under which not all insolvent institutions would be closed. Furthermore, the Congress took no action to provide the funds necessary to close all insolvent thrifts nor did it question the practice of deferring timely closure in order to minimize insolvency costs.

The limited financial resources of the FSLIC explain only partially the widening gap between the number of failed and the number of insolvent thrift institutions. As noted in Chapter 2, the FSLIC staff grew more and more inadequate to deal with the increasing number of insolvent institutions. From 1980 to 1985 the ratio of FSLIC employees to insolvent thrifts barely kept pace with the demand for their services, rising from two to just under three employees per insolvent thrift, while the number of examiners per troubled institution fell 50 percent during the same period. By 1984 the turnover rate for field examiners had risen to over 16 percent a year—60 percent higher than the 1981 rate. Due to high rates of attrition among examiners, moreover, the number of relatively inexperienced examiners rose dramatically. Of course, requests for additional staff and congressional response to the situation were lagging rather than coincident indicators of the developing problem.

As Chapter 2 also outlined, geographical expansion is now more accessible without merger, reducing the pool of bidders for insolvent institutions, and mergers have become more difficult to arrange. This can lengthen the time between an institution's insolvency and its closure, resulting in a higher cost to the FSLIC.

In 1984 the FSLIC reported that approximately 80 percent of its cases reflected deteriorated asset quality rather than the effect of high interest rates on the value of existing mortgage loans. The FSLIC further said that asset-quality problems accounted for approximately 20 percent of its caseload between 1980 and 1984. This shift from primarily interest-rate problems to asset-quality problems also contributed to the increase in FSLIC costs. Greater costs are associated with poorly performing assets, which are difficult to quantify, while the adverse effect of increases in interest rates on the value of a mortgage portfolio is calculated more easily. The longer insolvent institutions are permitted to remain open and to gamble for resurrection, the harder it becomes to evaluate the growing amount of deteriorating assets.

The growing FSLIC costs are reflected not only in the increasing present-value cost to the FSLIC presented in Table 2–9, but also in Table 3–2, which shows the attrition of FSLIC-insured institutions from 1980 through 1986. Since 1934 there have been only fifty-eight liquidations, of which fifty have occurred since 1981, forty-eight of them since 1983. This suggests that lower-cost mergers are increasingly being replaced by higher-cost liquidations. In addition, in April of 1985, the Bank Board began the MCP, which was designed to "warehouse" insolvent institutions, beginning with twenty-five in

Table 3-2. Attrition among FSLIC-Insured Thrift Institutions (1980-1986).

| | Number of Failed Institutions | | | | Attrition of Nonfailed Institutions | |
| | FSLIC Assistance Involved | | | No FSLIC Assistance Involved | | |
Year	Liquidations	Mergers and Other Types of Assistance Cases	Management Consignment Cases	Supervisory Mergers	Voluntary Mergers	Total
1980	0	11	0	24	82	117
1981	1	27	0	53	206	287
1982	1	69	0	182	262	514
1983	6	47	0	49	107	209
1984	9	18	0	14	33	74
1985	10	24	25	11	47	117
1986	23	27	29	4	36	119
Total	50	223	54	337	773	1,437

Source: Author's calculations based on data from Federal Home Loan Bank Board.

1985 and followed by twenty-nine more in 1986. The development of the MCP, discussed in more detail in Chapter 4, represents an acknowledgment of both the FSLIC fund's limitations and the increasing cost of disposing of the assets of insolvent institutions.

As if the risk-taking of insolvent institutions were not enough of a concern, the proliferation of opportunities provided by deregulated portfolios in combination with the strained resources of the FSLIC has encouraged more risk-prone individuals to enter the thrift industry. This phenomenon, by which insurance encourages those most likely to produce the insured-against outcome to purchase insurance, is called adverse selection.

The failures of privately insured thrifts in Ohio and Maryland provide two good case studies in how adverse selection can become a problem. The Ohio thrift crisis in the spring of 1985 was precipitated by the bankruptcy of a government securities dealer with whom one major Ohio thrift had government securities' repurchase agreements. About the same time, in Maryland, a real-estate syndication affiliate of one financially distressed, privately insured thrift went bankrupt, which may eventually impose over a billion dollars in losses on other thrifts, private mortgage-insurance companies, investment houses, and taxpayers. Fraud and substantial risk-taking appear to have played major roles. In these cases, inadequate private-insurance funds could not cover the costs associated with the closure of the institutions. Given the magnitude of the problem, it would seem that the examination and supervision did not properly monitor the institutions.

Overburdened insurance funds and inadequate examination and supervision attract and encourage those who take high risks and those who are willing to engage in fraud. The larger the number of insolvent federally insured thrifts and the more it appears that the FSLIC and other regulatory resources are limited, the more attractive federally insured thrifts become to these individuals.

These individuals have also been attracted by the unusually large leverage afforded thrifts due to the relatively small net worth they have been required to maintain. As already mentioned, net-worth requirements were indirectly lowered when accounting definitions were changed in 1981 and the minimum net-worth requirements were lowered from 5 to 4 percent in 1980, then to 3 percent in 1982. The net effect of these changes was to increase the maximum amount an institution could invest per dollar of a redefined and thus broader measure of net worth from twenty to thirty-three dollars. Requirements were actually lower for the institutions that until 1985 could use the phase-in and averaging techniques. Since capital requirements for a given year were based on the previous year's liabilities, institutions could maintain even lower minimum net worth. Many institutions were thus freed of potentially intense Bank Board scrutiny. At a time when an increasing number of institutions were in distress and when the capacity constraints of the FSLIC were obvious, the opportunities to take risks were accumulating. The growing ability to leverage off of declining net-worth requirements worsened not only the moral-hazard problems but also the adverse-selection problems.

THE CONTAMINATION OF SOLVENT THRIFTS BY THE SURVIVAL TACTICS OF INSOLVENT THRIFTS

Insolvent institutions' gambling for resurrection has usually involved attempts to grow. Growth provides them with additional funds to acquire assets with a greater expected return than those they currently hold. Without growth, they must rely on the repayment or sale of assets in their portfolios to fund new higher-yielding, but also higher-risk assets. The sale of assets at below book-value prices is relatively unattractive, of course, because regulatory net worth would immediately decline, thus increasing the likelihood of regulatory intervention.

The nature of the risk-taking can be seen by looking at the recent growth rate of the industry and where this growth has occurred. In 1984 the industry was growing nearly 20 percent a year, a rate at which it would double in size every three-and-one-half to four years. By contrast, commercial-bank deposits were growing less than 10 percent a year. The significance of rapid growth for risk-taking is apparent when one contrasts the asset composition of institutions growing rapidly to that of the industry as a whole. In 1984, construction lending, which historically has had far greater credit risk than mortgage lending, accounted for less than 6 percent of the industry's assets, but almost 25 percent of the assets of institutions doubling their size in one year or less. Acquisition and development loans—the lending category with the highest associated credit risk—accounted for approximately 2 percent of the industry's assets in 1984, but almost 13 percent for institutions growing rapidly. Direct investment equity securities, real estate, and service corporations also accounted for only about 2 percent of the industry's assets in 1984, but over 10 percent for rapidly growing state-chartered institutions in California and Texas, the states with the most liberal asset regulatory provisions. Throughout 1984 direct investments by the industry increased close to 100 percent annually.

One way for unhealthy institutions to grow is to offer rates on liabilities that exceed the rates paid by other thrifts and commercial banks. Table 3–3 provides data that insolvent institutions were paying higher-than-average rates for thrifts. As this table shows, the average cost of funds for thrifts was 32 basis points above the average for commercial banks in 1980. This differential reflected Regulation Q differences, which allowed thrifts to pay rates higher than banks, and rates paid on unregulated accounts. In 1981 rates for both banks and thrifts rose substantially, but the overall bank-thrift differential remained constant at 32 basis points. But the thrift institutions with the lowest net worth were paying as much as 311 basis points more for funds than the highest net worth associations. This pattern, which was maintained through 1985, suggests that insolvent institutions were pulling up the average for thrift rates for the period.

The number of basis points that the highest net-worth institutions paid over commercial banks also grew from 1980 to 1985. One interpretation of these data is that the growth tactics of insolvent institutions directly contaminated solvent thrifts by forcing them to pay more for funds in order to maintain their market share. There is skepticism about this interpretation, because solvent thrifts could maintain profitability over a range of withdrawals by drawing down on liquidity or selling assets. Why, then, some ask, would they sacrifice profitability or be forced to select higher-risk, higher-yielding assets in order to maintain profitability while maintaining market share?

Another interpretation is that depositors were demanding a risk premium to place funds in thrifts because they perceived a greater risk of failure for thrift institutions. Even insured depositors may demand a premium over commercial-bank rates in order to cover the possible inconvenience of a thrift being closed. More likely, a greater premium may be demanded by those with uninsured deposits. This

Table 3-3. Average Cost of Funds (COF) for Commercial Banks and for FSLIC-Insured Thrift Institutions (1980–1985).

Year	Average COF for Commercial Banks	Average COF for All Thrift Institutions	Average COF For GAAP-Insolvent Thrift Institutions		Average COF for Thrift Institutions Where $0 < \dfrac{GAAP\ NW}{TA} < .03$	Average COF for Thrift Institutions Where $.03 \le \dfrac{GAAP\ NW}{TA} < .05$	Average COF for Thrift Institutions Where $\dfrac{GAAP\ NW}{TA} \ge .05$
			Those Earning Negative Net Income for the Year	Those Earning Positive Net Income for the Year			
1980	8.47	8.79 (32)	8.78 (–1) (31)	8.86 (7) (39)	9.19 (40) (72)	8.82 (3) (35)	8.72 (–7) (25)
1981	10.54	10.86 (32)	12.20 (134) (166)	13.61 (275) (307)	11.25 (39) (71)	10.83 (–3) (29)	10.50 (–32) (–4)
1982	10.42	11.24 (82)	11.40 (16) (98)	11.28 (4) (86)	11.27 (3) (85)	11.30 (6) (88)	10.89 (65) (47)
1983	8.65	9.54 (89)	9.86 (32) (121)	9.41 (13) (76)	9.54 (0) (89)	9.54 (0) (89)	9.48 (6) (83)
1984	9.11	9.59 (48)	9.90 (31) (89)	9.50 (–9) (49)	9.69 (10) (58)	9.48 (11) (37)	9.43 (–16) (32)
1985	8.07	9.12 (105)	9.42 (30) (135)	8.95 (–17) (88)	9.29 (17) (122)	9.05 (7) (98)	8.82 (–30) (75)

a. The cost of funds for commercial banks is calculated by dividing the dollar interest expense for the following funds by the dollar volume of the funds averaged over five quarters: 1) deposits, excluding demand deposits; 2) federal funds; 3) interest-bearing demand notes and other borrowings; and 4) interest on subordinated notes and debentures. Data source: FDIC. The average cost of funds for thrift institutions is calculated by dividing the dollar interest expense of the following funds by the average annual dollar volume of the funds (1985 averaged through September): 1) deposits; 2) advances from Federal Home Loan Banks; 3) other borrowed money; and a) commercial bank loans; b) reverse repurchase agreements; c) consumer retail repurchase agreements; d) overdrafts in demand deposits; e) commercial paper issued; f) subordinated debentures; g) mortgage-backed bonds issued; and h) other borrowings. Data source: FHLBB.

b. The average COF for commercial banks includes the cost of deposits at foreign offices as well as deposits of domestic U.S. offices. The foreign cost of deposits was 13 percent in 1980, 16 percent in 1981, 13 percent in 1982, 9 percent in 1983, 10 percent in 1984, and 9 percent in 1985.

c. The number in parentheses is the number of basis points by which all thrift institutions' average COF is above or below (−) the average cost of funds for commercial banks.

d. The number in the first parentheses here and in the remaining columns is the number of basis points that institutions' cost of funds is above or below (−) the average cost of funds for all thrift institutions. The second number in parentheses is the same as in footnote c.

Source: Author's calculations based on data from the Federal Home Loan Bank Board and the FDIC. The author thanks Alan McCall of the FDIC for assistance in obtaining FDIC data and making the appropriate calculations.

would represent a more indirect contamination of solvent thrifts than that of solvent institutions directly matching insolvent thrift rates. A mark of the overall contamination is the 105 basis-point spread between thrift and bank cost of funds in 1985, an increase of 73 basis points over the differential prevailing in 1980, attributable to the higher rates of the insolvent institutions and whatever contamination of overall rates that was precipitated by the actions of the insolvent institutions.

REGULATORS ATTEMPT TO CONSTRAIN THE RISK-TAKING ACTIVITIES OF THRIFTS

In the thrift-industry crisis of the 1980s, largely unexpected events caught the Congress and the regulators off guard. The rise of interest rates in 1980 was unanticipated, and, as just described, having failed to close insolvent institutions, some of the regulatory responses from 1980 through 1982 had the unintended effect of fueling incentives for insolvent institutions to take excessive risks. These incentives were beginning to develop in 1982 and 1983. The mounting insolvencies coincided roughly with the resignation of the Bank Board chairman in March 1983 and the nomination of his successor.

For two years thereafter, not one major regulatory or congressional effort was made to deal with the growing number of insolvencies. In order to verify this, one may refer back to Table 2–3, which lists the significant regulatory changes affecting thrifts from 1980 to 1986. The one exception may have been the raising of capital requirements in 1983 for institutions receiving new charters. This regulatory effort, however, did nothing for existing institutions. Other regulatory initiatives were designed to fight the interest-rate risk problem by lengthening advances from ten to twenty years in 1983 and by requiring in 1984 that institutions establish policies for managing interest-rate risk. Simultaneously, the new Bank Board chairman encouraged institutions to protect themselves from interest-rate risk by using adjustable-rate mortgages. These efforts, however, were aimed at the targets of the past war rather than the new threat of insolvent institutions' risk-taking.

The new Bank Board began to focus formally on that problem in 1983, when it proposed to limit the use of brokered-originated deposits by thrifts. As first discussed in the Bank Board's 1983 report to Congress, new technology allowed brokers to place deposits any-where in the country in insured denominations of $100,000 or less.[3] Institutions could now garner large numbers of insured deposits merely by using the telephone. As Table 2–10 shows, broker-origi-nated deposits rose from 0.6 percent of thrift-industry assets in 1980 to 4.4 percent in 1984. This new capability added to the ease with which institutions could grow.

Fear of this growth led the Bank Board to limit broker-originated deposits in order to impede the high-growth rates of low net-worth institutions that posed a threat to the FSLIC. Critics pointed out that brokered deposits were merely one of many conduits for growth. They also emphasized that, although shutting off brokered deposits might impede deposit-pricing for growth and risk-taking, it could also drive these institutions to use more costly sources of funds, thus worsening the problem. Moreover, the critics noted, solvent thrifts used brokered deposits to improve the geographic flow of funds throughout the nation. Further, there would be no danger in providing solvent, well-managed institutions with new sources of potentially less expensive deposits. The Bank Board nonetheless pressed for the limitation of broker-originated deposits until a fed-eral district court declared the restriction illegal.

Major regulations designed to deal with excessive risk-taking were adopted in March 1985. The Bank Board adopted three regulations limiting the investment powers of federally insured thrifts on the grounds that these activities increase the overall risk of losses to the FSLIC. The Bank Board passed a regulation limiting an insured thrift institution's direct investment without supervisory approval to 10 percent of its assets or twice its net worth, whichever is greater. (With supervisory approval, an institution can devote more of its assets to direct investment.) The Bank Board also adopted a regula-tion that required additional net worth for institutions growing more than 15 percent per year. In addition, the board began to eliminate the phase-in and averaging techniques that allowed some institutions to lower their net-worth requirements and supported legislation that would impose a higher deposit-insurance premium on state-chartered institutions engaging in activities not allowed federally chartered institutions.

It may be helpful to recall that, as emphasized in Chapter 1, regu-lations limiting the investment activities of thrift institutions are part of a long-standing balancing act between government subsidies and restrictions. Thrifts were separated from commercial banks and provided federal deposit insurance and tax subsidies to promote housing finance, which Congress considered a merit good, one whose consumption should be enhanced by giving thrifts a competitive advantage over other lenders. Until the 1980s dramatically revealed the risks of asset portfolios dominated by long-term, fixed-rate mortgages, the assets of thrifts were narrowly proscribed. The relaxation of asset restrictions in 1980 under the Depository Institutions Deregulation and Monetary Control Act and in 1982 under the Garn–St Germain Depository Institutions Act provided thrifts the potential benefits of portfolio diversification that could strengthen their position while they continued to provide housing finance. Through regulatory action, the government has attempted to mimic the outcome that the market would produce if the moral-hazard and adverse-selection problems did not exist.

In 1986 the Bank Board continued to pass regulations designed to reduce the threat to FSLIC. In August 1986 it passed a regulation raising the minimum net-worth requirements for federally insured thrifts in an attempt to rebuild an adequate net-worth buffer to protect the FSLIC from losses and to help ensure that institutions conduct themselves sensibly by making sure they stand to lose money if their activities fail. All institutions must now meet progressively higher capital requirements, peaking at 6-percent RAP net worth.

They must also capitalize all growth at 6 percent in order to ensure prudent asset-selection strategies. The Bank Board also required higher incremental capital on all direct investments, land loans, nonresidential construction, and letters of credit. It perceived these assets to be inherently riskier than other assets and found them to be disproportionately represented in the portfolios of closed thrifts. Finally, the regulation provided for some offsetting reductions in net worth if institutions demonstrated reduced interest-rate risk exposure.

In December 1986 the Bank Board also extended the direct-investment regulation. The regulation had been due to expire at year-end 1986 and was extended for two-and-one-half months. Then, after public hearings held in January 1987, the Board extended the regulation further, with modifications that somewhat tightened it. The final regulation was adopted on June 10, 1987, and broadened to include certain land and nonresidential construction loans in addition to direct investments.

Having listed the regulatory responses of the Bank Board to part two of the thrift-industry crisis, an assessment of their likely effectiveness in reducing the risk-taking of insolvent institutions is in order. The defeated brokered-deposits regulation is a good starting point from which to begin to understand the validity and effectiveness of the current regulations. Brokered deposits have been used widely by insolvent and nearly insolvent institutions to grow at high rates. These institutions, reflecting moral hazard or adverse selection, have undertaken high-risk portfolio strategies that pose a threat to the FSLIC. Doing away with brokered deposits, however, would do nothing to diminish the incentives the institutions have to take risks. Moreover, the elimination of brokered deposits would have removed a tool that other solvent institutions could sensibly use.

So it is with direct investments, land loans, construction loans, and any other asset category one could select. Some institutions have used these assets in high-risk strategies, have failed, and have cost the FSLIC money. At issue, however, is whether the fault lies with the asset category *per se.* All the evidence suggests that it lies elsewhere. To understand the evidence, one must first understand that risk for a depository institution on the asset side of its balance sheet is not a function of a given asset but rather of the behavior of all the assets taken together.

An institution may have one asset—for example, a mortgage that has risks associated with borrower default and the fact that the value of the mortgage falls when interest rates unexpectedly rise—and can acquire another asset—for example, a direct investment in a firm that has risk of default greater than a mortgage but whose value rises when interest rates rise. A portfolio of both assets can be less risky than a portfolio of mortgages alone because the increased value of one can more than offset the decreased value of the other when interest rates change. The opposite movements in value mean that the assets have a negative covariance. A portfolio comprised of two assets, one of which has a higher variance, can be less risky overall than a portfolio comprised of only the lower-variance asset if the covariance of the two assets is negative.

In reality, financial institutions hold many assets with significantly different variances and covariances. An enormous number of theoretical and empirical analyses has found that well-capitalized firms are highly unlikely on average to select asset portfolios that pose excessive risks. Instead, firms tend to be risk adverse, choosing diversified portfolios to reduce overall risk. As discussed above, this is not true for insolvent or nearly insolvent thrift institutions. They may, in fact, prefer excessive risk and become risk plungers because they stand to bear little or no loss in the event of failure but may reap all gains from the success of risky tactics.

Thus, there is no theoretical or empirical evidence to suggest that direct investments in the portfolios of well-capitalized thrifts are a threat to the FSLIC; instead, direct investments may reduce the portfolio risk of these thrifts. Direct investments in poorly capitalized thrifts, however, may be used in extraordinary high-risk strategies. Thus, the problem lies not in the asset category, but in the portfolio strategies based on the perverse risk-taking incentives embedded in insolvency. Moreover, given the wide range of assets in which a thrift can invest, the limitation of one, or even several, of them does not pose much of an obstacle to designing a high-risk strategy.

The same arguments apply to the capital regulation that requires greater net worth for certain assets in another, less direct attempt to discourage the selection of certain asset categories. Direct investments and the other assets for which institutions must hold additional capital can be used to diversify portfolios and reduce risk. It is another unintended irony in the thrift-industry crisis that, by limiting portfolio diversification through the use of direct investments and other assets, overall risks may rise.

Moreover, the empirical evaluations performed to date of the effects of direct investments by thrifts do not justify limiting direct investments for all thrifts. The first econometric evaluation in 1985 of the determinants of thrift-institution failures found no relationship between the probability of failure and direct investment in thrifts' portfolios.[4] Subsequent empirical evaluations produced similar findings.[5] These and other econometric studies also evaluated the effect of direct investments in the portfolios of closed thrifts and costs to the FSLIC. Some of the studies found that direct investments were associated with higher costs.[6] Other studies found a similar association for small thrifts but not for large thrifts.[7]

These studies have been used—inappropriately—by the Bank Board as justification for direct-investment restrictions. The higher costs associated with direct investments in closed thrifts reflect the risk-taking incentives of insolvent but open thrifts, not a risk associated with direct investments *per se*. On average, the closed institutions in the 1986 failure-cost study were closed eleven months after they had become GAAP insolvent—it is no wonder that they were gambling with direct investments. However, their gambling does not suggest that industrywide restrictions are appropriate.

There is another issue raised by the ability of some thrifts to use direct investments. Holding all other things constant, the existence of federal deposit insurance allows thrifts and commercial banks to garner deposits from insured depositors at interest rates that do not reflect the risks taken by the institutions. This is not the case for financial firms with liabilities not insured by the federal government. For them, the rate of return paid to investors reflects the firms' risks. Some federally insured thrift institutions are now allowed to compete with uninsured financial and nonfinancial firms in an unprecedented range of activities. Unless the combination of the deposit-insurance premium and other costs associated with regulation raises the overall cost of deposits to levels commensurate with uninsured firms, and unless these costs fluctuate with the level of risk, a competitive advantage may be provided for thrifts.

THE FSLIC'S RECAPITALIZATION PLAN: ONCE MORE, TOO LITTLE, TOO LATE

The Bank Board's decision to raise overall net-worth requirements is unassailable, although, as developed in Chapter 5, the actual contribution of the current method to additional net worth is likely to be negligible. As net worth rises in the industry, moral hazard and adverse selection will become less of a problem. Net worth is like a deductible in a traditional casualty-insurance policy, wherein the higher the deductible, the less likely most individuals will be to take risks leading to a claim. But, alas, these requirements do not address the crux of the immediate problem—open, insolvent thrifts. It is astounding that from the time this problem was perceived in late 1982 and early 1983 no coherent strategy to resolve it has been devised by the Bank Board, the executive branch, or Congress. Basically, the strategy has been to use admittedly overwhelmed staffs of examiners, supervisory personnel, and enforcement attorneys to monitor, supervise, and, where necessary, to intimidate through enforcement actions open, insolvent institutions to behave in ways that will minimize the FSLIC's losses.

The inadequacy of this approach was inescapably demonstrated in the results of a series of analyses done by the Bank Board staff in December 1985 and January 1986, which led all concerned to conclude that a core of approximately 400 to 500 thrifts were insolvent. The studies used confidential data on examination ratings and therefore cannot be cited here, but the number of insolvent institutions and the size of their assets are of the order of magnitude described earlier in this chapter. Following these analyses, the Bank Board began to announce publicly that it could cost as much as $22.5 billion to dispose of the assets of these institutions.[8]

Simultaneously, meetings began to take place between the Bank Board and U.S. Treasury officials. From these meetings a plan developed to provide the FSLIC with additional funds. That plan, called the FSLIC recapitalization plan, which was proposed as legislation in 1986 but failed to get through Congress, became the Bank Board's, the Treasury's, and the administration's strategy to deal with part two of the thrift-industry crisis.

At the plan's base was the Federal Home Loan Bank System of twelve regional Federal Home Loan Banks that are owned by member thrift institutions. In 1986 the Banks had capital of approximately $9 billion. The proposed plan would have taken $3 billion of that capital to establish a corporation for the purpose of selling debt in an amount of approximately $15 billion or more. Repayment of the principal amount of the debt would be made by placing the $3 billion in zero coupon bonds whose value would equal the principal due as the bonds matured. The interest on the Bank's borrowings would be paid from the insurance premium, including the additional premium that has been levied since 1985. If the plan worked as conceived, approximately $5 billion per year would be raised and made available to the FSLIC to close insolvent institutions and dispose of their assets. Over time, the thrift industry would repay the borrowings, and the crisis would be resolved without expenditures from the federal government.

A variation of this plan was passed by Congress in legislation called the Financial Institutions Competitive Equality Act of 1987 and signed into law by President Reagan in August 1987. Instead of $15 billion, the legislation authorized $10.8 billion, a compromise between the administration's goal and an initial amount of $5 billion passed by the House of Representatives and a sum of $7.5 billion passed by the Senate. The legislation created the FSLIC Financing Corporation (FICO) to raise the funds, which are not to exceed $3.75 billion per year.

The plan can be questioned on the grounds that it is inequitable. Arguably, currently solvent institutions have done nothing to cause the plight of the insolvent institutions and, therefore, they should not be required to pay for FSLIC losses attributable to the insolvent institutions. To the extent that solvent institutions lobbied in behalf of the regulatory forbearance that worsened the problem, they may legitimately be asked to bear part of the burden but not all of it. Since no one fully perceived the consequences of the regulatory forbearance, and it was a product of both congressional and Bank Board policy, however, it may not even be in the nature of "rough" justice to make these institutions bear any of the burden. The wisdom of essentially taxing, through the supplemental premium, the income of solvent but struggling thrifts that could the source of retained earnings is questionable.

One should also keep in mind that, if priced properly, deposit insurance is not designed to benefit thrifts and banks but to protect society against the costs associated with widespread runs. Moreover, the deposit-insurance premium was never meant to be set at levels that would provide the FSLIC and FDIC with fund reserves adequate to deal with crises. As mentioned earlier, for example, the FSLIC's reserves have only risen above 2 percent of industry assets twice since 1934. Thus, there has been an implicit federal-government guarantee that to some extent it should bear part of the cost in times of crisis. Finally, considering this implicit guarantee and the fact that only the federal government has resources sufficient to close all institutions now, the government's responsibility grows as the costs mount from not closing the insolvent institutions immediately.

Regardless of who should pay, the conclusion is inescapable that the size of the plan is sufficiently flawed that an alternative or augmented plan should be sought. By conservative estimates, the cost of not closing the 229 institutions that were GAAP insolvent and earning negative net income in 1985 will grow by approximately $1 billion per year.[9] The growing number of insolvent thrifts, their declining net worth and income, and the escalating cost to close them as a percent of assets suggest rising costs. In addition, the costs stemming from the contamination of solvent thrifts by allowing insolvent institutions to operate are not included. The volatility of the economic conditions affecting the industry indicates that the cost could escalate substantially. Thus, if funds are made available in yearly increments of approximating $3.75 billion, a significant portion of the funds will be spent to deal with the future growth of the problem.

One must also consider the effect of the substantial delays in the development of the plan that have already occurred and appear likely to continue. The plan was conceived in spring of 1986, and Congress did not adopt a version of it until August 1987. It has taken time for the Banks to establish the funding corporation, to raise a portion the first year's funds, and to transfer them to the FSLIC. Still more time will pass before the FSLIC can employ the funds. In short, a delay of a year or more will probably occur in raising and using the first year's allotted funds. A plan that is so long delayed and, when operational, makes insufficient funds available in relatively limited yearly increments appears in itself inadequate.

The recapitalization plan was developed in part to avoid adding to the expenditures of the federal budget at a time of large budget deficits and the Gramm, Rudman, Hollings legislation requiring movement toward a balanced budget. Yet the government still bears a significant contingent liability because there is no certainty that the thrift industry will be able to pay the interest on the debt through premium payments.

As discussed in Chapter 4, the potential flight of the strongest thrifts from the FSLIC to the FDIC—despite attempts to stop them—may further reduce future premium income by reducing the industry's deposit base. Higher capital requirements on incremental assets and increased competition could further reduce growth. During the first half of 1987, deposits rose at an annual rate of only 1.6 percent. Following the October 19, 1987 fall in the stock market, there were significant deposit inflows—most likely seeking a temporary respite before seeking the higher yields from which they came. From 1982 to 1985 deposits at FSLIC-insured thrifts grew at an average annual rate of 12.6 percent.[10]

Based on the first issue of FICO bonds in September 1987, one can estimate the fragility of the industry's ability to meet its debt coverage responsibilities. The initial $500 million issue yielded 10.73 percent to maturity, approximately 90 basis points above comparable maturity treasury bonds. Future FICO issues may have lower yields, which would reduce future claims on deposit insurance premiums. Assuming a rate of 10.00%, annual interest on $10.825 billion is $1.083 billion. Total annual deposit insurance premiums for 1987, based on average deposits in insured institutions during the first six months of the year, will be $1.860 billion.[11] This provides an estimated debt service coverage (annual deposit-insurance premium income divided by annual interest payments) of 1.7, which would be ample. Even if interest rates decline, two critical assump-

Table 3-4.   Debt Coverage Ratio for the FSLIC Financing Corporation under Alternative Economic Assumptions.

Annual.Deposit Growth Rate	Annual Increase in FSLIC Costs as Percent of Deposits				
	0.00%	0.05%	0.10%	0.15%	0.20%
-10%	0.82	0.62	0.43	0.23	0.03
- 5	1.14	0.87	0.59	0.32	0.05
0	1.72	1.31	0.89	0.48	0.07
5	2.88	2.18	1.50	0.81	0.12
10	5.47	4.16	2.84	1.53	0.22
15	11.72	9.90	6.09	3.28	0.47

Note: This analysis is not adjusted for the more than $800 million in prepaid premiums that have already been spent, but that will be credited against future cash-premium requirements. Debt coverage ratios would be reduced by approximately 0.05 if these credits were taken into account.

Source: Calculations by R. Dan Brumbaugh and Andrew S. Carron based on FHLBB data. "Thrift Institution Activity in June" (August 11, 1987), reported in Brumbaugh and Carron, "The Thrift Industry Crisis: Causes and Solutions," *Brookings Papers on Economic Activity* (Washington, D.C.: The Brookings Institution, 2: 1987), pp. 1-29.

tions remain: first, that there will be no claims on deposit insurance premiums, other than for debt service, over the next thirty years; and second, that the level of deposits will not decline over the next thirty years. Both assumptions, as noted above, are questionable.

Table 3-4 shows the sensitivity of FICO debt coverage to these two assumptions.[12] (Debt coverage is defined here as the present value of projected insurance premiums divided by the present value of projected interest payments, both discounted at 10 percent annually.) The first column shows different possible deposit growth rates for the industry; the first row shows different possible levels of additions to the FSLIC caseload, expressed as a percentage of industry deposits. A $1 billion per year increase in the cost of resolving the problems of insolvent thrifts would represent approximately 0.11 percent of current deposits.

The table shows that the ability of deposit-insurance premiums alone to meet the debt service on FICO bonds is highly sensitive to these two assumptions. With an annual deposit growth rate of 5 percent, for example, a 0.15 percent increase in FSLIC costs as a percent of deposits (approximately $1.5 billion) would eliminate the ability of the industry to cover its interest costs. The coverage ratio is even thinner because the supplementary premium of 1/8 of one percent (assumed constant in Table 3-4) is scheduled to decline annually and reach 1/48 of 1 percent by 1991. Should premium collections fall short, the Congress would almost certainly have to step in to make additional resources available, either to pay bondholders directly or to defray competing FSLIC expenses to make the necessary funds available.

WILL WE RELIVE THE FIRST PART OF THE CRISIS?

By waiting to close the insolvent institutions, the government is running the risk that an increase in interest rates will greatly complicate the problem. Only the unexpected and precipitous decline in interest rates after 1982 prevented disaster for the thrift industry earlier in this decade. Two statements can be made with certainty about future interest rates: they will change, and no one can predict exactly how because interest rates embody expectations about future economic developments. How vulnerable is the thrift industry to interest rate increases? The answer depends in part on the duration—the time it takes to reprice—of the assets and liabilities in thrifts' portfolios. Traditionally, the long duration of assets in thrift portfolios and the shorter duration of liabilities have made them vulnerable to interest-rate swings because when interest rates rise, liability costs increase before the return on assets rises.

Table 3–5 uses interest-rate "gaps" to show what has happened in recent years with the portfolios of thrifts. An interest-rate gap is calculated by subtracting the dollar volume of liabilities repricing in a certain time—for example, in the next year—from the dollar volume of assets repricing in this same period and dividing that number by the total assets of an institution. The percentage amount is the percent of liabilities that reprice in the period that exceeds the assets that reprice over the same period.

March 1984 was the first time that data were collected that allowed for the calculation of interest-rate gaps for all thrifts. The numbers have negative signs because more liabilities reprice, for the one-year and the three-year period, than do assets. The larger the percent, the more damage will be done if future interest rates rise

Table 3–5. The One-Year and Three-Year Gaps of Federally Insured Thrift Institutions (1984–1986).

| Type of Gap | 1984 | | | | 1985 | | | | 1986 |
	March	June	September	December	March	June	September	December	March
One year	-40	-41	-38	-36	-34	-30	-29	-26	-23
Three years	-46	-45	-40	-38	-34	-29	-28	-25	-21
One year hedged	-40	-40	-37	-35	-33	-31	-29	-24	-21
Three years hedged	-45	-44	-40	-38	-33	-30	-28	-24	-20

Source: Author's calculations based on data from the Federal Home Loan Bank Board.

because thrifts will be paying more relative to what they are earning. The most notable phenomenon in Table 3–5 is the fall in the one-year gap by almost half and the more-than-50-percent fall in the three-year gap. Essentially, these gaps indicate that the interest-rate risk of the thrift industry has been halved since 1984.

Both the hedged and unhedged gap figures account for the effect of adjustable-rate mortgages (ARMs) in thrift portfolios.[13] This is done by using the time to repricing of ARMs as their term to maturity. The hedged gap accounts for the use of options and futures to reduce interest-rate risk. The small differences between the hedged and unhedged gaps reflects the negligible use of options and futures in the thrift industry. Thus, the data in Table 3–5 provides a useful insight into the interest-rate risk exposure of thrifts. Although the reduction of the gaps since 1984 has been substantial, the risk remains great. With a minus twenty one-year gap, an increase in interest rates of only 100 basis points would result in approximately $2 billion in losses to the industry. Referring back to Table 2–1, $2 billion in losses would wipe out all profits earned in 1986.

The increase in interest rates in 1987 (rates on one-year treasury bills, for example, rose from 5.4 percent in January to 6.7 percent in December) accounts for a significant part of the thrift industry's negative income for the period. Whether these losses pressage a third phase for the modern thrift crisis, no one can say because no one can predict interest rates. The 1987 performance, however, is a sobering reminder of the interest-rate danger.

NOTES

1. For another description of why insolvent institutions face substantial incentives to take risks, see Mark J. Flannery, "Deposit Insurance Creates a Need for Bank Regulation," *Business Review* (Federal Reserve Bank of Philadelphia) (January/February 1982): 17–27. For discussions involving the current condition of thrift institutions, see Mark J. Flannery, "Recapitalizing the Savings and Loan Industry" (presented at the Eleventh Annual Conference of the Federal Home Loan Bank of San Francisco, December 1985), and Stuart I. Greenbaum, "Reform of the Thrift Industry" (Banking Research Center working paper no. 123, March 1985).

2. According to a study done by the House Subcommittee on Commerce, Consumer, and Monetary Affairs, most of the thirty California thrifts closed in the three years preceding June 1987 involved "serious insider

misconduct." The study concluded that fraud in many thrifts has "reached epidemic proportions." See John Yang, *Wall Street Journal*, June 15, 1987, p. 5. Further study is necessary to distinguish between "misconduct and fraud" and greater risk-taking by institutions trying to recover before the FSLIC could close them.

3. See Federal Home Loan Bank Board, *Agenda for Reform, A Report to the Congress* (Washington, D.C.: Federal Home Loan Bank Board, March 1983).

4. James R. Barth, R. Dan Brumbaugh, Jr., Daniel Sauerhaft, and George H. K. Wang, "Thrift-Institution Failures: Causes and Policy Issues" (Proceedings of a Conference on Bank Structure and Competition Federal Reserve Banks of Chicago, 1985), pp. 184–216.

5. George J. Benston, "An Analysis of the Causes of Savings and Loan Association Failures" (Monograph Series in Finance and Economics, New York University, 1985); James R. Barth, R. Dan Brumbaugh, Jr., Daniel Sauerhaft, and George H. K. Wang, "Thrift-Institution Failures: Estimating the Regulator's Closure Rule" (research working paper no. 125, Federal Home Loan Bank Board, Office of Policy and Economic Research, August 1986), and George J. Benston, "Direct Investments and Losses to the FSLIC," testimony before the Federal Home Loan Bank Board, February 13, 1987.

6. Barth, Brumbaugh, Sauerhaft, and Wang, "Thrift-Institution Failures: Causes and Policy Issues"; and James R. Barth, R. Dan Brumbaugh, Jr., and Daniel Sauerhaft, "Failure Costs of Government-Regulated Financial Firms: The Case of Thrift Institutions" (research working paper no. 123, Federal Home Loan Bank Board, Office of Policy and Economic Research, Washington, D.C., October 1986).

7. George J. Benston, "An Analysis of the Causes of Savings and Loan Association Failures," and *Idem.*, "Direct Investments and Losses to the FSLIC."

8. Based on excerpts from Edwin J. Gray's address before the Ninety-Third Annual Convention of the United States League of Savings Institutions, Dallas, Texas, November 5, 1985.

9. See Barth, Brumbaugh, and Sauerhaft, "Failure Costs of Government Financial Firms." All the data on the rising FSLIC Costs—econometric evaluations, FSLIC costs as a percent of assets in closed thrifts, growing insolvencies, and negative income of the most insolvent thrifts—suggest that the present value of the costs is growing. Much less concern would be justified if the data suggested that the cost's present value were stable or declining.

10. Calculations by Brumbaugh and Carron in R. Dan Brumbaugh, Jr., and Andrew S. Carrow, "The Thrift-Industry Crisis: Causes and Solutions," *Brookings Papers on Economic Activity*, 2 (Washington, D.C.: The Brookings Institution, 1987), pp. 1–29.

11. *Ibid.*
12. *Ibid.*
13. The percentage of conventional home mortgage loans closed with adjustable rates was 37 in January 1983, then jumped to 64 in January 1985, but fell sharply to 27 and 28 in January 1986 and January 1987, respectively.

4 HOW TO RESOLVE THE CURRENT THRIFT-INDUSTRY CRISIS

Closing insolvent institutions is the only way to resolve the current thrift-industry crisis. Given the current anemic flow of income from the thrift industry, which is expected to continue, the industry itself will only be able to pay a fraction of the price of closing insolvent institutions. Even with the banking legislation of 1987, the burden of determining who will bear the cost still falls directly on Congress. Congress should establish, and soon, the distribution of cost among thrifts, banks (if the FSLIC and the FDIC are merged), and taxpayers. Ultimately, taxpayers will pay part—probably most—of the cost. Even if all the funds needed to close insolvent thrifts magically appeared overnight, it would take years to close them all. As a result, a triage mechanism must also be developed to help contain the risk-taking of open, insolvent institutions until they can be closed. This mechanism would also lead to a more orderly closure procedure with lower costs to the FSLIC. The most successful policy would be one in which substantially greater funding was combined with an expanded triage or damage-control mechanism.

The current policy, pursued by the Bank Board, the administration, and the Congress, has been to postpone both allocating the funds and developing a triage mechanism. The consequences of delay are not only rising costs but postponement of the implementation of the decision to the future, to a new president, to future Treasury secretaries and budget directors, a new Bank Board, and a new Congress. Postponement also means that the burden of payment may be redistributed in part from thrift institutions and their depositors to commercial banks and their depositors and to taxpayers.

In 1975 George Stigler wrote that "if an economic policy has been adopted by communities, or if it is persistently pursued by a society over a long span of time, it is fruitful to assume that the real effects were known and desired."[1] If this is so, we can conclude that shifting a larger future cost to future decisionmakers with a different distribution of individuals paying the cost has been the intention of current decisionmakers. This chapter shows how this shift is taking place.

FINDING THE FUNDS TO CLOSE INSOLVENT INSTITUTIONS

The Bank Board's strategy for handling the thrift-industry crisis has been an *ad hoc* patchwork of mostly ineffective measures. The Bank Board has, as discussed in Chapter 3, adopted a number of regulations designed to curtail risk-taking. The Board has also increased the number of examiners to approximately 2,000 at the beginning of 1988 and increased their compensation by placing them in the Federal Home Loan Banks. It has increased the number of lawyers and support staff in its Division of Enforcement who are responsible for enforcement of Bank Board regulations. In addition, in order to give it greater freedom to act, the Enforcement Division was made independent of the Office of General Counsel in 1986. The examiners and enforcement staff, along with the supervisory staffs of the Federal Home Loan Banks, are primarily responsible for containing the risk-taking of insolvent and nearly insolvent institutions as well as monitoring and supervising the rest of the thrift industry.

When containment fails, insolvent institutions are turned over to the FSLIC, where they become part of the FSLIC caseload that now includes Management Consignment Program cases. Conceptually, the MCP process is a form of triage, implemented when resolution of cases must be delayed because of the limited FSLIC fund—limited even after Congress established the FICO. As part of the failure-resolution apparatus, the Federal Asset Disposition Association (FADA), a federally chartered thrift institution created by the Bank

Board to help the FSLIC work out of its bad-asset portfolio, is also being used to obtain the best price for the poorest-performing assets of failed institutions acquired by the FSLIC.

The inadequacies of this approach are revealed by the growing magnitude of the problem. As shown in Table 3–1, the negative net income of GAAP-insolvent institutions more than tripled from the fourth quarter of 1985 to the fourth quarter of 1986. Over the same period, these institutions' negative GAAP net worth almost tripled. The significant jump in the rate of decline of these institutions from 1985 to 1986 is foreboding, and it occurred just before interest rates moved up for the first time since 1982. The 341 GAAP insolvent institutions earning negative net income are part of a group of 1,867 thrift institutions with assets of $743 billion that are financially weak, where weak is defined as having GAAP net worth of 5 percent or less. These institutions constitute 57 percent of all thrift institutions and hold 68 percent of all thrift-institution assets. Early reports of 1987 performance reveal continued deterioration.

Five-percent GAAP net worth was the major division used until 1981 to set the minimum net-worth level for the industry. If that level was appropriate until 1981, it certainly is appropriate now, when the economic environment is much more uncertain. The minimum primary capital requirement for commercial banks, moreover, is 5.5 percent, an indication that 5 percent may be low. Whether both of these measures are too low is also an issue, considering that between 1940 and 1970 average capital levels for thrift institutions were approximately 7 percent.

GAAP net worth is used not because it is the most appropriate measure, but because it is the most widely used book-value measure. At the moment GAAP net worth on average exceeds market-value net worth. The exaggeration is particularly pronounced when a thrift's major problem is asset quality rather than the interest-rate spread. The latter can be approached relatively straightforwardly by marking interest-sensitive assets to market based on existing interest rates. Neither problem is addressed by GAAP, however.

Ironically, GAAP has been widely used to obscure market value as asset quality has deteriorated—assets with positive value have been sold and booked on the balance sheet as a gain while underwater assets have remained on the books valued at historical cost. Thus, GAAP was a less reliable indicator of net worth in 1986 than it was in 1980. One would be justified in raising the threshold above 5 percent in order to set a minimum net-worth requirement consistent with that of 1980.

As a result, 5-percent GAAP net worth cannot be considered an unreasonable line of demarcation between institutions with a greater likelihood of failure and those with a substantially lower likelihood of failure. It is also a level below which one can reasonably begin to be concerned about risk-taking to ward off insolvency.

Until now, the book has focused on the incentives and behavior of insolvent institutions. This is also the focus of most public discussions about the thrift-industry crisis. The large number of institutions with net worth above zero but below 5 percent, however, greatly complicates the issue of what to do with insolvent institutions. In the best of worlds, one would want examination and supervisory staffs to concentrate on those institutions in addition to those with net worth at or below zero. These weak but solvent institutions would be especially targeted for examinations and preventive supervisory restrictions. As it is, the examiners—with approximately one federal examiner per troubled thrift—are overwhelmed by the most distressed insolvent institutions. It is also helpful for perspective to keep in mind that the remaining 1,385 institutions with GAAP net worth above 5 percent must also be examined, especially given the more complicated economic environment.

All the numbers suggest that the Bank Board's short-term strategy for dealing with the thrift crisis by using examination, supervisory, and enforcement staffs in coordination with the FSLIC to monitor, control, and punish insolvent institutions taking excessive risks or operating in other unsafe and unsound ways is woefully insufficient. By all estimates, the individuals on the Bank Board and Federal Home Loan Bank staffs are too few and too inexperienced to do the job. If they focus on insolvent institutions, other weak institutions cannot be adequately treated. If adequate attention is paid to weak but not insolvent institutions, as well as the remaining healthier institutions, moral hazard among insolvent institutions will become more rampant. There is no way for current staff, even with the planned additions to its numbers, to handle the three-tiered problem.

Before presenting in detail the solution to the immediate problem, a few more preliminary observations may be helpful. Imagine that a group of bank and thrift regulators, industry representatives, scholars, and business reporters had met in September 1979, just before the change in the Federal Reserve's monetary policy and the ensuing jump in interest rates. Imagine also that someone predicted that in about five years, 70 percent of thrift assets would be in institutions that were either insolvent or below their 5-percent GAAP minimum net-worth requirement and that the number of thrifts would have fallen approximately 25 percent from over 4,000 to little more than 3,000 institutions.

With only forty-three failures from 1970 through 1979 and with industry GAAP net worth at 5.6 percent, the individual probably would have been ridiculed. But, if the prediction were taken seriously, many at the meeting would have properly worried about whether such an event would precipitate runs that would damage the entire U.S. economy. That the fear of runs is not now prevalent is viewed by many as a triumph of the current system of deposit insurance and regulation. Thus, it is argued that we should be grateful that our deposit-insurance and regulatory system prevented possible runs, leaving us only with the problem of raising money to clear up the negative net worth of the thrift industry.

Raising and allocating that money is the crux of the solution to part two of the thrift crisis. In early 1985, based on the least-cost method of resolving FSLIC cases in 1984, the cost to close the 434 institutions insolvent at that time was estimated at $15.8 billion.[2] The chairman of the Bank Board objected, stressing that this estimate represented a worst-case scenario that was very unlikely to transpire.[3] He soon revised this statement and estimated publicly that the cost would increase to approximately $22 billion in three to five years, beginning in 1986.[4] In 1986, the GAO estimated the cost to be $22.3 billion.[5] Other estimates ranged as high as $50 billion.[6] Econometric techniques used in 1986 found that not closing the 229 institutions that were GAAP insolvent and earning negative net income in 1985 had resulted in cost increases of approximately $1 billion per year.[7] Most recently, the Bank Board announced that in 1987 the closure of 48 institutions cost the FSLIC $0.34 per dollar of assets. With nearly 500 institutions GAAP insolvent in 1987 with approximately $130 billion in assets, the estimated cost to close the institutions thus rose above $44 billion based on the FSLIC's 1987 experience. As discussed in Chapter 5, the cost to close the nation's second largest thrift—American Savings and Loan of California—which is insolvent but not counted among the 500 due to accounting treatment, has been estimated as high as $4.5 billion.

These cost estimates, moreover, do not include the indirect costs of allowing insolvent institutions to remain open. Thus, for example, the risk premium thrifts pay for deposits that is greater than that paid by banks is not included. The premium represents an income redistribution away from thrifts and will contribute to future thrift failures.

Unless anyone can convincingly argue that the present-value cost will remain the same or decline in the future—and no one is making that argument—the way to proceed to the least-cost solution is for Congress to appropriate funds that would allow the Bank Board to close insolvent institutions as quickly as possible. The Congress, however, has shown no willingness to appropriate any money from general revenues. Not until the spring of 1987 did either house of Congress approve any form of FSLIC recapitalization, and even then the funds were inadequate for the task at hand. Even the more generous recapitalization plan that was ultimately adopted has embedded in it the following implicit declaration: "We are going to postpone paying the price of insolvent thrift institutions in the hope that the thrift industry will be able to pay in the future, even though it is more than reasonable to conclude that the cost may be substantially higher as a result."

So any solution proposed in this book must contain a means to minimize the FSLIC's ultimate costs, subject to the political constraints whose economic significance is summarized in the above declaration. Given the uncertain future income stream of the thrift industry, this means that U.S. taxpayers will still face the contingent liability of FSLIC costs that are, to say it one more time, rising. It would be negligent, however, not to assert that the Bank Board, Congress, and the administration should evaluate more carefully the wisdom of making funds available directly and with all deliberate speed from general revenues. Based on available data and analysis, that would be the least-cost method of resolving the issue.

It appears unlikely, however, that Congress will make general revenues available, so we must turn to other existing ways to remove the need for direct expenditures from general revenues at this time. One approach builds on the net-worth and income-capital certificate programs. Essentially, these programs allow institutions to count as net worth promissory notes, the NWCs and ICCs, from the FSLIC. The notes are a contingent liability of the FSLIC, and by extension ultimately an implicit contingent liability of the taxpayer. These programs have been criticized, most prominently by the General

Accounting Office (GAO).[8] Notwithstanding the GAO's criticisms, Congress should explore an expanded variation of the program—if it chooses not to make direct appropriations.

The expanded program would, first, allow the FSLIC to close all insolvent institutions as promptly as possible and to provide the promissory notes as components of net worth. Second, by congressional action the notes could be backed by the full faith and credit of the U.S. government. Without such backing, the notes could be perceived as worthless because of the FSLIC's poor financial condition, which would cause both economic and legal problems. If backed by the U.S. government, however, another problem arises. The face value of the notes might have to be accounted for as outlays of the federal government and would hence affect the budget deficit. Concern about having to book the FSLIC recapitalization funds as U.S. budget expenditures led in part to the elaborate funding mechanism of that plan. It seems however, that worries about having to account for the promissory notes as immediate expenditures would constitute short-sightedness, given the contingent liability that already exists and is growing.

There is yet another approach. The FSLIC could take control of institutions and run them with FSLIC-appointed boards of directors and managers without any congressional action. This is the essence of the MCP. The role for the MCP—even if by another name—will expand under any solution scenario. For this reason, the next section of this chapter is an in-depth analysis of the MCP. For now, however, consider what the MCP's role would be even if the cost of closing all institutions were covered by an immediate appropriation from Congress.

It is impractical to think that the FSLIC or any other agency would be able to mobilize the forces necessary to close all insolvent institutions at once in the traditional manner. Traditionally, when an instituion is closed, many dozens of FSLIC employees, lawyers, and marshals descend simultaneously on it and all its branches near the close of business on a Friday. These individuals then reopen the institution on the following Monday to pay off insured depositors in the case of a liquidation, or the institution reopens after being merged with a healthy one. In either case, it is important to emphasize that a thrift closure does not mean that consumers are being deprived of a needed financial service, but rather that the service will no longer be provided by a specific thrift. Regardless of the amount of funds made available, such an operation could not be mounted simultaneously for all insolvent institutions.

Thus, some kind of orderly and expanded triage needs to be developed. It would include an evaluation by the Bank Board in order to rank institutions by degree of insolvency (insolvency being a proxy for the incentive to take excessive risk) and by the extent that institutions have acted on the incentive to take excessive risk. The Bank Board also has other ways to evaluate and rank institutions. The worst institutions would be the most likely targets for immediate closure. The next worst offenders would be the most likely candidates for the MCP, and the remainder would be candidates for continuing scrutiny by examiners, supervisory agents, and the Enforcement Division. Institutions in the third category, depending on an assessment of managerial behavior, could continue to operate without direct Bank Board intervention. The less funding was available for closure, the greater the burden of this program would be to the MCP.

From this analysis, one can distill specific recommendations:

Congress should appropriate general revenues immediately as part of the resolution;

If direct revenues are not forthcoming from the Congress, and perhaps if they are, Congress should guarantee that the full faith and credit of the U.S. government is behind all thrift and bank insured deposits in conjunction with an expanded NWC or ICC program;

The Federal Home Loan Bank System should expand substantially the examination, supervision, and enforcement staffs; and

The Bank Board should expand the MCP to take control of insolvent institutions whose managements are considered to be taking advantage of the overburdened system to indulge in excessive risk-taking.

The government agency most directly charged with the responsibility to act is the Bank Board. To date, its response to part two of the modern thrift crisis has been lamentable. Of the four-point program above, the Bank Board can implement items three and four by itself. The longer it takes Congress to appropriate general revenues and the less money that is made available through the current recapitalization plan, the more important points three and four become. Since, politically, direct appropriations seem unlikely anytime soon, and because the FSLIC recapitalization plan brings funds on line in relatively small increments, the MCP seems to take center stage. Its central role is to moderate risk-taking by open, insolvent thrifts and to use damage control to establish an optimal flow of funds for ultimate disposal of the thrifts.

TRIAGE UNTIL ALL INSOLVENT THRIFTS ARE CLOSED

Imagine that you were a member of the Bank Board in 1985. By year-end 1985, only 68 thrift institutions were able to be closed by the FSLIC in 1985 and 450 more institutions were insolvent. Although the FSLIC staff had grown from 34 in 1980 to 159 in 1985, the number of insolvent institutions was increasing at a much greater rate. The number of examiners was actually declining. Cases were becoming more time-consuming to resolve because more involved troubled assets rather than the problems of interest-rate spread. As nonbank banks continued to proliferate, it was becoming easier for financial institutions to expand geographically without acquiring failed thrifts. Therefore, it took FSLIC more time to arrange mergers, which potentially resulted in higher costs to the FSLIC.

In the midst of these developments, it is easy to understand why the Management Consignment Program was created in April 1985.[9] The goal of the MCP is to reduce FSLIC losses by taking control of those insolvent institutions that under current management pose the greatest threat of further deterioration. Instead of closing an insolvent institution immediately, however, the FSLIC allows it to continue operation under a new board of directors and new management. With selection criteria, instructions, contracts, monitoring, and the threat of enforcement, the FSLIC hopes that the new boards of directors and managers will minimize the deterioration of the institution and thus minimize the FSLIC's costs when a resolution is achieved. In this way, the FSLIC retains the ability to merge the problem institution and avoid the loss of its value as an ongoing concern, as would occur in a liquidation. This approach also postpones any cash outlay from the FSLIC's limited reserves. Furthermore, by delaying the resolution the MCP allows the FSLIC to gain better information on the specific value of the problem institution's assets. With such information, the FSLIC may reduce any risk premium that might be demanded by acquirers in return for acquiring an institution with assets of highly uncertain value. At year-end 1986 there were seventy-one institutions in the MCP.

There were precursors to the MCP. During the Bank Board chairmanship of Richard Pratt from 1980 to 1983, there were institutions called "phoenixes." The phoenix institutions were treated in much the same manner as the MCP institutions are today, but there were only three of them. They were considered insolvent but, given the limited FSLIC reserves and the relatively large size of the institutions, they were judged too large to close. As with the MCP institutions, the FSLIC replaced existing management and boards of directors. One of the institutions, Talman Home of Illinois, later converted to public ownership with FSLIC assistance.

Another variation involves American Savings and Loan of California, with approximately $34 billion in assets. In 1984 American experienced a severe withdrawal of deposits following a ruling by the Securities and Exchange Commission that accounting adjustments revealed a reported quarterly profit to be a loss. The institution had undertaken substantial interest-rate risk in the early 1980s and held significant assets that are below book value today. In this case, without declaring a receiver or conservator, the Bank Board insisted upon a change in management and essentially picked the new president. Because the net worth of the institution is below its regulatory minimum, the Bank Board monitors the institution closely and may approve or disapprove American's major decisions.

An institution is considered part of the MCP if it is a FSLIC case and some form of Bank Board action has been taken to replace either the institution's current board of directors or the current management or both. There are many GAAP-insolvent institutions that are not part of the MCP. While many of these institutions are under some form of supervisory control—generally either a supervisory agreement or operating under cease and desist orders—they are not part of the MCP unless the Bank Board takes formal action to replace their boards of directors or their management without arranging a final resolution.

The decision to make an institution part of the MCP depends primarily on the recommendation of the Bank Board's supervisory agent in the institution's Federal Home Loan Bank district that such a move is necessary. This decision reflects an explicit acknowledgment by the supervisory agent that the current management is unable

Table 4-1. An Overview of the Management Consignment Program.

Institution Characteristics	June 1985		December 1985		June 1986	
Number of institutions	6		25		40	
Average assets (in millions of dollars)	1,400		671		484	
Average GAAP net worth to total assets	-7.38		-15.21		-16.55	
Charter type	Pre MCP	Post MCP	Pre MCP	Post MCP	Pre MCP	Post MCP
Federal	4	5	8	19	9	26
State	2	1	17	6	31	14
Ownership form						
Stock	2	2	18	6	33	14
Mutual	4	4	7	19	7	26

Source: Author's calculations based on data from the Federal Home Loan Bank Board.

or unwilling to operate the institution in a manner consistent with containing the FSLIC's costs. Once such a decision has been made, representatives from the district Bank name a new board of directors and arrange for others to provide management services until a resolution can be arranged.

As Table 4-1 shows, the forty institutions in the MCP in June 1986 (ranging in size from $12 million to $2.3 billion in assets) had an average of $500 million in assets. The average GAAP net worth as a percent of total assets was negative 16.6 percent. Table 4-1 also indicates that a number of MCP institutions switched either charter type or ownership form or both upon joining the MCP. Twenty-six of the forty institutions in the MCP in June 1986 were federally chartered; only nine of these institutions had federal charters prior to joining the MCP. Nineteen of the thirty-three stock institutions became mutuals after joining the MCP. Many of these charter and ownership changes resulted from the use of a receivership to place an institution in the MCP. The use of a receivership for MCP cases has an advantage over a conservatorship because it eliminates any stockholder claim as well as any commitments made under the previous owners.

Table 4-2 summarizes the portfolio and performance characteristics of MCP institutions before they became part of the program and six months after they joined the program. As this table shows, the average asset portfolios of institutions in the MCP deviate substantially from the industry norm. While the thrift industry as a whole had 50 percent or more of their portfolios in residential mortgages and mortgage-backed securities, MCP institutions averaged less than 45 percent. MCP institutions averaged over 15 percent of their portfolios in commercial real estate mortgages, whereas the industry averaged less than 10 percent. Furthermore, MCP institutions averaged almost 10 percent of their portfolios in direct investments, while the industry averaged less than 3 percent.

Data in Table 4-2 also indicate a large increase in Federal Home Loan Bank advances for MCP institutions after joining the program, in part to offset the decline in deposits. This decline may be attributable to the difficulty with which MCP institutions retain uninsured liabilities. Since these institutions will be liquidated or merged in the future, uninsured creditors risk losing their investments and so may remove their deposits as early as possible. The loss of these deposits potentially raises the cost of the MCP above the cost of a liquidation, in which the cost is shared by both the FSLIC and the uninsured depositors. The large increase in ICCs stems from the efforts of the FSLIC to raise the regulatory net worth of MCP institutions to zero. While this was the initial strategy in the MCP, the FSLIC no longer purchases ICCs from new MCP institutions. One difficulty with the FSLIC's purchase of ICCs is that, in the event of a liquidation, the FSLIC note used to purchase the ICC becomes part of the receivership estate, and the FSLIC's liquidation cost is increased to the extent that unsecured creditors other than the FSLIC gain a pro rata share of the FSLIC note.

The bottom section of Table 4-2 reveals that MCP institutions, on average, are still losing money six months after joining the program. Institutions in the MCP for at least six months were losing annually an average of 400 basis points on their operations and another 300 basis points on the sale of assets. These losses may reflect accounting recognition of the deteriorated condition of the institution that led it to be placed in the MCP and thus should not necessarily be construed as indicating poor performance by the MCP. The performance

Table 4-2. Characteristics of Institutions in the MCP (*Percentage of Total Assets*).

Portfolio Composition	1 Year Prior[a]	6 Months Prior	Entry Date[b]	6 Months After[c]
Selected Assets				
Residential mortgages and motgage-backed securities	50	45	42	44
Commercial real estate mortgages	17	17	16	16
Land loans	10	10	9	7
Direct investments[d]	8	9	10	9
Selected Liabilities and Capital				
Deposits	86	89	95	89
Advances	6	6	7	14
Other borrowed money[e]	5	5	3	3
GAAP net worth	1	-2	-9	-7
Income capital certificates[f]	0	0	1	6
Performance				
Return on assets	-.5	-5.4	-8.3	-15.0
Net operating margin[g]	-.9	-2.8	-5.1	- 4.0
Net non-operating margin[h]	.4	-2.6	-3.2	- 3.0

a. Data are averaged for each institution for the nearest quarter at least one year before it entered the program. For example, data for an institution entering on August 1, 1985, would be from the June 30, 1984, quarterly report. Forty-four institutions are included.

b. Data are averages for the nearest quarter just prior to entry into the program.

c. Data are for those institutions in the program before December 1985 and not resolved by June 1986 and include twenty-four institutions.

d. Includes investment in real estate and equity in service corporations.

e. Includes commercial loans, reverse repurchase agreements, consumer retail repurchase agreements, overdrafts in demand deposits, commercial paper issued, subordinated debt not qualifying for net worth, mortgage-backed bonds issued, and other borrowings.

f. ICCs are promissory notes purchased by the FSLIC and count toward RAP net worth.

g. Operating income minus operating expenses minus interest expenses.

h. Non-operating income minus non-operating expenses minus taxes.

Source: Author's calculations based on data from the Federal Home Loan Bank Board.

of the management contracted by the FSLIC can be evaluated only after the embedded decisions of the former management are fully incorporated into the institution's financial statements.

Admittedly, the MCP is a second-best solution. Because of this, to determine whether the program has any merit, one would need to know how the institutions would have performed had they been allowed to continue operating as they had been before they were placed in the MCP. Empirical answers to that question would require a comparison of a peer group of institutions to the MCP group—a difficult task, since according to the FSLIC, the MCP institutions are by definition the worst performers, which frustrates the selection of a peer group. *A priori*, one must assume that if competent boards and managers are selected, the absence of the incentive to take risks for resurrection leads to an improvement or to less deterioration.

Other criticisms of the MCP focus on the disparity between the initial objectives stated in April 1985 and the actual realization of the plan. The MCP was designed to provide a short-term warehousing of institutions, which would be liquidated or merged after a few months in the program. Critics cite the fact that some institutions have been in the program since its inception in 1985 as a sign of failure. Yet the nature of the program changed because FSLIC funds were not available to allow for liquidation or merger. Given the closure rule and other constraints, mainly regulatory and congressional, it is actually a strength of the program that the MCP's role has been able to expand.

Another criticism is that the MCP institutions sometimes continue to operate as they did before they were in the program. A major example is the way MCP institutions price deposits. Critics accurately assert that MCP institutions offer rates above those competing solvent institutions, which gives them a competitive edge over privately owned solvent institutions. This criticism misses the point. MCP institutions' deposit rates generally reflect the failed strategies of the previous owners and managers who attempted to grow their way out of their problems, leaving assets whose market value is below book value. A sudden reduction in deposit rates would lead to withdrawals that would drain liquidity and exert pressure to sell the assets. The real cause of the problem is the lack of FSLIC funds to handle the underwater assets of insolvent institutions, not the MCP pricing strategy. Nonetheless, there remains the valid point that solvent institutions are forced to compete with institutions that should not be open for business.

Although these criticisms tend to miss the mark, they highlight that the FSLIC must monitor the MCP institutions continually to ensure that the board of directors and management that it selects will operate the institutions in a manner consistent with its goal of loss minimization. More generally, while the MCP provides the FSLIC with an opportunity to eliminate the inconsistencies between its goals and those of the new management, it must still anticipate potential conflicts with the new board of directors and management.

A related issue is how the FSLIC can ensure that the managing institution will provide an accurate evaluation of a problem institution's initial financial condition and its continuing operation, information that is absolutely essential if the FSLIC is ultimately to liquidate or merge an MCP at the least cost. The willingness of the managing institutions to supply the FSLIC with this information depends, in part, on the managing institutions' economic incentives. The incentives could include the possibility of gaining some future regulatory benefit in return for perceived meritorious service as an MCP manager. However, if the managing institution is a potential acquirer of the MCP institution, it may have an incentive to conceal information about the managed institution's financial condition: By understating the actual value of the institution's assets, the potential acquirer could reduce its cost of acquisition. In so doing, however, the managing institution raises the costs to the FSLIC of resolving the insolvent institution.

Management might also have an incentive to conceal information in order to prolong a resolution. This might occur if the managing institution is able to manage the MCP institution at a cost significantly less than its compensation from the FSLIC, for example, if it uses less senior staff to run the MCP institution.

The managing institution's willingness to provide the type of management that minimizes resolution costs for the FSLIC also depends on other economic incentives. For example, if the MCP case is a potential competitor, there may be less incentive to pursue a value-maximizing strategy. Such a value-maximizing strategy could actually hurt the managing institution if the MCP institution were to become a formidable competitor. Likewise, the managing institution may be reluctant to use its senior staff to run the MCP case because such a talent drain could hurt its operation. Without such talent, however, the MCP institution might not be operated as effectively as possible.

In another scenario, if the managing institution is a potential acquirer, it has an incentive to prevent further deterioration of the firm but may not choose to maximize the value of the institution as a separate entity. Instead, it may operate the institution so as to maximize the value of the future combined entity, exploiting any synergies that arise between it and the problem institution. For example, if the MCP case has a well-developed construction-loan department and the managing institution is in need of such a department, it may expend excessive resources in this area while neglecting the rest of the problem institution. Such a strategy may benefit the managing institution, but it will not necessarily reduce the FSLIC's cost. If such management reduces other potential acquirers' willingness to acquire the problem institution, the FSLIC may not ultimately obtain the most cost-effective resolution.

This discussion outlines a number of ways that the interests of the FSLIC and the directors and managers of an MCP institution can diverge and how what are termed "agency" problems can arise. The FSLIC has taken steps to control its agency problems. First, the supervisory agents look for managing institutions whose own performance appears to reflect a consistency between their goals and those of the FSLIC. Table 4–3 provides information on the characteristics of the managing institutions. They average over 60 percent of their portfolios in residential mortgages and mortgage-backed securities and approximately 6 percent of assets divided evenly between land loans and direct investments. These institutions thus hold portfolios that the FSLIC and the Bank Board consider appropriate in terms of risk. Whether these portfolios are actually less risky to the FSLIC than those that are heavily weighted with land loans and direct investments clearly depends on the variance and covariance of the returns on the assets and the capital levels of the institutions that hold them.

The managing institutions have also had an average GAAP net worth above 4 percent for the last three years and have demonstrated a consistent pattern of profitability. Table 4–3 shows that the annualized second-quarter return on assets (ROA) for the managing institutions was a negative 4 basis points in 1986. If three institutions that suffered abnormal nonoperating losses in the second quarter are eliminated, however, the average ROA rises to 75 basis points.

Table 4-3. Characteristics of Managing Institutions in the MCP[a]
(*Percentage of Total Assets*).

Portfolio Composition	1982	1983	1984	1985	1986[b]
Selected Assets					
Residential mortgages and mortgage-backed securities	70	70	66	64	63
Commercial real estate mortgages	6	8	9	10	10
Land loans	1	2	3	3	3
Direct investments[c]	2	2	3	4	3
Selected Liabilities and Capital					
Deposits	76	79	77	75	74
Advances	11	9	8	10	10
Other borrowed money[d]	8	6	8	7	9
GAAP net worth	3	4	4	5	4
Income capital certificates	0	0	0	0	0
Performance					
Return on assets	.52	.52	.64	.91	-.04[e]
Net operating margin[f]	-1.07	.22	.32	.52	.72
Net non-operating margin[g]	1.59	.30	.32	.39	-.76

a. Includes only thrift institutions. Uses data from the thirty-one thrift institutions that were managing institutions in June 1986.

b. Through June 1986. Performance data are annualized.

c. Includes investment in real estate and equity in service corporations.

d. Includes commercial loans, reverse repurchase agreements, consumer retail repurchase agreements, overdrafts in demand deposits, commercial paper issued, subordinated debt not qualifying for net worth, mortgage-backed bonds issued, and other borrowings.

e. Three institutions had very low earnings in the second quarter of 1986. Without these, the average ROA was 0.75.

f. Operating income minus operating expenses minus interest expenses.

g. Non-operating income minus non-operating expenses minus taxes.

Source: Author's calculations based on data from the Federal Home Loan Bank Board.

The boards of directors for MCP institutions, which are independent of the managing institutions, provide another layer of monitoring. Directors are selected based on past accomplishments and represent a cross section of academicians, former industry officials, and former regulators. In addition, managing institutions are required by the Management Service Agreement (MSA), the contract between the FSLIC and managing institutions, to prepare a condition report for the supervisory agent within ninety days of taking control of a problem institution. While in the past these reports have tended to vary, the FSLIC is currently standardizing the requirements for the initial and all subsequent reports to ensure that all relevant information obtained by the Bank Board is timely and consistent. These reports consist of an overview of the current situation, an analysis of the problem institution's strengths and weaknesses, a summary of the interim management's activities and accomplishments, and a review of the institution's overall business plan.

The FSLIC may also attempt to limit its potential agency problems by requiring that interim management obtain prior approval for business decisions that materially affect the operations of the problem institution. The FSLIC has recently discussed establishing various layers of approval: For certain decisions, management would only need approval from the board of directors; more important decisions would require the approval of the supervisory agent; and critical decisions would require the approval of the FSLIC and possibly the Bank Board. Depending on the skill and efficiency of the FSLIC's representatives, however, the required reporting and approval processes could become self-defeatingly slow or unresponsive.

Other techniques to limit agency conflicts have also been discussed but have not been adopted to date. For example, managing institutions could be prohibited from acquiring the MCP cases they manage. Yet, while such an approach would reduce potential conflicts, it would also reduce the incentive to supply value-enhancing management. Part of the motivation for managing these institutions likely comes from the ability to gain extensive information about them; a ban on acquisitions would remove the opportunity to trade on this inside information.

Another technique to limit conflicts would be to base compensation on performance. Compensation to institutions managing MCP institutions is currently based on a negotiated flat rate. This rate averages approximately 135 percent of the salary and benefits of individuals supplied to the MCP institution plus a monthly fee of approximately $30,000 for the managing institution. A performance-based compensation plan, however, requires a definition of acceptable performance, which in turn requires some measure of a starting point. Since part of the purpose of the MCP is to gather information on the current condition of the problem institution, judging performance becomes very difficult. However, many institutions are currently being placed in the MCP by means of asset-backed transfers (ABTs). In an ABT, the insured deposits of an insolvent institution are placed in a newly federally chartered mutual institution. These deposits are offset with the "good" assets of the problem institution and with assets from the FSLIC's own portfolio. For institutions in the MCP as a result of an ABT, the performance of the managing institution becomes easier to judge, since the FSLIC has a relatively accurate measure of the starting point. From the first such transfer in August 1985 through December 1986, eleven institutions with $5.6 billion in assets have been placed the MCP in this manner.

Finally, MCP institutions are subject to the same examination that all FSLIC-insured institutions undergo. In addition, MCP institutions are scrutinized by FSLIC staff specifically assigned to the MCP program. Further attention arises from the public awareness of the MCP. Both the financial press and competitors are aware of which institutions are in the MCP, and this provides yet another layer of vigilance that would be somewhat less acute if the institutions remained open but under less public control, in the form, for example, of supervisory agreements. Compatibility between the FSLIC's goals and institutions' behavior is also maintained by the threat of possible dismissal against particularly malfeasant boards of directors or management.

COST-AVOIDING STRATEGIES AVAILABLE TO SURVIVING THRIFTS

The program set forth here to solve the current thrift-industry crisis consists of two main parts, raising money and establishing a triage mechanism to contain the risk-taking of insolvent thrifts that cannot be closed immediately. After fifty-three years during which FSLIC reserves have been raised from a deposit-insurance premium, it is uncertain whether thrift institutions paying the premium can bear the burden of paying the difference between the value of the assets and the insured deposits of insolvent thrifts. Given this uncertainty and the growing costs caused by delaying the closure of insolvent institutions, dividing the cost between the thrift industry and general revenues makes the most sense. This course, however, appears unpalatable to most of those who would be affected directly. The solvent institutions in the thrift industry want to avoid the cost, and so does Congress, presumably because it wants to avoid increasing the deficit, reducing spending, or raising taxes. There is, moreover, the issue of responding to the requests and perceived problems of constituents. In 1986, for instance, the Speaker of the House of Representatives was from Texas, a state in which approximately 20 percent of the GAAP-insolvent thrifts losing money were located. In the spring of 1987, he was widely reported in the press as being opposed to closing all insolvent thrifts in Texas.

The issue of how willing the industry should be to pay the price is complicated for the firms involved. The longer the issue remains unresolved and the larger the cost becomes, the less likely it becomes that the solvent institutions of the thrift industry will be asked to pay all of the cost. Whether their future share will be more or less than it would be now is uncertain, but some prospect exists for avoiding most of the cost. Delay, however, increases the possibility of a merger between the FSLIC and the FDIC. The FDIC is a tempting source of funds to a Congress that wants to avoid spending general revenues. Opposition to a merger of the funds among commercial banks is unanimous. If a merger evolves, one can only conclude that pressure would be exerted by the banks to erode any perceived advantages that thrifts have over them. Thrifts could thereby face stiffer competition than they otherwise might. The price of stiffer competition could be higher than the additional premium that could be required.

For thrifts that can meet FDIC standards and convert to bank charters, the potential strategies become even more complicated and interesting. From their perspective, opposition to paying for the FSLIC recapitalization while preparing to switch charters may make the most sense, if the cost of charter conversion, including forgoing whatever relative benefits are embedded in a thrift charter, is less than the benefits of gaining a bank charter, which would include not having to pay to eliminate insolvent thrifts. For these thrifts a merger of the two insurance funds, which could potentially arise from the delay in recapitalization caused by their opposition, would mean that, even as newly chartered commercial banks, they might have to bear the higher premium that they tried to avoid.

Year-end 1986 data indicate that about 1,200 thrifts were able to switch charters based on their ability to meet the FDIC's 5.5-percent minimum primary capital requirement. The FDIC capital definition was approximated by subtracting goodwill (not allowed by the FDIC) and adding all subordinated debt (allowed by the FDIC) to the institutions' GAAP net worth. The assets of the institutions were approximately $200 billion, or 17 percent of 1986 industry assets. Of the 1,200 institutions, only four had assets exceeding $1 billion, and the largest had assets of $2.5 billion. Criteria other than net worth are also used by the FDIC to assess whether an institution can convert. Thus, it is uncertain how many thrift institutions could contemplate switching to a bank charter and which of these would be successful.

It is interesting to speculate about why qualifying institutions might flee the thrift industry and what the consequences of such flight would be. The incentive to switch is significant for large institutions for whom the conversion cost is small compared to the cost of the special insurance premium of 1/8 of 1 percent of total deposits that is being charged annually to support part of the recapitalization plan. The additional premium in 1987 cost institutions $1,250 per million dollars of deposits. That amounts to $1.25 million per year for an institution with $1 billion in deposits. Along with the additional direct deposit-insurance premium, the institutions are paying more than banks for deposits and other nondeposit liabilities. The premium cost may rise even more as current and perhaps future recapitalization plans consume thrift income, making the future income stream of the industry appear more uncertain to investors. Investors will demand more return for the additional risk, and the return will have to be borne by the thrifts through premium increases. Uncertainty about the industry has also pushed up the cost of Federal Home Loan Bank advances to thrifts. In general, with a rising number of insolvent institutions that are more costly to close, there is little reason to think that these costs will fall.

The costs, moreover, should rise with the number of institutions that show an interest in exiting or that actually exit the FSLIC for the FDIC, because the exit of strong institutions further weakens the FSLIC's ability to handle problem institutions by shrinking its revenue base. The potential of rising costs caused by the exit of some institutions in turn motivates other institutions to get out as fast as they can. The current fee demanded by the Bank Board to exit—two years' worth of regular deposit-insurance premia and special assessments ($4.2 million per billion in deposits)—plus raising the needed net worth, plus the cost of additional FDIC restrictions may be less costly than future FSLIC-related costs. Looking only at deposit-insurance costs, an institution could switch to the FDIC, pay the exit fee, and within three years and four months be better off because it would not have to pay the special assessment. Thus, the sentiments of a senior executive of one of California's five largest thrifts, who said privately "we want out of FSLIC as fast as we can get out," are hardly surprising. Fulfillment of that desire must be deferred, however, because the August 1987 banking legislation prohibited FSLIC to FDIC switches for a year.

Once again, the cause of all this jockeying is the failure to close insolvent institutions. Regardless of whose avoidance strategy is ultimately most successful, the battle is over the future distribution of a growing burden among thrifts, banks, their depositors, and taxpayers. In the meantime, an expanded program of containment for insolvent thrifts is essential. The centerpiece of the containment program should be a variant of the MCP. The MCP should take control of the worst of the worst institutions—those that are insolvent under management demonstrably taking excessive risks. Even if Congress were provided all the funds necessary to close all insolvent institutions, the MCP would still be necessary because not all insolvent institutions could be closed swiftly. Expansion of the MCP is within the control of the Bank Board, which should make it a top priority. This is especially true now because no direct funding appears to be forthcoming, and the recapitalization will bring funds on line in relatively small amounts over a period of years.

The Bank Board's reluctance to date to expand the MCP is not puzzling. Since 1983, the Board has been extremely slow to respond to the current crisis. The responses have never been comprehensive and, since January 1986, have focused intensively on FSLIC recapitalization. That in itself is fine, but this narrow focus has overlooked the need to gain better control over insolvent thrifts. Moreover, the MCP, which, aside from examination, supervision, and enforcement, is the major tool available to contain risk-taking, has been volubly criticized. Much of this criticism, however, mistakenly blames the MCP for problems caused by the FSLIC's depleted reserves. One must also keep in mind that many thrift institutions, and their trade associations, may have economic incentives to prolong resolution and therefore may have little motivation to support the MCP.

Regardless of how soon money is made available to the FSLIC and regardless of the ultimate form of the risk-containment program for currently insolvent thrifts, the solution to the current crisis does not contribute much to the prevention of future crises. Prevention of a future crisis depends on how well one can control the moral hazard created by deposit insurance priced at a flat rate regardless of the risks taken by institutions. Moral hazard, as the current crisis has demonstrated, will prevail as long as net-worth levels remain low and the FSLIC continues to delay the timely closure of institutions.

NOTES

1. George J. Stigler, *The Citizen and the State: Essays on Regulation* (Chicago: Chicago University Press, 1975), p. 140.
2. James R. Barth, R. Dan Brumbaugh, Jr., Daniel Sauerhaft, and George H. K. Wang, "Insolvency and Risk-Taking in the Thrift Industry: Implications for the Future," *Contemporary Policy Issues* (Fall 1985): 1–32.
3. Testimony of Edwin Gray before the Senate Banking Committee reported by the Associated Press, July 26, 1985.
4. From Edwin J. Gray's address before the Ninety-Third Annual Convention of the United States League of Savings Institutions, Dallas, Texas, November 5, 1985.
5. U.S. General Accounting Office, "Thrift Industry Problems: Potential Demands on the FSLIC Insurance Fund" (Washington, D.C.: U.S. Government Printing Office, February 1986).
6. Edward J. Kane, *The Gathering Crisis in Federal Deposit Insurance* (Cambridge, Mass.: MIT Press, 1986); Bert Ely, "Private Sector Depositor Protection Is Still a Viable Alternative to Federal Deposit Insurance," *Issues in Bank Regulation* (Winter 1985): 40–47.
7. James R. Barth, R. Dan Brumbaugh, Jr., and Daniel Sauerhaft, "Failure Costs of Government-Regulated Financial Firms: The Case of Thrift Institutions (research working paper no. 123, Federal Home Loan Bank Board, Office of Policy and Economic Research, Washington, D.C., October 1986).
8. U.S. General Accounting Office, "Thrift Industry: Net Worth and Income Certificates" (Washington, D.C.: U.S. Government Printing Office, June 1986).
9. For a more detailed description, see Donald J. Bisenius, R. Dan Brumbaugh, and Ronald C. Rogers, "Insolvent Thrift Institutions, Agency Issues, and the Management Consignment Program" (presented at the Financial Management Association Annual Meeting, October 1986).

5   HOW TO AVOID ANOTHER THRIFT-INDUSTRY CRISIS

About the only aspect of proposed reforms that most, if not all, economists will agree on is the need to reduce the moral hazard caused primarily by deposit insurance priced at a fixed rate. It may be that the solution is to develop a variable, or risk-sensitive, deposit-insurance premium that increases with the level of portfolio risk within an institution. Another closely related option would be the development of a risk-sensitive capital requirement. Movement toward a risk-sensitive insurance premium has been a major recommendation in reports to Congress by both the Bank Board and the FDIC.[1] The Bank Board even indicated in its 1983 report that a risk-sensitive insurance premium ought to be part of any program to end the thrift-industry crisis. In addition, the Bank Board has adopted what has been called a risk-sensitive capital requirement, and the FDIC has proposed a type of risk-sensitive deposit-insurance premium.

Whether a risk-sensitive deposit-insurance premium or capital requirement will contribute much to reducing moral hazard is doubtful. Because it is so appealing to say that a variable-rate premium or capital requirement is the solution to a problem caused by a flat-rate premium, this conclusion may be displeasing initially. There are, nonetheless, substantial reasons to question whether implementation of a practicable risk-sensitive deposit-insurance premium or capital requirement can contribute to controlling risk-taking or reducing the cost to insurers of resolving the problem of troubled institutions. This is not to say that a risk-sensitive deposit-insurance premium or capital requirement should be rejected as a possible source of assistance in curtailing risk-taking. Rather, effective implementation of such a program will require a thorough evaluation of a large number of issues that until now have only been partially identified and, as yet, remain largely unanalyzed.

The questionable value of a risk-sensitive insurance premium or capital requirement is emphasized here because of the relative prominence of these options in the public debate over what reforms are needed. These and other reforms, such as lowering federal deposit-insurance coverage from the current level of $100,000 per account or abolishing it altogether, with or without private insurance to take its place, are addressed in more depth later in this chapter. The chapter, however, focuses on three specific reforms, the successful implementation of which would reduce the problems associated with excessive risk-taking and delayed closure of insolvent institutions and, in the process, tend to diminish the need for additional reforms like a risk-sensitive insurance premium. Stated as ukases, the reforms are the following:

Impose substantially higher capital requirements;
Establish a specific closure rule that allows the Bank Board to close barely solvent thrifts, thus minimizing the possibility that closure will result in a loss for the insurer; and
Force the Bank Board to use the market-value accounting tools it has available now and to move as close to full market-value accounting as possible.

THE ROLE OF MINIMUM CAPITAL REQUIREMENTS FOR INSURED DEPOSITORY INSTITUTIONS

To understand the purpose of minimum capital requirements, it is helpful to discuss how they can help to reduce excessive risk-taking and the likelihood of a loss to the FSLIC or the FDIC should excessive risk-taking or another event lead to a life-threatening problem for a thrift or bank.[2] In the process, it will become clearer how the reforms advocated here interact with each other, lessening the need for other reforms.

One of the fundamental tenets of economics is that unrestricted entry and exit of firms in an industry is the best way to ensure that customers' demands are met at the lowest cost.[3] The harsh side of this dictum is that free exit is a euphemism for the freedom to fail without recourse to government assistance. When firms that would otherwise fail are propped up by the government, this constitutes a federal subsidy to the firms' stockholders and employees. Consumers, who could be paying lower prices to more efficient firms, pay for the subsidy instead. The principle of "freedom to fail" ought to apply more to thrifts and banks than it has been, and the minimum capital requirement plays a role in this process.

"Wait a minute," you may be thinking, "are you saying that the government ought not to discourage thrift and bank failures?" The answer is yes, as long as a thrift or bank failure does not set off a run or impose a cost on the deposit insurer. This conclusion is based in part on the effect of the hundreds of thrift failures since 1980. As Chapter 2 points out, deposit insurance and regulation were intended to reduce the probability that individual thrift and bank failures would lead to difficulties for solvent thrifts and banks, which could harm the entire economy if the contagion extended far enough. The current thrift-industry experience suggests that worries about contagion are exaggerated. As these words are being written in 1987, almost one-quarter of the FSLIC-insured thrift institutions existing in 1980 have already been closed or are currently insolvent and targeted for closure. The Bank Board has acknowledged that an additional several hundred thrifts are insolvent but open because the Bank Board does not have money to close them. Yet thrift depositors are not queuing up to withdraw funds. Why?

There have been no runs because insured depositors know that the U.S. government has sufficient financial resources to resolve the problem of failed thrifts and they also appear to have faith that the government will provide those funds if necessary, even though there is no explicit requirement that it do so. Indeed, most depositors are probably unaware that the U.S. government is not explicitly required by law to pay insured depositors if the FSLIC or the FDIC cannot. If there were doubts about whether the government would live up to the implicit obligation to stand behind the FSLIC or FDIC, they would most certainly surface and spread rapidly given the intense scrutiny and exposure such issues receive by professional observers.

It would require a cataclysmic economic upheaval for widespread runs to develop. If such a catastrophe occurred, it would be the financial strength of the U.S. government and the depositors' faith that the government would act that would forestall runs—not the regulatory and deposit-insurance apparatus. Even if runs were to occur, so long as depositors merely fled insolvent institutions to put their funds in solvent institutions, even runs would not have the disruptive effect that was feared at the time the current regulatory and deposit-insurance systems were created.[4]

These observations bear directly on what ought to be the government's attitude toward the freedom to fail for thrifts and banks and the required minimum capital or net-worth levels set by the relevant government agencies. Fundamentally, the government should not be concerned with whether a given bank or thrift will need to be closed but whether its closure will cost the insurance funds anything.[5] The primary goal of capital should be to provide a buffer large enough so that, within the limits of the insurer's ability to monitor the condition of institutions, problem institutions can be closed with little or no cost to the insurer. If the insurer incurs no cost, neither will any insured depositor. Thus, protecting the FSLIC and the FDIC against losses is synonymous with protecting insured depositors against losses and guaranteeing that runs do not occur.[6] The major goal in setting a capital requirement ought to be to establish a capital buffer for the insurer.

The government should not shore up inefficient thrifts or banks, but rather should accept the closure of such institutions as long as it does not impose a high cost on the insurer. However, the government cannot acquiesce to the deteriorating condition of an institution because the deterioration does carry the potential of a cost to the insurer. Here, again, capital as a buffer plays an important role. Recent statistical studies have found that there is a statistically significant relationship between a thrift's or bank's capital buffer and the probability of failure or closure.[7] The studies find that higher capital levels are associated with a greater chance of avoiding failure, suggesting that higher net-worth institutions have more time to adjust when unexpected problems arise, while lower net-worth institutions have little or no time to do so. In addition, when unexpected difficulties arise, the incentives to take great risk develop faster for an institution with low net worth.

As discussed in Chapter 3, capital in a depository institution is similar to the deductible that is used in casualty-insurance policies to reduce moral hazard. Buying time with higher capital levels and reducing incentives for risk-taking when crises hit are extremely important objectives because, as the modern thrift-industry crisis has proven, economic difficulties can arise unexpectedly and affect the entire thrift and banking industries.

IN TROUBLED PERIODS, DO NOT LOWER CAPITAL REQUIREMENTS—INCREASE EXAMINATION AND SUPERVISION

The most important question to answer is at what level the minimum regulatory capital or equivalently net-worth requirement provides an adequate buffer to the FSLIC and FDIC. Table 2-7 presents selected average capital or net-worth levels for the thrift industry during the deposit-insurance period. Aside from two years in the 1930s when it fell slightly below 6 percent, net worth in the thrift industry was above 6 percent until 1975. From 1942 to 1970 net worth fluctuated within a range from approximately 6½ to 7¼ percent. With the narrowing of interest-rate margins caused by rising interest rates and greater competition, net worth began to fall in 1970 and continued to drop almost continuously until 1985.

As Table 1-2 in Chapter 1 shows, the period of relatively high and stable average net worth from 1934 to 1970 was accompanied by considerable exit of thrift institutions. There were over 10,000 institutions in 1935, approximately 7,500 in 1940, and about 5,600 in 1970. Although all exiting firms were not failures, a substantial number of failures did occur—as shown in Table 1-2, for example, over 1,000 institutions, primarily privately insured thrifts that were not granted FSLIC insurance in 1934, failed from 1935 through 1939. Although the number of institutions declined, the assets of thrifts grew steadily through the period. As Table 1-3 demonstrates, from 1945 to 1975 thrift assets as a percentage of all assets held by major financial intermediaries also grew, while the assets in banks declined as a percentage of all assets held by major intermediaries.

The most important point in the context of this chapter is that the ratio of net worth to a rising amount of assets in insured institutions remained stable and relatively high. The contrast in net-worth behavior in the post-1970 period is stark. Approximately 1,000 insured institutions exited the industry between 1970 and 1980. Another 1,300 exited between 1980 and 1985. Again, assets grew substantially in the industry and by 1985 were six times what they had been in 1970. However, unlike the period from 1940 to 1970, net worth fell 25 percent, from 6.98 percent in 1970 to 5.26 percent in 1980—in retrospect, a powerful warning signal. The slide continued with GAAP net worth falling more than 50 percent further, from 5.26 in 1980 to 2.37 percent in 1984.

Falling net worth is both a symptom of a disease and a disease itself: a symptom because whatever erodes net worth is generally a problem; a disease from the perspective of the FSLIC and the FDIC because it is an erosion of the capital buffer that protects the insurance funds against losses. Furthermore, when net worth falls to zero or near zero, incentives to take risk soar. The Bank Board's decision to lower the minimum regulatory net-worth threshold from 5 to 3 percent in 1981 and 1982 and to liberalize what could be allowed as qualifying net worth aggravated the problems caused by an eroded capital buffer.

A better approach would have been to keep the minimum capital standards as they were in 1980 and to have focused on the conduct of the institutions. This approach would have allowed well-capitalized institutions with higher net worth to use the greater powers provided by various states and by federal legislation in 1980 and 1982 to diversify their portfolio risks while increasing the ability of the Bank Board to rein in institutions with lower net-worth that had an incentive to take excessive risks.

A recent study cites evidence that the lowering of net-worth requirements has distorted the relationship between thrift common-stock returns and changes in thrift asset and liability values, reporting a "significant decrease in the comovement of S&L stock returns with the returns in S&L portfolio holdings following the reduction of net-worth requirements in 1980."[8] Thus, the study stuggests that the change in accounting practices inhibits the market from evaluating accurately the risk and risk-adjusted rate of return of thrifts. Bank regulators are now allowing selected commercial banks, primarily those in trouble due to regional economic downturns, to continue operating with lowered net-worth requirements. The 1987 FSLIC-recapitalization legislation lowered minimum net-worth requirements for thrifts under some circumstances to 0.05 percent. The thrift industry's experience in the 1980s, however, strongly suggests the error of these approaches.

RAISE THE MINIMUM REQUIRED CAPITAL LEVEL TO 6-PERCENT GAAP NET WORTH AND RAISE IT NOW

In August 1986 the Bank Board adopted new minimum capital requirements that were imposed on January 1, 1987. Appendix D presents a summary of the regulation, showing how complicated it is. The minimum capital requirement for most thrifts was set at a "base level" of 3 percent of the liabilities on a thrift's books on January 1, 1987. This part of the regulation is called the "liability component" (the specific form is summarized in Appendix D). The base level is lower for some thrifts because of accounting techniques such as the five-year averaging and twenty-year phase in discussed in Chapter 2. In addition, the minimum base level of capital is determined by RAP, not GAAP or tangible asset components of capital.

The minimum capital requirement will increase each year by a fraction of the previous year's thrift-industry profitability until it reaches 6 percent. The regulation ties the rate of increase in the minimum capital requirement to a thrift's initial base level. An institution with a base level below 3 percent must increase capital by 90 percent of the industry's average return on assets or 90 percent of its own return on assets, whichever is higher. For institutions at the 3-percent base level, the "standard group," the annual percentage increase is 75 percent. An institution whose regulatory capital exceeds the 3-percent base level does not need to raise its capital level until the standard group catches up. Then its capital must match the standard group's increase. The regulation also requires institutions to hold capital equal to 6 percent of their liabilities in excess of the level of liabilities on their books on January 1, 1987. Thus, all future liability growth in the industry must be capitalized at 6 percent.

Additional provisions of the regulation, called the "contingent component," require additional capital on recourse liabilities, standby letters of credit, scheduled items, and selected assets like direct investments, land loans, and nonresidential construction loans. These represent either troubled assets or assets considered by the Bank Board to represent high risk. Still other maturity-matching credit provisions allow institutions to lower their capital requirement, though not below 3 percent, if their one-year and three-year cumulative hedged maturity gaps are below a specified level.

The selected-asset and maturity-gap aspect of the regulation constitute what some term its "risk-sensitive" quality. As discussed in Chapter 3, "risk" is a portfolio concept involving the variances and covariances of all assets, not an asset-specific concept involving only the variances of some assets. Therefore, it is inappropriate to term the Bank Board's regulation as a risk-sensitive net-worth requirement.

Complaints from the thrift industry about this new minimum capital requirement were muted for the most part. Some slight criticism centered on how the 6-percent requirement on new liabilities would retard growth. But, as Chapter 3 explained, problems surrounding high-growth rates in the earlier 1980s and the disparity between the thrifts' far greater ability to leverage growth relative to commercial banks during that period tended to dampen the criticism. Additional minor criticism arose because of concern that the hedged maturity gap was not the appropriate index to use to measure interest-rate risk. The major criticism was directed at the "direct-investment" provisions of the regulation by a small but voluble group funded by a single thrift institution whose portfolio of direct investments was approximately 25 percent of its total assets.

There were virtually no complaints about what ought to have been the core of the regulation, the overall raising of the minimum capital requirement: The reason, thrifts could hardly have hoped for a regulation that would affect them less. Using the formula described above and based on annualized net income and asset data from fourth-quarter 1986, the standard group of institutions would need to raise their minimum net worth from 3 to approximately 3.004 percent the first year. Only in a boom period would any institution need to be concerned that substantial additional capital would have to be found. Implicit in the Bank Board's approach was the assumption that the minimum capital requirement could only be increased at a rate that would allow extremely poorly capitalized institutions to raise capital. The approach also means that poorly capitalized thrifts do not fail the capital requirement.

From the perspective of public policy, this approach fails both to demand the development of an adequate capital buffer and to restore to the Bank Board its former authority over thinly capitalized thrifts. The 1,300 institutions with regulatory net worth above 3 but less than or equal to 6 percent are under-capitalized in terms of the FSLIC's need for a capital buffer. Based on annualized September 1986 income data, these firms earned $3.8 billion in 1986, a significant percentage of which ought to have been required as a contribution to net worth. The capital buffer provided by institutions with regulatory net worth less than or equal to 3 percent is smaller still. Additions to net worth out of income are even more important in these cases, and, as a result, it is reasonable to propose that 100 percent, rather than 75 and 90 percent of return on assets, be contributed to capital. These institutions should have been required to retain all their net income.

In addition to providing a capital buffer, the minimum net-worth requirement also gives the Bank Board enormous supervisory power over an institution's behavior when it fails to meet the requirement. By setting the ultimate requirement at 6-percent RAP net worth, the Bank Board was implicitly stating that it must have the right to exercise supervisory power when an institution's net worth falls below that level. That is correct, and that is why the Bank Board should have then and should now raise the minimum capital level to 6 percent for all institutions. Moreover, the requirement should be based on GAAP to provide an additional buffer.

If the minimum net-worth level were raised to 6-percent GAAP net worth, it might well be below the 5-percent level of 1980 because, as discussed in Chapter 4, GAAP allows institutions to book gains on sales of appreciated assets but does not force institutions to book losses on unsold underwater assets. Based on September 1986 data, 2,105 institutions with $916 billion in assets would fail to meet a minimum requirement of 6-percent GAAP net worth. Approximately 586 institutions with assets of $219 billion fail the current requirement. If the threshold were based on 6-percent RAP net worth, 1,903 institutions with $813 billion in assets would not meet the requirement.

If minimum required capital levels were raised in this manner, the already overburdened staff of supervisory agents and examiners, and the Federal Home Loan Banks in general, would acquire an enor-

mous additional workload. Concerns would arise about the Banks'
ability to discern which of the institutions failing the higher net-
worth requirement were the most troubled and what kinds of new
reporting and additional restrictions ought to be placed on which
institutions. To respond properly, supervisory and examination staffs
would have to be enormously augmented with unprecedented speed.
What the Bank Board and the industry confront today is an economic environment just as perilous as that of 1980, with the indus-
tey's net worth far more depleted than it was then. Thus, as already
emphasized, even without a higher minimum net-worth requirement,
an extraordinary increase in the supervisory and examination staffs is
justified. Given the thin earnings and the poor capital buffer provided by the approximately 2,000 institutions with net worth below
6 percent, the Bank Board needs both to regain the authority it re-
linquished by lowering net-worth requirements and simultaneously
to conscript a larger, fully professional army of supervisory agents
and examiners.

Although this chapter is devoted to designing programs to avoid
a future thrift-industry crisis, the success of the effort to avoid a
future crisis is tied directly to the speed with which the current crisis
is overcome by closing currently insolvent but operating institutions.
The faster the closures occur, the sooner the new army of supervisors
and examiners could attack the problem of the 1,300 to 1,600 remaining institutions with low net-worth.

An important issue in raising the minimum required capital level is
whether this would create an incentive for institutions to take greater
risk. Would stockholders demand a greater return on assets if, for
example, rather than being paid out as dividends, earnings had to be
retained as net worth? To increase the return on assets, greater risks
might be taken. One way to approach this issue is to examine the
behavior of institutions whose net worth is already at 6 percent by
GAAP or at intermediate levels above 3 percent. The data from the
thrift-industry crises do not suggest a pattern of greater risk-taking
by solvent institution whose expected income can maintain their solvency. Greater risk-taking by lower-net-worth institutions under a
higher capital requirement would reflect attempts to ward off insolvency. The great dividing line separating risk junkies from prudent
risk-takers appears to be whether stockholders and managers feel
their institution is or is about to become insolvent.

A famous proposition in finance, moreover, is that a firm's investment—and hence risk-taking—and its financing decisions should be independent of each other.[9] A firm's asset selection should not depend on its level of capital or debt. Applied to the thrift industry and the issue of a minimum capital requirement, the proposition suggests that for a given level of assets—say $100—a thrift should be ambivalent about whether it has $97 in deposits and $3 in capital or $94 in deposits and $6 in capital. If the cost is the same, the thrift should be indifferent between paying interest on $3 of deposits or dividends on $3 of capital. But because a thrift can deduct interest payments on deposits from its taxes, and it cannot deduct dividend payments, it would rather pay interest than dividends. Since subordinated debt can in some cases count as net worth, and interest on subordinated debt is deductible, the issue of tax-adjusted costs may not be as important as it otherwise would be. Subordinated debt, however, is more expensive than insured deposits. Thus, a thrift could pay more for subordinated debt.

Another major consideration involves bankruptcy costs. If stockholders can increase debt relative to their stock, they shift the cost of bankruptcy more toward debt holders. Thus, if subordinated debt is raised as capital, it creates an incentive for subordinated debt holders to scrutinize thrift operations. Their scrutiny could offset the incentives to take risk caused by the higher cost of subordinated debt. Finely calibrating the net effects of raising capital levels on risk-taking, however, is difficult. On balance, thrift risk-taking thus far in the 1980s suggests that leaving thinly capitalized thrifts open without a higher minimum capital requirement is far more dangerous.

EXPLICITLY EMPOWER THE BANK BOARD
TO CLOSE BARELY SOLVENT THRIFTS

The FSLIC's (and the FDIC's) closure rule works in concert with regulatory capital, adequate supervision, examination and enforcement, and the availability of funds from the Congress when significant unexpected shocks occur, like the spike in interest rates in 1980. When unexpected shocks develop, the minimum net-worth requirement should be high enough to allow institutions to respond without the immediate pressure and incentives to take great risks that come with insolvency or near insolvency. Simultaneously, the capital buffer allows the Bank Board and the Federal Home Loan Bank system, with its supervisors and examiners, to evaluate the relative effect of the shocks on individual institutions. Since 1980 the Bank Board has been following a closure rule that guarantees that by the time the Bank Board closes an institution the institution will be market-value insolvent and thus, with no capital buffer losses will be borne by the FSLIC, which, with mounting bank insolvencies, could deplete the FDIC fund much as the FSLIC fund has been depleted.

A recent study of the costs associated with 324 thrift closures found that an average of nearly one year of GAAP insolvency preceded closure, thus imposing costs on the FSLIC.[10] The study also found that by following the rule that delays closure until an institution's book net worth—generally based on RAP—is negative, the estimated costs to the FSLIC of not closing the 229 GAAP-insolvent institutions earning negative net income in 1985 were rising by approximately $1 billion per year. Based on the 341 GAAP-insolvent institutions taking losses in 1986, that cost has risen to approximately $1.5 billion per year. These estimates are probably low because at year-end 1986 there were 460 GAAP-insolvent institutions, and further estimates suggest that the cost of failing to close them is about $2 billion per year. Ironically, only the deposit-insurance guarantee allows these institutions to remain open, continuing to increase the FSLIC's cost of closure.

In general, the closure rule can be viewed as a form of call option held by the Bank Board.[11] The strike price that allows the Bank Board to take control of an institution—merge it with another institution, liquidate it, or place it in a program like the MCP—is set by statute and regulation. Generally, when the Bank Board sees that an institution has zero net worth, it can exercise its option and take control of the institution. Under the National Housing Act, the grounds for appointing a receiver (in essence, closing an institution) include insolvency, unsafe and unsound practices, and dissipation of assets, although in the overwhelming number of instances, negative regulatory net worth has been the cause of closures. When a large number of insolvent or nearly insolvent institutions exist, it is the ability of the insurer to exercise the call option when it is "in the money" and the perception that the insurer will exercise the option that determine whether the insurer will be able to control risk-taking by those institutions. By following its current rule of closing institutions with no RAP net worth, however, the Bank Board almost always exercises its call option only when it is "out of the money," that is, when it will sustain a loss. Moreover, as is the case today, an adequate staff of examiners and supervisors will not be available to control large numbers of insolvent institutions when unexpected crises develop. Even if the unexpected crisis continues for years as the thrift crisis has, it would be difficult for the government to muster adequate numbers of examiners and supervisors.

The effectiveness of other often-suggested risk-reducing reforms, such as risk-sensitive deposit insurance premiums or lowering deposit-insurance coverage levels, also depends on the insurer's ability to exercise its call option. If the insurer is unable or perceived to be unable to exercise the call option, potential risk-reducing techniques in themselves will do nothing to control the tendencies of insolvent thrifts to take risks in a bid for resurrection. Indeed, the techniques would actually tend to increase risk-taking incentives for depository institutions. For example, unlike a fixed-rate premium, a risk-sensitive premium that would raise premium costs for these institutions would create a further incentive to take greater risk in order to recover the additional premium costs.

Similar effects arise if the level of deposits covered by deposit insurance is reduced. Decreasing the coverage level, and thereby putting additional depositors at greater risk should the insurer exercise its call option, increases uninsured depositor scrutiny of depository institutions' conduct and performance. The institution's performance and condition decline faster because, in reaction to the diminished performance, uninsured depositors will tend to withdraw funds among other actions. Proposals to decrease the coverage level generally also include increasing disclosure of information on the financial condition of institutions. Greater disclosure would tend to increase the speed with which uninsured depositors would withdraw funds from troubled institutions.

Under these conditions, if the insurer is, or is perceived to be, reluctant to exercise its option, and if little capital and income are at risk, the decreased coverage will tend to increase risk-taking. Although newly uninsured depositors may still respond with withdrawal to any deteriorating performance associated with increased risk, the institution—at least for a while—may use higher interest rates to attract new insured and uninsured depositors or hold old ones. To pay higher rates, greater risk must be taken. Clearly, without an effective call option, decreased coverage could stimulate risk-taking.

When the number of insolvent and nearly insolvent FSLIC-insured institutions is as large as it is today, increasing the number of uninsured depositors and providing them with better information also increases the probability of runs. Depositors in jeopardy for the first time of losing funds would likely be highly skittish. Depositors who had been uninsured before the coverage level was reduced and who expected that the insurer would make uninsured depositors whole if an institution failed would reassess their expectation as the number of uninsured depositors grew. As a result, they, too, would become more prone to withdraw funds.

In addition, if the insurer cannot, or is perceived to be unable to exercise its call option, a risk-sensitive premium and lower coverage levels will also tend to increase risk-taking among solvent institutions. The reasons why are similar to those discussed in Chapter 3, especially in explaining Table 3-4, showing how the cost of funds for thrifts has risen relative to banks' cost of funds. Some insolvent institutions taking greater risk will grow and in order to do so will offer higher interest rates on liabilities. The most aggressively growing insolvent depository institutions will offer whatever interest rates on insured deposits that are necessary to sustain the desired rate of growth.

Competing solvent institutions must then react to a shrinking market share of deposits. If they wish to maintain their market share, they must match the interest rate paid by the insolvent institutions. Depositors who are unable to distinguish between insolvent and solvent thrifts may also demand a risk premium to keep their funds in any thrift. In order to maintain profitability, both the insolvent and the solvent institutions competing with rate increases must select assets with greater expected return and, hence, greater risk. The ceiling on the level of risk taken will be set by insolvent institutions, according to the risk-return preference of the insolvent institutions and their perception of how much risk can be taken before the insurer exercises its call option.

Regardless of the nature of the insurance premium or the level of coverage, a properly designed closure rule would allow the Bank Board to close an institution before its market-value net worth becomes negative. The Bank Board should be able to strike when an institution's capital buffer is so eroded that it is reasonable to conclude that it will reach zero. A properly designed strike price would, in other words, allow the Bank Board to close an institution with positive but relatively low market net worth.[12] With contemporary book-value accounting, RAP and GAAP net worth would almost certainly be positive when market-value net worth was zero.

With an effective closure rule of this type, moreover, the need for a risk-sensitive insurance premium or capital requirement and lower deposit-insurance coverage—from the perspective of imposing market discipline—disappears. As long as the insurer closes an institution before it is insolvent, the institution's risk-taking cannot affect insured depositors and thus impose the social costs that deposit insurance was designed to avoid. With such a closure rule, regulation of allowable activities also becomes irrelevant to the avoidance of excessive risk-taking. Finally, the appropriate deposit-insurance premium would cover the insurer's administrative and monitoring costs.

Probably the most significant monitoring cost arises from examination and supervisory staffs. Market-value accounting would tend to reduce the need for these staffs because there would be less need to validate reported income and balance-sheet data. To the extent that market-value accounting facilitated the closure of thrifts and banks without insurer losses, it would reduce the need for costly expansion of examination and supervisory staffs during crises.

To some, closure of thrifts and banks may appear to eliminate these institutions' services. This would only be the case if institutions' assets were liquidated and the proceeds paid to the depositors. Even then, depositors could redeposit their funds in the remaining multitude of thrifts and banks. With liquidation, however, most deposits are sold to other institutions. In addition, only a few insolvent institutions have been liquidated; most have been merged with other thrifts. Although the number of thrifts in the United States has fallen from nearly 13,000 in the 1920s to almost 3,000, the percentage of assets held by thrifts has risen substantially.

The idea of closing an institution with positive net worth may seem like government confiscation of private shareholder wealth. It is not. First, in noncrisis periods, when failures are relatively rare, history suggests that normal monitoring allows the FSLIC and the FDIC to close institutions with relatively little or no loss to the insurance funds. In a crisis, however, the volatility of economic events is great enough to cause large numbers of institutions to deteriorate rapidly overwhelming the insurer's reaction time. In short periods of time, they can become so deeply insolvent that the insurance funds' cannot cope with the losses. If the insurer does not have the power to close an institution with positive net worth in these circumstances, the cost of further declines in the institution's value shifts to taxpayers and to solvent thrifts which will pay a higher premium. In other words, the loss is not limited to the shareholders of the insolvent thrift, although they, not taxpayers or shareholders of solvent thrifts, ought to bear the costs. If some capital remains after institutions are closed, it should be dispensed to the stockholders of the closed institutions.

The level of positive net worth at which the Bank Board ought to be authorized to close an institution will vary according to the nature of the economic difficulties confronting the industry. In general, the more volatile the situation, the greater the Bank Board's power should be. The level will also vary with the quality of information available to the Bank Board. In turn, the quality of information depends on how much time the Bank Board has to react to the deteriorating situation, and that will depend on how serious the economic threat is and how much capital there is in the industry as a whole and in the most heavily damaged institutions.

DEVELOP MORE ACCURATE MARKET-VALUE ACCOUNTING AND APPRAISAL PRACTICES

The quality of information available to the Bank Board hinges on how well institutions are monitored before and during a crisis. The size and quality of the supervisory and examination staffs and the quality of information available to them will determine the effectiveness of monitoring. In an unexpected economic downturn, the supervisors and examiners need to know the effect of the economic changes on the income flows and, with a lag, on the stock of net worth of the thrift institutions. Two primary categories of information are needed: the effect of changes in interest rates on the value of an institution's assets and liabilities or their cash flows; and the market value of direct investments and the assets that make up the collateral held by an institution. The value of the assets can be tangible, as in the value of property collateralizing mortgages or owned by an institution, or intangible, as in the charter value of the institution or the quality of its management.

Table 5-1. Selected Balance-Sheet Data from Financial Corporation of America.[a]

	March	September
Selected Assets		
Total assets	27,952	27,591
Total mortgages	22,681	22,447
ARMS	6,190	6,168
Mortgage-backed securities	5,778	6,656
Net REO	853	1,003
Delinquent mortgages	812	1,004
Selected Liabilities		
Total deposits	19,070	18,211
Jumbo CDs	12,065	12,549
Advances	2,760	2,834
Repurchase agreements	4,986	5,343
Net worth	327	315

a. In millions of dollars as of 1985.
Source: Author's calculations based on data from the Federal Home Loan Bank Board.

In principle, the Bank Board would like to know that the market value of all the institution's assets and liabilities at all times. The difference between the two would constitute the institution's market-value net worth.[13] To understand the importance to the Bank Board of knowing the market-value net worth of an institution, let us consider the case of American Savings and Loan of California, the second largest insolvent thrift in the country. American is owned by Financial Corporation of America and is known generally as FCA. As mentioned in Chapter 4, FCA's financial difficulties surfaced in August 1984, when the SEC forced FCA to reduce its reported profitability. The day after the public announcement of the SEC's position, depositors began to withdraw funds. Hundreds of millions of dollars per day, primarily in maturing Jumbo CDs, flowed out of FCA. FCA's vulnerability to hair-trigger withdrawals is highlighted in Table 5-1, which displays selected items from FCA's balance sheet, where Jumbo CDs represent over 70 percent of total deposits in September 1985. Collateralized borrowings from the Federal Home Loan Bank of San Francisco were used to meet the extraordinary withdrawal demands. Ultimately, the withdrawals subsided, following the replacement of the chairman of FCA with a person hand-picked by the Bank Board.

At any time since the summer of 1984, the Bank Board would have been justified in appointing a receiver for FCA under provisions of the National Housing Act. Table 5-1 presents a synopsis of why this was so in 1985. In March 1985, FCA's RAP net worth was $320 million, about 1.2 percent of its total assets of $28 billion. By the end of 1985, FCA had negative 2.9 percent net worth based on commercial-bank standards (GAAP net worth minus goodwill, plus subordinated debt). These book-value measures almost certainly camouflage a deep market-value insolvency.

What to do about FCA has been a constant, frequently reassessed issue at the Bank Board. At the end of 1985, the data in Table 5-1 were reviewed. The primary question was whether FCA had managed to reduce the truly enormous potential costs it signified for the FSLIC. The answer was "not really." FCA's six-month and one-year gaps, already large by industrywide standards, had risen slightly, and FCA's strategic plan at the time called for the origination of significant amounts of fixed-rate loans.

With FCA's net worth below 3 percent, the Bank Board had the power to veto the strategic plan and also to decide whether FCA should grow or shrink. With falling interest rates, FCA's plan called for growth and profits from originating mortgages at rates higher than would prevail in the future if rates continued downward. Like the hundreds of other insolvent thrifts gambling for resurrection, FCA wanted to grow out of insolvency. From the perspective of protecting the FSLIC, the universal Bank Board staff view was that FCA should shrink and all possible gains from the sale of existing assets that had appreciated with the fall in interest rates should be taken. The staff estimated that $8.5 billion of FCA's $16.4 billion in fixed-rate mortgages could have been sold for a gain in January 1986. That number could be high, it was understood, because some of the mortgages were nonconforming (that is, they did not meet standards for sale to the Federal Home Loan Mortgage Corporation, the Federal National Mortgage Association, and the Government National Mortgage Association). In addition, the staff speculated that the $6.6 billion in mortgage-backed securities could be sold at a gain.

A sense of quiet urgency pervaded these deliberations. At the time, in addition to FCA's interest-rate risk, its interest-earning assets were only $23.3 billion, less than its interest-paying liabilities of

$26.6 billion. The $150-million growth in REO (real estate owned through repossession) from March to September 1985 represented almost half of reported net worth. As Table 5-1 reflects, the combined growth of REO and delinquent mortgages from March to September exceeded FCA's total reported net worth.

From what the Bank Board knew about the market values of FCA's assets, there were gains to be made from their sale, but the level of precision was inadequate. The Bank Board staff urged the board to seek much more and better information on the yield and maturity distribution of FCA's mortgage-backed securities, conforming whole loans, and nonconforming whole loans. The staff was struggling to interpret imperfect market values and almost pleading for the Bank Board to get better data.

Interest rates continued to fall throughout 1986. FCA's interest-rate risk declined as well but remained substantially higher than industry averages. Rather than shrinking, however, FCA was allowed to grow by more than $7 billion while continuing to hold a substantial portfolio of REO. The big fear was that the interest-rate window would not be open forever. In February 1987, interest rates began to rise. The window may now be shut, and the enormous potential costs to the FSLIC embedded in the growing FCA balance sheet may be increasing substantially.

In 1987 the Bank Board began to acknowledge FCA's insolvency when in negotiations with potential acquirers FSLIC assistance of between $1.0 and $4.5 billion was openly discussed. If closure of FCA costs the FSLIC its 1986 average as a percent of assets, the cost would approach $8 billion. Given that any resolution will probably include indemnification for the next owners against imbedded but difficult-to-calculate losses, years will pass before FCA's full cost to the FSLIC emerges.

The most prudent course for the Bank Board to have taken in 1984 and 1985 with FCA was to use the available market values to force FCA to sell selected appreciating assets. Hamstrung by inadequate market-value accounting, however, it was unable to be as specific about sales as it should have been. FCA is a metaphor for the entire industry: The Bank Board needs to use what it knows about market values and it needs to demand better overall market-value accounting.

At any point in time, however, there may be disagreements about the market value of a thrift. The calculation of the market values of mortgage assets presented in Table 2-7 indicates some of the reasons for this. The calculation takes the tangible net worth of the institutions and adjusts it for the "marked-to-market" value of the fixed-rate mortgage portfolios of the institutions. The adjustment is based on an assumption backed by historical experience that the mortgages will be paid off in a shorter period than the full number of months to maturity by contract. The length of that period fluctuates, increasing when interest rates rise. In addition, the current market rate for mortgages is used to calculate the present value of the stream of payments from the mortgage and the lump sum payment at the estimated date of prepayment. The negative market values shown in Table 2-7 show how rising mortgage interest rates lower the market value of existing mortgages with lower coupon rates than those prevailing.

Notwithstanding the disputes surrounding this technique for calculating the present value of a thrift's mortgages, if it reveals that—holding all other influences constant—an institution's net worth is zero, the Bank Board should have the power to close the institution. If this rule had been followed between 1980 and 1982, many more institutions would have been closed. One might object that it would have been incorrect to close thrifts based on market interest rates in 1981 because rates came down in 1982, and, thus, the institutions were not really insolvent. However, this observation contains a fundamental error—it allows a onetime Bank Board judgment (or, better, act of prayerful anticipation) to determine the closure rule for thrifts, rather than the market's judgment of future interest rates.

In essence, the Bank Board was saying that its expectations of future interest rates were more accurate than the market's, even though, on average, the market's estimates will be more accurate. When market-value estimates of the value of assets are available, they should be used by the Bank Board. Fluctuations in asset values due to fluctuation in interest rates should be reported to the Bank Board. As a result, changes in the values of mortgages, mortgage-backed securities, and other interest-rate sensitive assets would be marked-to-market for the Bank Board. In this way, the Bank Board's assessment of institution's net worth would resemble more closely the values the FSLIC would receive if it closed the institution.

Along with marking interest-rate sensitive assets to market, the Bank Board can rely on other market evaluations. An area where huge gains in accuracy are possible and enormously helpful is the appraisal of real property. As one who has managed a thrift institution, I can testify to two facts. First, relatively accurate market-value appraisals of even the most complicated property are possible at reasonable expense. Prudent thrifts do not lend funds or invest directly in real estate without an appraisal they think is accurate. Moreover, the additional effort and cost to make results available to the Bank Board are trivial. Second, bogus appraisals are a dime a dozen. In reaction to these two facts, in 1986 the Bank Board began sending "R" memoranda demanding better appraisals to thrifts. The most recent R memorandum, promulgated in September 1986, followed the Bank Board's December 1985 adoption of the classification of assets regulation that allows examiners and supervisors to classify thrifts' assets as substandard, doubtful, and loss, and to demand that reserves be established where appropriate.

Vocal thrifts have complained that the R memoranda are excessive and that the classification of assets regulation gives examiners too much discretion. Closer to the truth, is an observation made by an industry analyst that the most recent R memorandum "could force institutions to make sweeping reductions in the appraised value of real estate collateralizing existing mortgage loans. This, in turn, would reduce their net worth—something that troubled thrifts can ill afford."[14] A similar debate surrounds the FASB's December 1987 proposal (open for comment until March 1988) that all financial institutions be required to report the market value of their assets and liabilities. The issue, however, should be accuracy. For its part, the Bank Board—representing the interests of taxpayers and solvent thrifts—must demand it, regardless of the consequences to individual troubled thrifts. If the Bank Board backs away from the classification of assets regulation and the R memoranda because of misguided thrift-industry pressure, the future cost of resolution of failed thrifts will rise.

NOTES

1. See Federal Home Loan Bank Board, *Agenda for Reform, A Report to the Congress* (Washington, D.C.: Federal Home Loan Bank Board, March 1983) and Federal Deposit Insurance Corporation, "Deposit Insurance in a Changing Environment," Washington, D.C., April 15, 1983.

2. For a summary of issues in regulating depository institutions' capital, see Tang D. Wall, "Regulation of Banks' Equity Capital," *Economic Review* (Federal Reserve Bank of Atlanta) (November 1985): 4–18.

3. For a treatment of this issue in the context of depository institutions, see George J. Kaufman, "Implications of Large Bank Problems and Insolvencies for the Banking Industry and Economic Policy," *Issues in Banking Regulation* (Winter 1985): 35–42.

4. *Ibid.* for an elaboration of the point in the context of the closure of large banks.

5. See Paul M. Horvitz, in "The Case Against Risk-Related Deposit Insurance Premiums," *Housing Finance Review* (July 1983): 253–264; and *Idem.*, "Deposit Insurance after Deregulation: A Residual Role for Regulation" paper presented at the Ninth Annual Conference of the Federal Home Loan Bank of San Francisco, December 1983). Horvitz was among the first to observe that the failure of a thrift does not necessarily have to impose a cost on the insurer and to point out some implications for deposit-insurance reform.

6. If the threat to the banking system's stability when thrifts and banks fail is exaggerated, there are other flaws in the traditional theory according to which regulators have set minimum capital levels. The theory is that banks and thrifts, if left on their own, would set capital levels too low, basing them solely on the private cost of failure to stockholders and not taking into account the potential social cost associated with the bank-system and economywide disruption that bank failures could cause. As a result, market-determined capital levels would be too low because they would ignore the negative externality of bank-system disruption. The negative externality today is so negligible that its use as a principle in setting minimum regulatory capital levels is unjustified.

7. See James R. Barth, R. Dan Brumbaugh, Jr., Daniel Sauerhaft, and George H. K. Wang, "Insolvency and Risk-Taking in the Thrift Industry: Implications for the Future," *Contemporary Policy Issues* (Fall 1985): 1–32; *Idem.*, "Thrift Institution Failures: Causes and Policy Issues" (proceedings of a conference on bank structure and competition, Federal Reserve Bank of Chicago, 1985); and *Idem.*, "Thrift Institution Failures: Estimating the Regulator's Closure Rule" (research working paper no. 125, Federal Home Loan Bank Board, Office of Policy and Economic Research, Washington, D.C., August 1986).

8. See James A. Brickley and Christopher M. James, "Access to Deposit Insurance, Insolvency Rules, and the Stock Market Returns on Financial Institutions," *Journal of Financial Economics* (in press): 37.

9. See F. Modigliani and H. M. Miller, "The Cost of Capital, Corporate Finance, and the Theory of Investment," *American Economic Review* (June 1958): 261–297, and *Idem.*, "Corporate Income Taxes and the Cost of

Capital: A Correction," *American Economic Review* (June 1963): 433–443. These are summarized in Richard Brealey and Stewart Myers, *Principles of Corporate Finance* (New York: McGraw-Hill, 1984).

10. See Barth, Brumbaugh, Sauerhaft, and Wang, "Thrift Institution Failures: Estimating the Regulator's Closure Rule."

11. Options theory has been used by Robert C. Merton, "An Analytic Derivation of the Cost of Deposit Insurance and Loan Guarantees: An Application of Modern Option Pricing Theory," *Journal of Banking and Finance* (June 1977): 3–11, to estimate the value of deposit insurance based on the perception that deposit insurance conveys a put option to the insured institution to sell its assets to the insurer in the event of insolvency. The call option discussed by R. Dan Brumbaugh, Jr., and Eric I. Hemel, "Federal Deposit Insurance as a Call Option: Implications for Depository Institutions" (research working paper no. 116, Federal Home Loan Bank Board, Washington, D.C., October 1984), is the same option viewed differently. Viewed as a call option, it is helpful in evaluating the insurer's closure rule and the incentives for risk-taking by insured institutions.

12. For another discussion of such a closure rule, see Jack M. Guttentag and Richard J. Herring, "Restructuring Depository Institutions" (paper prepared for the Thirteenth Annual Conference of the Federal Home Loan Bank of San Francisco, December 10, 1987).

13. One of the earliest proponents of market-value accounting was Ed Kane; see particularly *The Gathering Crisis in Federal Deposit Insurance* for a review. Also see Brumbaugh and Hemel, "Deposit Insurance as a Call Option"; Barth *et al.*, "Insolvency and Risk-Taking in the Thrift Industry" and "Thrift-Institution Failures: Estimating the Regulator's Closure Rule"; and Guttentag and Herring, "Restructuring Depository Institutions" for the use of market values in determining an appropriate closure rule.

14. Kenneth Leventhal & Company, *Real Estate Newsline* 4, no. 3 (March 1987): 1, 6.

6 REGULATION OF THRIFTS AND BANKS

Thrift institutions and commercial banks, though private firms, are among the most heavily, probably the most heavily, government-regulated firms in the United States. Chapter 1 outlined the evolution of thrifts and banks as private business firms, emphasizing balance-sheet differences and keeping the description of government intervention to a minimum. Chapter 6 fills in the gaps by presenting in detail the development of government regulation of thrifts and banks from its start after the Revolutionary War through 1986. The chapter is designed to set the stage for Chapter 7's proposed radical overhaul of deposit insurance and thrift and bank regulation.

WHAT JUSTIFIES THE EXISTENCE OF THRIFTS AND BANKS?

If asked what justifies the existence of thrifts and banks, many people would respond by saying that the answer is obvious: Consumers, for example, need checking accounts, savings accounts, and loans. Yes, but these needs derive from more fundamental needs. Individuals maximize their utility, or satisfaction, by choosing paths of consumption and leisure or work constrained by their income and other endowments. Individuals actually maximize expected utility because the future is not known. Since expected utility is being maximized over time, expectations about future income, for example, affect decisions made today. This means that guesses about future events, not just knowledge of current and past events, drive individual consumption and the economy.

Individuals typically prefer a smooth consumption path over time to an irregular one. Income, however, tends to be irregular due to the inevitable shocks to which it is subjected. For consumption to follow a smooth path, it will exceed income in some periods and fall below it in others. The relevance of these basic ideas for financial firms is that individuals will have to save some of their income in some periods and borrow in others in order to maintain smooth consumption and to maximize intertemporal expected utility. Furthermore, some individuals will borrow for investment on some occasions in order to increase their income in the future and, in turn, increase their future consumption.

If savers and borrowers knew each other and if relevant financial information about them were widely available at low cost, there would be little need for thrifts and banks. But there are so many savers and borrowers with so much financial information about them unavailable except at high cost that there is a need for someone to "intermediate" between savers and borrowers. Mainly because of informational asymmetries, savers have imperfect information about the soundness of loans to borrowers for consumption and investment. Financial-service firms survive profitably by specializing in information acquisition and the processing and monitoring of credit transactions.

One can see why both efficient operation and efficient government regulation of intermediaries are important. Lost efficiency can limit the ways in which individuals can save and borrow in order to smooth consumption. It can also raise the cost to save and borrow and in the process reduce consumption. Lost efficiency can also limit investment opportunities, raise the cost of investment, and thereby reduce economic growth and future consumption. When market-driven efficiency is thwarted by thrift and bank opposition to change, sometimes abetted by compliant government regulators, consumption and investment opportunities are lost. The cost to individuals and the economy of accumulated inefficiencies can be significant and could be astronomical if inefficient thrifts and regulators failed to cope with an economic crisis and runs developed as a result.

Thus, it is important to establish in detail what might cause such runs.

RUNS: THE MAJOR MODERN REGULATORY CONCERN

What could cause widespread depositor withdrawals that might halt the intermediation process and freeze the payment mechanism? In intermediating between borrowers and savers, financial-service firms transform liquid assets, convertible on demand into currency at face value, into illiquid assets and vice versa. A depositor's demand deposit (liquid asset), for example, helps to finance a farm (illiquid asset) through a mortgage. Liquid assets like demand deposits exist because they facilitate low-cost exchange. Illiquid assets or a range of financial assets with varying degrees of riskiness represent the desire to save and to borrow over time by heterogeneous individuals in a risky world.

The intermediation process may suffer when guesses about the future in a world of uncertainty—like farm income—turn out to be wrong, and the underlying real assets—like farms—do not generate the income necessary to prevent declines in the values of various financial assets. The effects of insufficient income can be made far worse, however, by runs on solvent institutions.

Solvent depository institutions are vulnerable because, in contrast to nondepository financial-service firms, they agree contractually to accept deposits that are payable on demand at face value. The essential difference is that creditors of depository institutions believe they are extending virtually risk-free credit of known value and the creditors of nondepository firms know they are extending credit whose value, determined by market forces, can rise or fall from its initial level. If demand deposits, the most volatile credit extended to thrifts and banks, were backed by 100-percent reserves or assets like short-term Treasury securities (which have virtually no interest-rate or default risk), depository financial-service firms offering the service of currency convertibility to their customers would always be able to meet any demand-deposit withdrawal at face value. Demand deposits, however, become liabilities for firms without an equivalent amount of reserves or Treasury bills held as assets. Usually, neither of these extremes is practiced; instead, firms operate on a fractional reserve system, which means that the value of a firm's demand deposits is based on the value of assets with both interest-rate and default risk. The assets mainly include loans whose market value can vary widely at any time.

Since demand deposits are payable in the order in which the demands are made, those holding such deposits have an incentive to withdraw them whenever they believe the assets of an institution cannot cover the deposits, that is, when an institution appears to be approaching insolvency. This feature of demand deposits in a world of uncertainty arouses concerns about the "safety and soundness" of the financial system. If depositors thought that only a few institutions were insolvent, withdrew funds from those institutions, and redeposited them in other institutions perceived to be solvent, there would be no threat. But widespread depositor runs throughout the entire financial system might lead to the forced sale of illiquid assets at depressed prices, which could drive otherwise healthy firms into insolvency. Although this would damage the intermediation process, the major fear seems to be the prospect of a collapse in the payments mechanism. With the Great Depression cited as a vivid example, the fear of widespread runs is used to justify governmental intervention to protect the payments system by assuring that depository financial firms engage in safe and sound practices.

What might precipitate a run large enough to disrupt the payments mechanism? A major economywide event like a national depression could render the solvency of all depositories questionable. Depositors might be unable to distinguish between solvent and insolvent institutions and run on both. The key to a nationwide run is a nationwide economic problem that creates nationwide uncertainty, brought on by imperfect information, about the solvency of most or all depositories.

A run of lesser magnitude could be based on regional economic difficulties. For example, depositors could observe declining farm prices and farm land values, conclude that thrifts and banks in agricultural areas must be headed for trouble, and rush to withdraw their deposits. This sequence can be extrapolated to any area where the economy is dominated by a single industry, such as oil, timber, or a certain type of manufacturing, whose activities have been hit by falling prices or new competition. Such regional runs are unlikely to spread nationwide due to the varying asset mixes across thrifts and banks in different regions of the country.

Various suggestions—all based on the premise that financial-service firms should provide demand deposits and should intermediate between savers and borrowers—have been made concerning how to deal with the potential for runs. One approach recommends the provision of federal deposit insurance to instill sufficient confidence in depositors to eliminate runs. Another involves backing demand deposits with 100-percent reserves or Treasury securities so that the payments-provision (or liquidity-transformation) service is completely separated from the more information-based intermediation service between saver and borrower. Some have advocated coupling private deposit insurance with a lender of last resort that will always stand ready to avert runs by lending to solvent but illiquid depository financial-services firms whenever frenzied withdrawals start mounting. Much more dramatically, some have recommended a laissez-faire system in which financial-service firms would issue the payments medium, like demand depositors, competitively in an unregulated system. Before discussing the strengths and weaknesses of these various alternatives, it is useful to review the evolving role of the government in the financial-services market.

U.S. GOVERNMENT REGULATION OF THRIFTS AND BANKS: REACTION TO CRISES

Because of the need to finance the Revolutionary War, the federal government understood the importance of money and banking from the beginning. The U.S. Constitution, however, explicitly gave the federal government power only "to mint coin and regulate its value," making no mention of federal chartering and regulation of banks. In the 1800s, however, various Supreme Court decisions established the principle that minting coin and regulating its value could be broadly interpreted referring to both coin and currency and to banks issuing currency or demand deposits.

The federal government became directly involved in banking when it provided twenty-year charters to the First Bank of the United States (1791–1811) and the Second Bank of the United States (1816–1836). Since there was no express prohibition against state-chartered banks, they too appeared and, indeed, flourished after the disappearance of the Second Bank of the United States. Because of the relative ease with which state charters were granted and the attendant growth in the number of state banks, 1837 to 1863 is called the "free-banking" period.

Following the free-banking period, federal regulation of thrifts and banks has been characterized by periods of crisis followed by congressional action that changed the balance sheets of depository financial institutions in some significant fashion. As Figure 6-1 shows, legislative changes have taken place mainly during wars and severe recessions. First, during the Civil War, the national banking system was established. The creation of the Federal Reserve followed the panic of 1907, and, in the wake of the Great Depression, legislation was passed that essentially created today's federal deposit-insurance and financial regulatory system. We are now in the midst of a fourth period of legislative change that began with alterations to thrift-institution balance sheets in 1980 and 1982. (See Appendix E for a summary of major and related legislation.)

In 1863 and 1864 two acts were passed by Congress that are collectively referred to as the National Banking Act. The act permanently established the federal government's more direct role in banking by setting up the Comptroller of the Currency to charter federal, or national, banks. With the National Banking Act, national currency was issued for the first time by the newly created nationally chartered banks. The new system was established to help finance the Civil War—it was the emergency of war that began federal regulation of depository institutions.

Under the National Banking Act, banks could issue currency but were required to back it with Treasury securities. Effective in 1866, a tax was levied on state banks' note issuance in an attempt to drive them and their currency out of existence. Although the number of state banks did initially decline quite sharply as the number of national banks grew, the state banks managed to survive as demand deposits continually grew in importance relative to currency as a payments medium. Since the Civil War, the United States has had a dual banking system, with federally and state-chartered banks operating side by side.

The so-called "bank panics" in 1893 and 1907 led to even more consolidation of federal government control over banking by providing the impetus for the establishment of the Federal Reserve System in 1913. Banks that became members of this system, which included all national banks by law and any state banks that elected to join, were given the "privilege" of borrowing from the Federal Reserve

Figure 6-1. History of United States Regulation of Depository Financial Institutions.

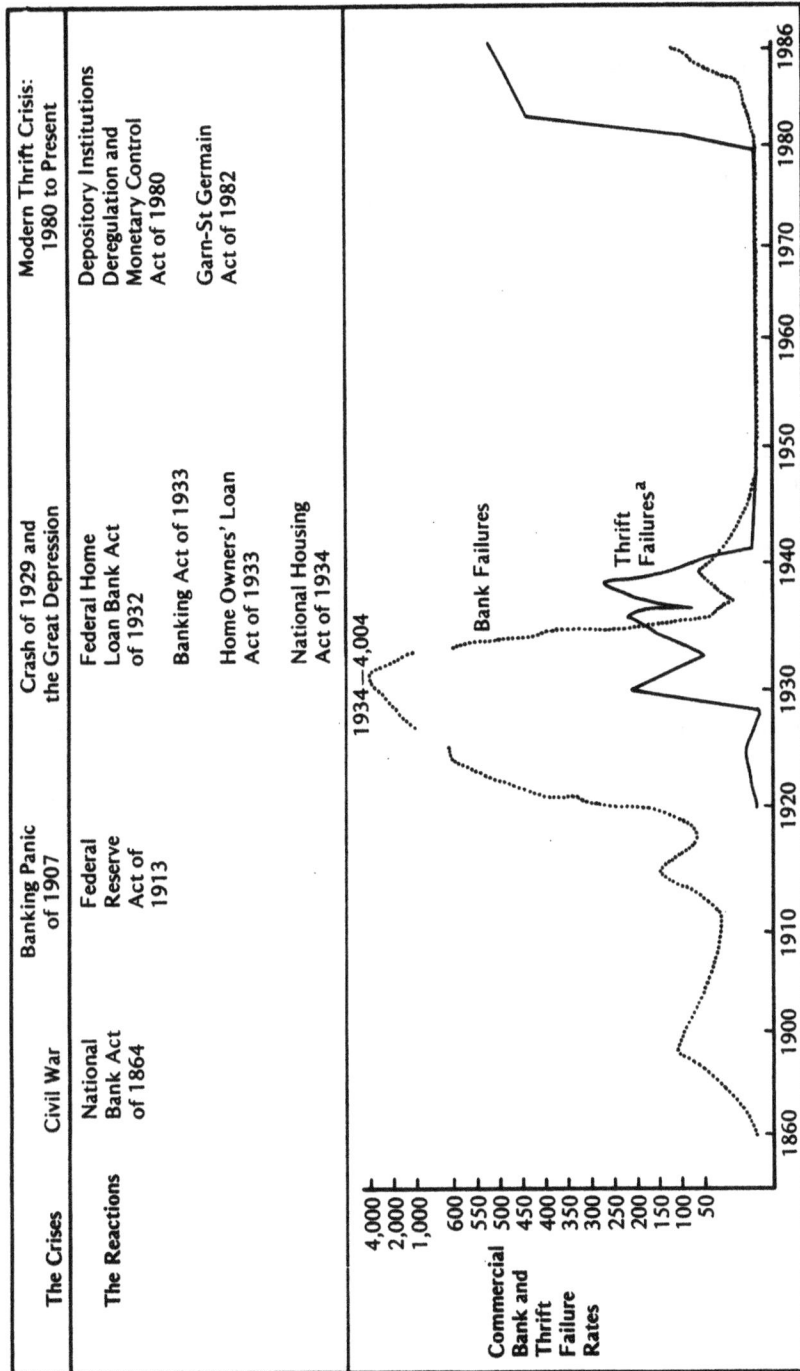

The Crises	Civil War	Banking Panic of 1907	Crash of 1929 and the Great Depression	Modern Thrift Crisis: 1980 to Present
The Reactions	National Bank Act of 1864	Federal Reserve Act of 1913	Federal Home Loan Bank Act of 1932 Banking Act of 1933 Home Owners' Loan Act of 1933 National Housing Act of 1934	Depository Institutions Deregulation and Monetary Control Act of 1980 Garn-St Germain Act of 1982

a. Includes insolvent but open thrifts after 1980.

Source: Based on data from U.S. Department of Commerce, Bureau of the Census, *Historical Statistics of the United States: Colonial Times to 1970* (Washington, D.C.); author's calculations from data from the FDIC; and Table 1-2.

when confronted with liquidity problems caused by unexpectedly heavy deposit withdrawals. The Federal Reserve was not intended to provide liquidity to insolvent banks, but rather to provide liquidity to solvent banks suffering from deposit withdrawals and thereby to prevent widespread bank runs or panics based on an erroneous perception that solvent banks were insolvent.

The Great Depression, however, proved that the existence of the Federal Reserve was insufficient, at least at that time, to prevent widespread bank panics. Several state insurance funds for banks had been established after the panic of 1907, but all of these had failed or were inoperative by the time of the Great Depression. Only the federal government, it was believed, could instill complete confidence in the safety and soundness of deposits throughout the entire banking system. As a result, federal deposit insurance was established for commercial banks in 1933, with the dual aim of protecting small depositors and providing depositors with confidence in the safety of the banking system in order to limit, if not actually eliminate, any future destructive runs on both solvent and insolvent banks.

Since 1789, then, the federal government has consolidated its control first over coin and currency, then over demand deposits, and more recently and generally over transaction accounts by chartering national banks, establishing the Federal Reserve System, and providing federal deposit insurance. Through court cases, legislative acts, and regulations, the federally established agencies overseeing these functions have attempted to contain the activities of all financial-service firms offering transaction accounts in an effort to protect the payments system. Protection of the small depositor resulted as well.

The containment system has involved geographical constraints, restrictions on the type and amount of assets and liabilities, limits on interest rates paid on deposits and charged on loans, and capital and liquidity, or reserve, requirements. Competition among the states and between the states and the federal government has resulted in some differences in the regulatory environment in which state and federally chartered financial-service firms operate. The exploitation of these differences, however, has generally been controlled either by federal law or regulations issued by the appropriate federal regulatory or insurance agency.

EARLY REGULATION OF THRIFTS: PRECURSOR
TO THE MODERN CRISIS

Before about 1850, savings and loans were primarily unincorporated firms that collected savings from local groups of individuals and over time rechanneled these funds back to the same individuals in the form of mortgage loans. After incorporation in 1850, savings and loans continued making local mortgage loans but also began accepting deposits from individuals who had no explicit interest in obtaining mortgage loans. In this way, the link between savers and borrowers began to weaken, despite the mutual form of organization under which savings and loans typically operated.

Due to the resulting informational asymmetries between savers or depositors and borrowers, managers became more important but, at the same time, more distant from both depositors and borrowers. Savings and loans could still intermediate between saver and borrower and specialize in residential mortgage loans, but monitoring the institutions to protect the depositors was increasingly considered to be a potential problem once the two sides of the balance sheet represented different individuals.

Since savings and loans, unlike commercial banks, were not involved in issuing currency or demand deposits from their inception in 1831 through the remainder of the century, the federal government showed little interest in their activities, with the important exception of providing them with tax concessions beginning in the late 1800s. Before the 1880s, the involvement of state governments was largely confined to granting charters—and to the restrictions inherent therein—although New York did pass legislation for the first time in 1875, requiring the filing of annual reports. Because relatively few savings and loans appear to have failed before 1890, relatively limited attention from the government resulted.

In the 1890s, however, savings and loans did fail, and the result was the establishment in 1892 of the U.S. League of Local Building and Loan Associations, now the U.S. League of Savings Institutions. As discussed in Chapter 1, one of its early accomplishments was to lobby successfully for state legislatures to prohibit the establishment of national savings and loan associations, a trend that had developed in the 1880s. Local savings and loan associations attributed most of their troubles in the 1890s to improper loans made by the "nationals" that harmed the "locals" because customers were unable to distinguish between the two types of firms during the panic of 1893. By seeking to enforce homogenization as well as localization, thrifts were attempting both to remain separate from other financial competitors and to limit competition within their own industry.

Commercial banks and savings and loan associations remained compartmentalized throughout the 1800s. As income and wealth grew, however, the two industries began to compete for business. Competition was facilitated in the early 1900s, when national banks were informed that they were no longer prohibited from offering savings deposits and when the Federal Reserve Board set much lower reserve requirements on savings than on demand deposits. Commercial banks now had an incentive as well as the right to compete with savings and loan associations for savings deposits. This opened the door for limited competition on the liability side of the balance sheet.

On the asset side, competition began to develop over residential mortgage loans, but to a much more limited degree. Without active secondary markets and with regulations that were still somewhat restrictive, the two types of depository institutions found that each had its own particular strengths in information collection and processing that maintained fairly identifiable balance-sheet differences. This was especially so because of the favorable tax treatment afforded the thrifts.

The Great Depression finally changed the role of the federal government in the thrift industry. Thus far, the federal government had devoted all its efforts to chartering and regulating banks; it now expanded its range of operations to include saving and loan associations. Finally, in 1932, the Federal Home Loan Bank Board was established to charter federal savings and loan associations and to make advances (loans) to its members, which included all federal associations and those state associations that wished to join.

The chartering of federal savings and loan associations did not represent an attempt to drive state-chartered thrifts out of business. For this reason, federal thrifts were to be chartered only where no state thrifts were located or where they existed in insufficient numbers and size to service all consumers. Furthermore, the federal thrifts were to be only mutual-type thrifts and would operate as local institutions like almost all of the state thrifts. In addition, the Federal Savings and Loan Insurance Corporation was established in 1934 to provide insurance for savings deposits at all federally and state-chartered FHLBB member thrifts as well as any remaining state-chartered thrifts that wished to join.

With the establishment of the FSLIC, thrifts were placed on the same competitive level regarding federal deposit insurance as commercial banks. When the FDIC was created in 1933, the insurance limit was $2,500 but this rose to $5,000 in 1934 to match the limit for deposits at thrifts. Since then, the maximum insurance limits for all federally insured depository institutions have been the same, rising to $10,000 in 1949, $15,000 in 1966, $20,000 in 1969, $40,000 in 1974, and $100,000 in 1980.[1] Furthermore, the premiums paid by the two types of insured institutions have been based upon a non-risk-adjusted calculation that is a fixed percent of total deposits. The premium has been the same 1/12 of 1 percent since the 1930s, although partial rebates have been common FDIC-insured institutions. Since 1985 a special assessment of 1/8 of 1 percent per annum has been levied on thrifts, due to the record costs incurred by the FSLIC because of troubled institutions. This recent differential has induced some thrifts to switch to bank charters in order to obtain federal deposit insurance at lower cost.

After the Great Depression, additional legislation was passed to fortify the FSLIC against any potential heavy demands for insurance payments. This included authority in 1950 to borrow up to $750 million from the U.S. Treasury, the establishment in 1961 of a secondary reserve (to be phased out during those periods when the ratio of FSLIC reserves to insured deposits is above 1.25 percent), and the authority in 1965 to borrow from thrifts. The FSLIC may also borrow from the Federal Home Loan Banks, which it did for the first time in 1984.

Tax law began to affect the thrift industry in 1951. Before the Revenue Act of 1951, thrifts were exempt from federal income tax. Although this act terminated their tax-exempt status, thrifts were nonetheless able to avoid paying taxes by being permitted to deduct up to 100 percent of taxable income through a bad-debt reserve. Based on its estimate of bad loans, an institution could establish a bad-debt reserve and deduct the amount of the reserve from taxable income. In 1962, however, a Revenue Act was passed that reduced the bad-debt deduction to 60 percent of taxable income, subject to a qualifying-asset restriction. This restriction stated that 82 percent or more of the assets had to consist of cash, U.S. government securities, and passbook loans, plus one-to-four-family residential property loans to be eligible for the maximum deduction. The bad-debt deduction was reduced by ¾ of 1 percent for every 1 percent the qualified assets fell below 82 percent of total assets. The deduction was zero if these assets fell below 60 percent.

The Tax Reform Act of 1969 modified this by permitting a thrift to base its bad-debt deductions on taxable income, loss experience, or percentage of eligible loans. Since the vast majority of thrifts used the taxable-income method, the result was that the portion of taxable income that may be excluded from income as an addition to a reserve for bad debts was reduced in scheduled steps from 60 percent in 1969, to 40 percent in 1979. The Tax Equity and Fiscal Responsibility Act of 1982 further reduced the bad-debt deduction to 34 percent in 1982 and then to 32 percent in 1984. More recently, the Tax Reform Act of 1986 reduced the bad-debt deduction as a percent of taxable income to 8 percent in 1987.

At the same time, the 1986 act reduced the maximum corporate tax rate from 46 to 34 percent provided for an alternative minimum tax, and extended the time of the loss-carryforward provision, all of which, unlike the reduced bad-debt deduction, benefit savings and loan associations. To be eligible for the maximum deduction under the 1986 act, a savings and loan only had to have 60 percent or more of its assets in qualifying assets (largely those mentioned above). Thus, over time, the tax laws have provided a large but diminishing incentive to invest in eligible mortgage-related assets.

Apart from tax laws, there are other important laws and regulations pertaining to FHLB System thrifts, FSLIC-insured thrifts, federal thrifts, and state thrifts. One law concerns the rate paid on savings deposits and the other addresses member thrifts' liquidity (where liquidity refers to the minimum amount of assets such as cash and U.S. Treasury securities that must be held as a percentage of savings deposits). The power to set liquidity requirements was granted in 1950. The Interest Rate Control Act of 1966 gave the FHLBB the authority to set rate ceilings, nonexistent until then, on member thrifts' savings deposits. To provide thrifts with a competitive edge in garnering funds for the residential housing sector, this ceiling was set initially at ½ of 1 percent (later reduced to ¼ of 1 percent) above the ceiling rate that commercial banks were permitted to pay on savings deposits. This differential was abolished in January 1984, and all such rate ceilings for all financial depository institutions were eliminated in March 1986.

As far as FSLIC-insured institutions are concerned, the regulations are quite comprehensive and subject to change. They involve asset and liability restrictions, closure procedures, and net-worth, or capital, requirements. Since these regulations have been discussed, it will suffice to make two short points. First, the Financial Institutions Supervisory Act of 1966 allows the FHLBB to issue cease-and-desist orders whenever an insured thrift is engaged in "unsafe and unsound practices." This law, passed to curtail perceived harmful practices by troubled thrifts, requires member thrifts to comply immediately with FHLBB orders, leaving legal challenges until later. Second, the net-worth regulation was designed to provide a buffer against asset-value declines and thereby to protect the insurance fund from losses due to failures. It was also used in 1984 to discourage fast-growing thrifts from engaging in risky loan policies.

The federal thrifts are subject to the most control by the Bank Board. The reason, of course, is that they are subject to three sets of regulations as federal, member, and insured thrifts all in one. Interestingly enough, "there are cases where the FHLBB has given federal associations certain powers . . . and then set tighter restrictions (for insured associations) taking away these powers."[2]

The regulations covering federal thrifts were initially intended quite specifically to limit lending to local home-mortgage loans (loans secured by houses within fifty miles of the thrifts' home office). In 1964 federal thrifts were permitted to make unsecured, personal loans for college or educational expenses—the first time thrifts had been allowed to make loans for any purpose other than acquiring real estate. In the same year, the geographical limit for mortgage loans was extended to one hundred miles. In later years Congress extended the limit to encompass a thrift's home state, and even beyond, for the largest thrifts. Then, in 1983, the FHLBB permitted federal thrifts to make loans nationwide. Unless prohibited by state law, state thrifts with FSLIC-insurance were permitted to do the same. As in the 1880s, thrifts were again "nationals." In 1986, however, the FHLBB proposed restricting thrifts' ability to make nationwide loans but subsequently dropped the proposal after considerable opposition.

In 1964 federal thrifts were also permitted to issue mortgages and buy property in urban-renewal areas and to buy securities issued by federal, state, and municipal governments. Then, in 1968, these thrifts were allowed to make loans for mobile homes, second or vacation homes, and housing fixtures. Thus began thrifts' entry into business areas long viewed as the exclusive domain of commercial banks.

GOVERNMENT REGULATION OF THRIFTS
IN THE TURBULENT 1970s AND 1980s

The high and volatile interest rates of the 1970s and 1980s finally drove home the point that the balance sheets of thrifts dominated by fixed-rate mortgage loans and passbook savings deposits were creating major problems for these institutions. The response was to grant thrifts nationwide expanded depository powers beginning in 1981 through the negotiable order of withdrawal (NOW) account, after private initiative, which began in Massachusetts in 1972, and lengthy and protracted legal, regulatory, and congressional action. Another significant innovation was the money-market certificate, introduced in 1978. This and other types of accounts enabled thrifts to compete for savings more effectively with the expanding range of financial-service firms.

On the asset-side of the balance sheet, thrifts finally began to move more heavily into variable-rate mortgages. In 1974, however, Congress initially rejected proposals for this type of mortgage on a national basis, with the result that only state-chartered thrifts in a few states began to experiment with these mortgages in the 1970s. But in 1977 Congress authorized the Department of Housing and Urban Development to insure graduated-payment mortgages nationwide, and on January 1, 1979, the Bank Board authorized variable-rate, graduated-payment, and reverse-annuity mortgages for federal thrifts.

At first, the variable-rate mortgages were allowed only in states where state thrifts were authorized to offer them, but on July 1, 1979, the authorization was extended to federal thrifts in all states. Furthermore, with the introduction of pass-through securities and mortgage-backed bonds, thrifts began to turn to the secondary market as source of mortgage funds. In the process, thrifts began seeking more of their income in the origination and servicing of mortgages while simultaneously reducing their risk in holding individual mortgages. In short, thrifts began acting more like mortgage bankers.

The federal government was not involved in a direct and significant way in most of the regulatory changes in the 1970s. This changed dramatically in the 1980s because of the severe problems of thrifts during this period. First came the passage of the Depository Institutions Deregulation and Monetary Control Act in March 1980, which provided for the gradual elimination of interest-rate ceilings on deposits by March 1986. As Appendix E indicates, it also granted new powers to federal thrifts, including the authority to operate remote service units, offer credit cards, engage in consumer and commercial lending, and offer NOW accounts. Thrifts were also given equal access for the first time to the Federal Reserve System services and the Federal Reserve discount window for borrowing purposes in emergency situations, in exchange for being subjected to reserve requirements on their deposits.

Following the passage of this legislation, the Bank Board began to loosen its regulatory grip over the thrift industry through a number of actions in 1980, 1981, and 1982. The Bank Board allowed federal thrifts to negotiate any type of fixed- or variable-rate mortgage instrument with borrowers. FSLIC-insured thrifts were permitted to borrow outside the FHLB system without limit and to accept more liabilities maturing within a three-month period. Federal thrifts were given authority to invest in mutual funds and up to 3 percent of their assets in service corporations. FSLIC-insured thrifts were permitted to make real-estate loans without regard to geographic constraints. Federal thrift service corporations were allowed to engage in a wider range of activities without prior approval and to deal with a broader range of customers. FSLIC-insured thrifts were also authorized to issue variable-rate savings accounts and certificates.

The second major change was the passage of the Garn–St Germain Depository Institutions Act in October 1982. In broad terms, this legislation gives the Bank Board the authority to arrange mergers of failing thrifts with other thrifts, commercial banks, savings and loan holding companies, bank holding companies, and nondepository companies. More specifically, a program of capital assistance was established for thrifts with seriously low net worth. Under this program, the FSLIC would issue promissory notes to purchase net-worth certificates from qualified thrifts. If the qualified thrifts recovered from their troubles, the promissory notes and net-worth certificates would be retired. Otherwise, the FSLIC would be forced to pay off the promissory notes, thus incurring losses. In addition, the FHLBB received authority to approve interstate transactions by permitting the FSLIC to override any state or federal law that would prevent a financially troubled FSLIC-insured thrift from merging with any other FSLIC-insured thrift or FDIC-insured bank or being acquired by any person or company, including a bank holding company. The approval of a significant number of transactions of this kind, of course, increases the pressures to remove all banking restrictions as well as the walls between difference types of financial firms. The act also expands the balance-sheet powers of thrifts and grants greater freedom for thrifts to operate in stock rather than mutual form. Several of these provisions dealing with financially troubled thrift institutions expired on December 31, 1986, and have not been extended by Congress as of June 1987.

The "permanent" changes made by the 1982 act were indeed historic. These involved additional asset and liability powers as well as greater freedom pertaining to organizational form and capital generation. Existing law had been biased against the stock form of organization that restricted access to capital markets, but this act allowed the creation of new federal thrifts—whether on a *de novo* or a conversion basis or in the mutual or stock form—nationwide and permitted any federal thrift to convert from the mutual to the stock form or the reverse, also without geographic restriction.

The Garn-St Germain Act also specifically provided for federal thrifts to make secured and unsecured loans for commercial, corporate, business, or agricultural purposes. Investment in such loans was limited to 10 percent of assets as of January 1, 1984. Complementing this new commercial-lending power, federal thrifts were authorized to offer demand deposits to individuals and to corporations to which they had already made corporate, commercial, business, or agricultural loans. Corporations could also establish demand deposits at federal thrifts into which individual customers could pay their bills. These particular changes permitting federal thrifts to accept demand deposits and to make commercial loans essentially transformed them into banks, although they are exempt from being classified as such under the Bank Holding Company Act. Instead, these thrifts are regulated exclusively by the Savings and Loan Holding Company Act as it regards acquisitions or control by companies other than bank holding companies.

Under the 1982 legislation, federal thrifts were permitted to invest up to 40 percent of their assets in loans for nonresidential real estate, up from 20 percent. They were also permitted to invest as much as 30 percent of assets (again, up from 20 percent) in consumer loans, which for the first time could include inventory and floor-planning loans. Federal thrifts could also invest up to 10 percent of their assets in tangible personal property for lease or sale, thus enabling them to compete with commercial banks in the commercial leasing business. Table 6–1 lists the various asset limitations for thrifts, and Table 6–2 shows the change in asset composition that has developed since the late 1970s.

In sum, the Garn-St Germain Act enables a federal thrift to invest up to 90 percent of its assets in commercial-type investments. It also permits these thrifts to invest up to 100 percent of their assets in state or local government securities and, for the first time, to invest in other thrifts' time and savings deposits and use such investments to help meet liquidity requirements.

As Table 6–2 reveals, home mortgages have declined 45 percent and mortgage-backed securities have nearly doubled. Mortgage loans for commercial real estate, land and land development, and non-mortgage commercial loans have increased, as has direct investment in real estate and service corporations. Since 1980 thrift assets have more than doubled, and most of the growth has been in "nontraditional" assets not permitted before regulatory reform.

Table 6–3 takes both balance-sheet and income-statement data to show the major categories of asset diversification from 1980 through 1986. For each activity there are two measures: one based on assets and one based on income. This is necessary because for certain activities (such as leasing) the investment precedes the income, while for other activities (such as mortgage banking) the value of the earning "asset" does not appear on the balance sheet. Although the categories selected and the measures of activity used are somewhat arbitrary, they represent broad asset-diversification trends in the industry.

Mortgage-banking activity has increased, and fee income from origination and servicing has become an important source of revenues. Another measure of mortgage banking is the value of loans serviced for others, net of loans serviced by others. As a share of total loans held, this measure of mortgage-banking activity has increased nearly 500 percent.

Some thrifts have shifted their asset mix away from mortgage loans toward investment securities. They earn income from the spread between asset yield and the cost of liabilities and from gains when appreciated investments can be sold at a profit. Income from

Table 6-1. Thrift Institution Asset Limitations.

Federals

Nonresidential real estate	40% of assets
Investments in personal property for rent or sale	10% of assets
Consumer loans and corporate debt	30% of assets
Commercial loans	10% of assets
Education loans	5% of assets
Community development investments	2% of assets
Non-conforming residential loans	5% of assets
Unrated corporate debt securities	1% of assets
State housing corporation loans	30% of assets
Service corporations	3% of assets
Manufactured homes	100% of assets

All Insured

Direct investment	PSA review when in excess of the greater of 10% of assets or twice capital
Loan-to-value (major loans) (proposed)	PSA waiver when greater than 100% of capital
Nationwide loans (homes) (proposed)	PSA waiver when greater than 200% of capital
Nationwide loans (major loans) (proposed)	PSA waiver when greater than 100% of capital
Participations (proposed)	100% of assets
Earnings-based accounts	5% of assets; up to 20% with PSA approval
Brokered deposits	5% of deposits if the institution fails net-worth requirements; PSA waiver possible
Rated obligations of one issuer	1% of assets

Source: Based on data from the Federal Home Loan Bank Board.

Table 6-2. Percentage Distribution of Assets Held by FSLIC-Insured Institutions (1977-1986).

Type of Asset	1977	1978	1979	1980	1981	1982	1983	1984	1985	1986
Mortgage-backed securities	2.8	3.1	3.5	4.3	5.0	8.5	10.8	11.0	10.3	13.5
Home mortgages	67.4	67.8	67.7	66.2	64.7	55.7	49.3	44.5	42.0	38.1
Subtotal	70.2	70.9	71.2	70.5	69.7	64.2	60.1	55.5	52.3	51.6
Multifamily mortgages	6.7	6.6	6.2	5.8	5.4	5.3	5.8	6.3	6.8	7.1
Mortgages on commercial real estate	7.3	6.8	6.5	6.2	6.2	6.3	7.2	8.4	9.1	9.0
Mortgages for land and land development	0.9	0.8	0.9	0.9	0.9	0.9	1.5	2.3	2.8	2.8
Nonmortgage commercial loans	0.1	0.1	0.2	0.3	0.1[a]	0.1	0.4	1.1	1.5	2.0
Nonmortgage consumer loans	2.2	2.1	2.6	2.7	2.7	2.8	3.0	3.4	4.0	4.3
Repossessed assets	0.3	0.2	0.1	0.2	0.2	0.4	0.5	0.5	0.9	1.1
Investment real estate	0.1	0.1	0.2	0.2	0.3	0.4	0.5	0.5	0.6	0.7
Cash, deposits, and securities	9.2	9.2	8.9	9.8	10.1	12.0	13.4	13.3	12.8	14.1
Fixed assets	1.7	1.7	1.7	1.8	1.8	1.9	1.8	1.2[a]	1.2	1.3
Equity in service corporations/ subsidiaries	0.3	0.3	0.4	0.5	0.6	0.8	1.0	1.6	1.9	1.8
Goodwill	b	b	b	b	1.8	0.2	2.3	3.6	3.9	2.1
Other	1.0	1.2	1.1	1.1	1.8	2.6	2.3	3.6	3.9	6.7
Total assets (in billions of dollars)	450	513	568	618	651	393	819	979	1,070	1,165
Number of institutions	4,065	4,053	4,039	4,002	3,779	3,343	3,183	3,167	3,246	3,220

a. Change in definition.
b. Less than 0.05 percent.
Source: Author's calculations based on data from the Federal Home Loan Bank Board.

Table 6-3. Thrift Industry Diversification Trends (*Amounts in percent*).

Diversification Activity	End of Year	
	1980	1986
Mortgage Banking		
Net loans serviced/held	3.2	18.7
Mortgage fee income share	4.8	9.6
Trading		
Investment assets share	0.5	4.2
Investment income share	9.9	11.1
Real-Estate Development		
Real estate assets share	13.6	22.6
Real estate income share	0.5	0.5
Commercial Banking		
Nonmortgage loan assets share	1.4	5.6
Nonmortgage loan income share	3.6	7.3

Source: Calculations based on data from the Federal Home Loan Bank Board by R. Dan Brumbaugh and Andrew S. Carron in "Thrift Industry Crisis: Causes and Solutions," *Brookings Papers on Economic Activity* (Washington, D.C.: The Brookings Institution, 2: 1987), pp. 1-29.

trading activities exceeds income from the other diversification activities, although trading is the smallest share of assets.

Relaxation of regulations permitted thrifts to engage directly in real-estate development. The share of assets devoted to this activity has increased 66 percent since 1980. Gross revenues from real-estate activity are not reported separately, nor are revenues from service corporations engaged in real-estate development identified. Only net income is shown, and that is down due to substantial losses in many areas.

Thrifts are also beginning to offer a full range of nonmortgage loans, paralleling the services provided by commercial banks. The share of nonmortgage loan assets has increased by 300 percent, while the revenue share from those sources has doubled.

Although the Garn–St Germain Act gives federal thrifts many bank-like powers, it also imposes bank-like branching restrictions under certain circumstances. A federal thrift may have interstate branches only if it qualifies as a savings and loan assocation according to the Internal Revenue Code by meeting the "thriftness test" of having a minimum of 60 percent of its assets in home-ownership financing or other qualifying assets such as mortgage-backed securities, cash, certain government securities, student loans, and passbook loans. Also, if a FSLIC-insured institution that is a subsidiary of a unitary savings and loan holding company no longer qualifies as a savings and loan association under the Internal Revenue Code, the parent must either divest the association or come into compliance with the restrictions applicable to multiple savings and loan association holding companies.

Following the Garn-St Germain Act, the Bank Board continued to issue a number of regulations affecting thrifts. In 1983 Federal Home Loan Banks were permitted to make advances for terms of up to twenty (rather than ten) years. Federal thrifts were permitted in 1984 to establish finance subsidiaries to issue securities for their parent institutions. In the same year, FSLIC-insured institutions were required to establish policies to manage interest-rate risk in their operations. New net-worth and direct-investment requirements were imposed in 1985 and again in 1986 and early 1987. As discussed in Chapter 5, FSLIC-insured thrifts must increase net worth according to their rate of growth. Those thrifts with more than $100 million in assets must seek permission from the FHLBB to grow more than 25 percent a year. Greater net worth is also required for thrifts with direct investments. And, finally, the five-year averaging and twenty-year phase-in used to calculate net worth will be gradually eliminated.

If their direct investments, or investments in equity securities, real estate, and service corporations exceed 10 percent of assets or twice regulatory net worth, whichever is greater, thrifts must undergo a process of supervisory review and approval and post a 10-percent reserve against all direct investments made after December 10, 1984. This particular asset restriction was quite controversial and therefore had a sunset provision to expire on March 15, 1987, unless it was extended by the FHLBB. It was extended, and further modifications were made that effectively resulted in more curtailment of direct and other equity-risk investments.

The recent legislation and regulatory changes have caused thrifts to resemble commercial banks more than at anytime since their development in 1831. Until relatively recently, thrifts' balance sheets consisted almost entirely of passbook saving accounts, on the liability side and home mortgage loans on the asset side. Tables 6–2, 6–3, and 6–4, show just how much both sides have changed since 1977. At the end of 1986, passbook accounts constituted only 6.8 percent of deposits, down from 33.0 percent in 1977. Home mortgage loans accounted for only 38.1 percent of assets (or 51.6 percent when mortgage-backed securities are included). The rationale for government regulation of thrifts seems to be changing in kind, its focus shifting from their role in thrift and home financing toward their role in the payments mechanism, which is also the regulatory approach to commercial banks. (Before continuing, the reader may find it useful to refer back to the discussion of thrift organizational form and government regulation in Chapter 1).

IMPLICATIONS FOR THE FUTURE REGULATION OF THRIFTS AND BANKS

Government regulation of thrifts and banks has rested on two cornerstones since the Great Depression. First, for the past fifty-five years deposit insurance has provided the bulwark against runs on thrifts and banks. Because deposit insurance is priced by law at a flat rate, regulation of balance sheets has been necessary to combat moral hazard. Second, as part of a congressional commitment to promoting home ownership, thrifts have been provided with subsidies to make home loans. As a result, until the 1980s, thrift and bank portfolios have been compartmentalized.

The two cornerstones are now crumbling at an ever-increasing rate. Deposit insurance worked well only as long as interest rates were relatively stable and the economy was largely immune from inflation and deflation. With volatile interest rates, inflation, and deflation in the 1970s, and especially in the 1980s, the deposit-insurance system for thrifts could not cope with rising numbers of insolvencies. Deregulation, beginning in 1978 with greater freedom to price liabilities, was a reaction to market forces that might otherwise have rapidly destroyed the thrift industry. But deregulation, in combination with those same market forces (such as the development of mortgage-backed securities), began to homogenize thrift and bank balance sheets. The growing homogenization of balance sheets is undermining the rationale for government sponsorship of thrift institutions as specialized housing-finance lenders. In fact, the few remaining dif-

Table 6-4. Percentage Distribution of Liabilities Held by FSLIC-Insured Institutions (1977-1986).

Type of Liability	1977	1978	1979	1980	1981	1982	1983	1984	1985	1986
NOW, Super NOW, and other transaction accounts	a	0.1	0.1	0.2	1.3	2.1	2.9	3.0	3.5	4.5
Fixed-maturity accounts	53.9	57.3	61.8	65.0	64.7	62.0	57.0	59.8	57.4	53.2
Money-market deposit accounts	0	0	0	0	0	} 16.0	} 22.0	11.1	12.1	11.9
Passbook and other accounts without fixed maturity	33.0	27.3	21.2	17.5	14.3	{ 16.0	{ 22.0	6.4	5.9	6.8
FHL bank advances	4.5	6.4	7.2	7.7	9.8	9.3	7.0	7.3	7.9	8.6
Commercial bank loans	0.3	0.2	0.3	0.2	0.1	0.1	0.1	0.1	0.1	0.1
Reverse repurchase agreements	0.9	1.2	1.2	1.4	2.5	3.4	3.4	4.9	4.3	5.1
Commercial paper issued	b	b	b	b	a	a	a	a	0.1	0.1
Subordinated debentures	a	a	a	a	a	a	a	0.1	0.1	a
Mortgage-backed bond issues	0.3	0.4	0.6	0.6	0.5	0.5	0.4	0.5	0.8	1.0
Other liabilities	7.1	1.4	1.9	2.1	2.5	2.9	3.2	3.0	3.4	4.1
Regulatory net worth	5.6	5.7	5.7	5.3	4.3	3.7	4.0	3.8	4.4	4.6
Total liabilities and net worth (in billions of dollars)	450	513	568	618	653	693	819	979	1,070	1,165
Number of deposit and savings accounts	79	85	88	92	97	99	103	112	114	110

a. Less than 0.05.
b. Not reported separately.
Source: Author's calculations based on data from the Federal Home Loan Bank Board.

ferences between thrift and bank portfolios are the legacy of past regulation that no longer serves a useful economic purpose.[3]

NOTES

1. Some analysts have argued that market discipline by uninsured depositors was eroded by the increase in insurance coverage from $40,000 to $100,000 in 1980. Seen in a historical context, the increase in the insurance level was another episode in a cycle that has been repeating since 1939 (the earliest date for which data are available). In 1949, when uninsured deposits reached 6.6 percent of total deposits, the insurance level was doubled from $5,000 to $10,000. This caused uninsured deposits to decline to 1.9 percent of total deposits. Similar cycles were repeated in 1966, 1969, and 1974. In 1979, uninsured deposits had again increased to 6.6 percent of deposits. Increasing the insurance level in 1980 reduced uninsured deposits to 4 percent of total deposits. By year-end 1984, the level of uninsured deposits had increased to a historical high of 7.8 percent. It is thus difficult to make the case that increasing insurance coverage in 1980 altered the market discipline that had traditionally been exerted by uninsured depositors.
2. See Thomas Marvell, *The Federal Home Loan Bank Board* (New York: Praeger Publishers, 1969), p. 137.
3. For another discussion of the issues examined in this chapter, see James R. Barth and Martin A. Regalia, "The Evolving Role of Regulation in the Savings and Loan Industry," in *The Financial Services Revolution: Policy Directions for the Future*, ed. Catherine England and Thomas F. Huertas (Norwell, Massachusetts: Klurver Academic Publishers, 1988), pp. 113–161. This paper draws in part on earlier work done by Barth and Brumbaugh.

7 BEYOND THE THRIFT-INDUSTRY CRISIS
The Redesign of Thrift and Bank Regulation and the Rollback of Deposit Insurance

This chapter explains why there no longer exists an economic rationale for government separation of specialized housing lenders called thrift institutions from other depository institutions. As a result, there is also no economic rationale for a separate regulatory agency for thrift institutions. The chapter therefore calls for the consolidation of the balance sheets of insured financial depository institutions and the consolidation of the thrift and bank regulatory agencies.

Ultimately, economic policy must be judged by how it affects individuals. For the stockholders, directors, managers, and staff of the 3,200 existing thrift institutions and for the Bank Board and staff, this chapter's conclusions and recommendations may seem threatening. Some of these individuals may lose wealth and income, although consolidation of thrifts and banks and their regulation will itself impose few losses on thrifts because those that survive the current crisis will adopt new balance sheets and will be able to adapt to changes in regulation. The greatest losses will be suffered by individuals associated with insolvent thrifts that will not survive to be consolidated. For taxpayers and the consumers of financial services, benefits from consolidation will far outweigh the costs to individuals associated with consolidating thrifts. Some individuals associated mainly with troubled thrifts will exclaim: "Prove it! Prove that the benefits and costs are what you say they are." Anything short of a definitive study before consolidation of dollar-denominated benefits and costs will not satisfy some vocal thrift-industry advocates of the *status quo*.

A more reasonable standard of proof has two components. First, because congressional support for thrifts continues to be based on subsidizing housing finance as a merit good, justification for the consolidation of thrifts and banks requires that the supply of housing finance continue unchanged. Second, consolidation should not undermine the goals of deposit insurance: protection against the externalities, or social cost, of runs. These tests, as this chapter will show, are easily met.

The rationalization of thrift and bank balance sheets and regulation is an important reform, needed to enhance stability in financial markets. It is, however, a by-product of the failure of the deposit-insurance system created in the 1930s. Failure does not refer only to the bankruptcy of the FSLIC and the financial distress of the FDIC. It also alludes to the changes in fundamental economic phenomena that have rendered intermediaries inherently more volatile and risky and have undermined the ability of the deposit-insurance system to provide the financial stability it was designed to ensure.

MORTGAGE-BACKED SECURITIES HAVE FOREVER BLOWN APART THRIFT BALANCE-SHEET COMPARTMENTALIZATION

As lenders to mortgage borrowers, thrifts have traditionally served three functions. They have originated mortgages, financed and held the mortgages in their own portfolios, and in the process serviced the mortgages by, for example, collecting monthly payments. Financing and holding the mortgages created the particular interest-rate risk that faces thrifts and that commercial banks largely avoided by both originating and holding relatively few mortgages.

When the Bank Board was created in 1932, the need to hold mortgages was inescapable because there was no way to separate origination from financing and holding mortgages. Now, however, any thrift can separate the origination and service functions from the need to finance and hold mortgages. Recent institutional innovations, primarily the development of a secondary market for mortgages, have created an array of mechanisms that allow thrift institutions to earn a return on originations and service without holding the mortgages in their portfolios.

Table 7–1 puts the thrift industry's role in holding mortgages into historical perspective. At the turn of the century, more than half of all mortgages were held by private individuals and other private financial firms. The sources forming the "other" column evolved over time.[1] For approximately the first half of the century, these sources eclipsed savings and loans as holders of mortgages. During World War II, a rough equivalency existed among commercial banks, mutual savings banks, and life-insurance companies in mortgage holdings. Savings and loan associations began to edge slightly ahead by 1940, signalling the beginning of a thirty-five year period of growth that culminated in 1975, when they held 42.3 percent of mortgages.

In 1975, however, savings and loan mortgage holdings and those of mutual savings banks and life-insurance companies began a sharp and steep decline. Commercial-bank holdings also declined, though less precipitously, between 1980 and 1985. The decline in mortgage holdings from these sources was made up for by the growth of holdings by firms in the "other" column. The shift in mortgage-holding shares occurred while the dollar volume of mortgage holdings nearly doubled between 1975 and 1980 and rose by over 50 percent between 1980 and 1985—substantial growth rates even after accounting for inflation.

The shift in holdings since 1975 was facilitated by the growth of a secondary market supplementing the primary market in mortgages.[2] In the primary market, borrowers arrange mortgage financing from a mortgage originator, generally a depository institution or mortgage banker, a private finance company specializing in housing finance. The secondary market comprises private credit agencies, financial intermediaries, and federal credit agencies—the Government National Mortgage Association (GNMA, also known as Ginnie Mae), the Federal National Mortgage Association (FNMA or Fannie Mae), and the Federal Home Loan Mortgage Corporation (FHLMC or Freddie Mac). Through these sources, investors buy mortgages originated in the primary mortgage market. The secondary market in mortgages has been crucial in "unbundling" thrift mortgage holdings from other functions and in integrating the mortgage market with the capital market, the market for long-term securities.

Although thrift-institution participation is relatively recent, the secondary market has existed for some time. In the 1950s, 1960s,

Table 7-1. Nonfarm Residential Mortgage Holdings by Type of Institution (1900-1985).

Year	Total Holdings (in millions of dollars)	Percent of Total Holdings				
		Commercial Banks	Mutual Savings Banks	Savings and Loan Associations	Life Insurance Companies	Other[a]
1900	1,917	5.4	21.7	12.7	6.3	53.9
1905	3,520	8.3	23.4	12.7	7.2	48.4
1910	4,426	10.1	25.1	15.6	9.1	40.1
1915	6,012	9.4	23.6	18.3	8.7	40.1
1920	9,120	8.8	19.5	20.4	6.1	45.2
1925	1,323	10.8	17.6	23.2	8.2	40.2
1930	27,649	10.3	15.9	22.2	10.4	41.2
1935	22,211	10.0	17.9	14.9	9.9	47.3
1940	23,810	12.6	16.4	17.1	12.1	41.7
1945	24,643	13.8	13.7	20.9	14.7	36.8
1950	54,362	19.2	13.0	24.1	20.3	23.4
1955	100,827	15.8	15.4	29.5	21.0	18.3
1960	161,540	12.6	15.0	34.9	17.8	19.7
1965	256,494	12.6	15.6	39.0	15.0	17.7
1970	354,464	12.9	14.1	38.3	12.0	22.7
1975	577,545	14.4	11.0	42.3	6.4	25.8
1980	1,097,512	15.8	7.6	40.9	3.4	32.5
1985	1,683,162	14.1	5.4	33.4	1.9	45.2

a. Includes individuals, private pension funds, government credit agencies, finance companies, mutual money market funds, and others.

Source: U.S. Department of Commerce, Bureau of the Census, *Historical Statistics of the United States Colonial Times to 1970* (Washington, D.C.), Part 2; and Board of Governors of the Federal Reserve System, "Flow of Funds" (various years).

Table 7-2. Growth of Securities Backed by One-to-Four-Family Mortgages
(1980–1986).

Year	Annual Flow of Mortgages, Originations Securitized (percentage)	Total Stock of Mortgages Securitized (percentage)
1980	17.4	11.7
1981	14.7	12.4
1982	20.5	16.6
1983	34.7	20.7
1984	19.1	22.1
1985	33.5	25.3
1986	58.3	34.1

Source: Kenneth T. Rosen, "Securitization and the Thrift Industry" (paper presented at the Twelfth Annual Conference of the Federal Home Loan Bank of San Francisco on Thrift Financial Performance and Capital Adequacy, December 11–12, 1986), pp. 6–7.

and early 1970s, 25 to 30 percent of mortgage originations were sold in the secondary market, primarily by mortgage bankers to life insurance companies.[3] In 1982 mortgage sales as a share of originations soared to 85 percent. This dramatic growth in the secondary market came with the development of mortgage-backed securities. From a fledgling 1 percent of the total stock of mortgages held in mortgage-backed securities in 1965, the volume grew to 34 percent in 1986, as shown in Table 7-2.

The most common mortgage-backed security is called a pass-through security. Generally, a bank, thrift, or mortgage bank originates a number of mortgage loans. The originator or an agency to which the loans are sold creates a security backed by the pool of mortgages and sells the security to capital-market investors as a public offering or a private placement. The original lender often services the loan. Borrowers' payments of principal and interest are "passed through" to holders of the security on a *pro rata* basis, after servicing and other fees have been deducted. The process transforms a mortgage with one set of characteristics into a more attractive security for investors. A typical mortgage pool contains a few dozen to several hundred loans, available to investors in units of $25,000. The investor, moreover, is freed from servicing the loan, payment is assured, and the security is standardized so that it is easily marketable.

Table 7-2 summarizes the phenomenal growth of mortgage-backed securities. In 1986 $257 billion, or 58 percent, of the $380 billion in one-to-four-family mortgage originations were securitized.[4] $518 billion, or 34 percent of the total $1.5 trillion stock of one-to-four-family mortgages were securitized in 1986. The decade began with only 17 percent of the one-to-four-family mortgage flow and 12 percent of the one-to-four-family mortgage stock securitized.

Through mortgage-backed securities, the capital market is supplanting thrifts as the holder of mortgages. The extraordinary speed with which mortgage-backed securities are developing, moreover, promises further rapid improvement in the securities for capital-market purchases. One of the original problems of the standard mortgage-backed security was that *pro rata* pass-through of principal and interest payments led to uncertain cash flows, primarily due to unexpected prepayments of principal. To reduce this problem, a "second-generation" mortgage-backed security was marketed for the first time in the second quarter of 1983. The security was called a CMO, for "collateralized mortgage obligation." The CMO separates the principal repayments of pools of mortgage loans to holders into fast-pay tranches, or classes, and slow-pay tranches. A typical CMO has four tranches. The first three tranches receive interest payments, with principal payments going first to the fast-pay tranch. After the first tranch is repaid, principal payments are used sequentially to retire the remaining tranches. The fourth tranch does not receive any interest or principal payments until all previous tranches are retired.

Table 7-3 shows the rapid expansion of CMOs since their introduction in 1983. From 1983 to the first quarter of 1987, the total number of CMOs went from zero to 433, and the dollar volume rose from zero to almost $100 billion. Moreover, CMOs are growing at an increasingly faster rate, with the dollar amount of issues in the first quarter of 1987 greater than the amount of those issued in 1983, 1984, and 1985. The average size of a CMO in 1983 was $388 million but has fallen since then to an average of $231 million. This is an indication that CMOs are becoming more efficient financial instruments.

Thrifts, banks, insurance companies, pension funds, and other firms can buy mortgage-backed securities. These firms can buy different tranches of securities or buy interest-only or principal-only parts of securities. Thrifts and banks can also create mortgage-backed

Table 7-3.   Issuance of Collateralized Mortgage Obligations *(1983-1987)*.

Year	Total Number of CMOs	Total Amount (in millions of dollars)	Average Size of CMOs (in millions of dollars)
1983	12	4,660	388
1984	38	10,594	279
1985	87	15,401	177
1986	226	48,035	213
1987 Q1	70	21,291	304
Total	433	99,981	231

Source: Derived from First Boston Corporation, Fixed Income Research, "Mortgage-Related Securities CMO Quarterly," May 1987, Exhibit 1, p. 1.

Table 7-4.   Major Institutional Buyers of CMOs in First Half of 1986 *(percentage of sales)*.

Tranch	Thrifts	Commercial Banks	Insurance Companies	Pension Funds
A	9.4	30.4	9.3	48.3
B	14.4	19.3	16.0	46.4
C	5.0	3.3	21.5	61.7
D	4.2	1.5	21.0	63.0

Source: Kenneth T. Rosen, "Securitization and the Thrift Industry" (paper presented at the Twelfth Annual Conference of the Federal Home Loan Bank Board of San Francisco on Thrift Financial Performance and Capital Adequacy, December 11-12, 1986), p. 13.

securities out of the mortgages that they originate. The same is true of securities that are not backed by mortgages.

Table 7-4 shows how the development of CMOs has broadened the investor base in mortgage-backed securities. Commercial banks and pension funds bought nearly 80 percent of the fastest-paying CMO tranches in the first half of 1986. This suggests that CMO securitization has created a mortgage instrument whose short duration is attractive to banks, thereby increasing the number of banks likely to hold mortgages in a securitized form. In contrast, thrifts and commercial banks together purchased only a small portion of the slowest-paying tranches, while insurance companies and pension funds bought more than 80 percent of the slowest-paying tranches. Thus, through CMOs, pension funds and insurance companies are buying the long-duration mortgages that have caused thrifts' interest-rate risk problems in the past.

With the CMO, the residential mortgage-backed security market has demonstrated a remarkable ability to adapt and expand. The same is true of other debt-backed securities. Mortgages on office buildings, hotels, shopping centers, and industrial buildings are part of a developing commercial mortgage-backed securities market. Issues of securities backed by automobile and light-truck loans (CARS) grew from $900 million in 1985 to $8.9 billion through November 1986. Securities backed by multifamily mortgages came into being in 1985, and by November 1986 $3 billion of the $170 billion of multifamily mortgages were securitized.

Securities backed by adjustable-rate mortgages also exist but are, as yet, a small part of the market. A current strategy of many thrifts is to hold adjustable-rate mortgages in portfolio and sell fixed-rate mortgages in the secondary market. As the secondary mortgage market has developed in the past few years, the relative heterogeneity (for example, the use of different indices to adjust interest-rate caps) of adjustable-rate mortgages has slowed their entry into the secondary market. Also a problem is the secondary market's perception that the thrift industry has widely mispriced the mortgages—charged borrowers too little primarily to promote adjustable-rate mortgage origination. As the pricing improves, the secondary market demand for adjustable mortgage will likely grow substantially.

The development of securities backed by other debt instruments is widely diversifying the risks associated with those debt instruments—single and multifamily mortgages, commercial mortgages, adjustable-rate mortgages, credit-card receivables, car loans, and so on. As a result, thrifts no longer need to be saddled with extreme interest-rate risk. Banks, moreover, can now originate mortgages without having to hold them.

In essence, the securitization of debt has dissolved the government-facilitated compartmentalization of thrift balance sheets. A wide and growing range of nonthrift investors can buy mortgage-backed securities without the interest-rate risk that once had to be borne by thrifts. Opening the capital markets to mortgages means the market-driven end of thrifts as mortgage holders. It also means an expanding, probably exploding, opportunity for nonthrift mortgage originators and servicers. Through the first quarter of 1987, for example, finance subsidiaries of builders had sold $14.2 billion in mortgage loans into CMOs. These sales represented 14.1 percent of the collateral behind CMOs.[5] The explosion of secondary markets in debt instruments is a major revolutionary force, not only for thrifts, but for all financial firms.

THE ROLE OF GOVERNMENT SUBSIDIES IN MORTGAGE-BACKED SECURITIES

The intense competition caused by securitization and the changes in thrift balance sheets comes at a time when thrifts' profitability is already squeezed. One important question is whether the federal government's involvement in the mortgage-backed security market is intensifying this by subsidizing mortgage-backed securities. At issue is whether the federal government is substantially increasing the mortgage security market by providing varying degrees of guarantees behind the securities. If this were the case, it would be the government subsidy, not the economic value of the securities, that is harming thrifts, and an argument could be made that mortgage-backed securities are not a threat to them.

The presence of the federal government is felt primarily through the GNMA, FNMA, and FHLMC, each of which is chartered by the federal government. Of the total outstanding mortgage-backed securities in 1986, GNMA securities accounted for 50 percent, FNMA for 19 percent, and FHLMC for 30 percent.[6]

GNMA securities are backed explicitly by the full faith and credit of the federal government. FNMA was established in 1938 to buy Federal Housing Administration (FHA) and later Veterans Administration (VA) loans, as well as conventional loans, primarily from mortgage bankers. By 1984 only about 40 percent of FNMA's mortgage portfolio was guaranteed by the FHA or VA. The FHLMC was established in 1970 to provide the same service for thrift institutions. The FNMA and FHLMC mortgage-backed securities carry an implicit backing by the federal government.

To estimate the cost advantage of an agency security, one can compare what it costs the agencies to make securities out of a pool of conventional mortgages carrying private mortgage insurance to what it costs a private intermediary to create an equivalent security.[7] The estimated cost difference is 0.1 percent of the loan balance annually. If this 10 basis-point cost advantage had been passed directly to borrowers in the form of a reduction in the interest rate on a typical mortgage, it would have accounted for approximately $400 million of the $300 billion spent on housing in 1985. That cost saving is .0013 percent of housing sales, and thus the subsidy embedded in agency securities appears minimal. These estimates suggest that complete elimination of the subsidies available to the federally chartered agencies would leave a thriving market in mortgage-backed securities. The estimates also suggest that the development of mortgage-backed securities represents an economic innovation that has increased the efficiency of the mortgage market.

The integration of the mortgage market with the capital market through mortgage-backed securities signals the end of the thrift industry's separation from commercial banks. Between 1980 and 1986, approximately one-quarter of all thrifts perished, and the industry contracted from approximately 4,000 institutions to slightly more than 3,000 institutions. When Congress finds the funding, another 500 institutions and perhaps more will likely perish. Voluntary mergers will consume many hundreds more in the near future. Those institutions that remain will have balance sheets free of exaggerated domination by mortgages. The already eroded rationale for a housing finance lender and a separate regulatory apparatus for the surviving thrifts will be gone. The time for Congress to begin the transition to regulatory consolidation is now.

ANY CONGRESSIONAL SUBSIDY OF HOUSING FINANCE SHOULD BE AS DIRECT AS POSSIBLE

Through direct and indirect subsidies, Congress has lowered the price of housing relative to the price of other goods and services. In economics jargon, this qualifies housing as a "merit good," the purchase of which society subsidizes. The tax system provides the largest subsidy to homeownership by directly lowering the after-tax cost of mortgage interest payments. Moreover, roughly 60 percent of the total credit furnished to the public by the federal government goes to the residential mortgage markets.[8]

Consolidation of thrifts and banks and their regulation does not mean the end of this deep, historic commitment to housing, but rather, a more efficient means of demonstrating it. Whatever congressional subsidies exist ought to be as efficient as possible. An efficient subsidy is generally one that goes as directly as possible to the targeted economic goal. The further away a subsidy is from the targeted activity, the more likely it is to be dissipated by going to non-targeted activities. In addition, the more widely distributed the subsidy is to the individuals making up the group engaging in the subsidized activity, the more efficient the subsidy. Here, the target is lower housing costs. Thus, government activities that most directly lower housing costs to the widest possible range of homeowners are the most efficient.

As Chapter 1 and 6 develop, thrifts were initially exempt from federal taxation. When taxed, favorable tax deductions were created and still exist, though greatly diminished from what they were only a few years ago. Some, probably most, of this subsidy never reached borrowers, but went instead to thrift shareholders in the form of higher returns and to thrift managers in higher salaries. Shareholders and managers have an economic incentive to redirect to themselves the subsidy designed for borrowers or depositors. Indirectly subsidizing housing by subsidizing thrifts through tax provisions, preferential accounting practices, net-worth forbearance, deferred closure, and other practices is extraordinarily inefficient and costly. To the extent that federal subsidies have lowered the cost of mortgage-backed securities, however, the lower cost reflects a more efficient subsidy.

A COMPREHENSIVE FRAMEWORK FOR REGULATORY REFORM OF INSURED DEPOSITORY INSTITUTIONS

The analysis of the previous section brings us to the point where we can summarize the framework for regulatory reform of depository institutions. Table 7–5 presents the framework. The reforms required in each of the four phases depicted in Table 7–5 can develop simultaneously, although Phase I is the most urgent and Phases I and II are more urgent than Phases III and IV. Phase I summarizes the recommendations made in Chapter 4 for ending the current thrift-industry crisis. The appropriate role for Congress is to raise the funds required to close insolvent institutions. The responsibility of the Bank Board as the operating head of the FSLIC is to use the funds to close insolvent thrifts. Because closure will require extensive triage over a relatively lengthy period of time, the Bank Board must also

Table 7-5. Framework for Regulatory Reform of Insured Depository Institutions.

| Phase | Required Congressional and Regulatory Action | |
	Congressional Action	Regulatory Action
I	Raise funds necessary to close insolvent institutions	Close insolvent institutions Control open insolvent institutions until they can be closed • Expand the MCP • Increase substantially the number of examiners and supervisory agents
II	Clarify the FSLIC and FDIC closure rule, allowing barely solvent institutions to be closed	Raise the minimum net-worth requirement Use and develop further market-value accounting Implement the new closure rule
III	Consolidate thrift and bank regulation	Implement consolidation Homogenize balance sheets
IV	Authorize federal deposit-insurance rollback Specify Federal Reserve responsibilities Create Treasury-backed transaction accounts Eliminate balance-sheet regulation	Roll back deposit insurance Phase out balance-sheet regulation Transfer closure responsibility to the Federal Reserve

take tighter control of insolvent thrifts that it cannot close immediately. This requires an expansion of the Management Consignment Program or a close variant of it and a substantial increase in the number of examiners and supervisory agents. The greater the expansion and the more efficient it is, the faster funds can be spent optimally and the lower costs will be.

Phase II reflects Chapter 5's analysis of the existing regulatory process and its recommendations for altering it to avoid another thrift crisis. The Bank Board should immediately raise the minimum net-worth requirement. Raising the requirement would give the Bank Board and its staff—primarily the examiners and supervisory agents—power to scrutinize more institutions more thoroughly and to establish appropriate restrictions for institutions failing the net-worth requirement. It would especially help the Bank Board to identify those nearly insolvent institutions acting on the incentive to take greater risks. Simultaneously, the Bank Board should both use available market values to evaluate thrifts' conditions and develop additional market-value accounting wherever possible. The Congress should define a new closure rule allowing the Bank Board to close an institution with low estimated market-value net worth. Neither the FSLIC nor the FDIC—as they now do—should close institutions based on book-value net worth, since this systematically means that market-value net worth is negative at the time of closure.

As the preceding sections of this chapter emphasize, the government-sponsored balance-sheet differences between insured thrifts and banks no longer make economic sense. As a result, in Phase III Congress should begin to develop a plan for the consolidation of thrift and bank regulation as a response to the market-driven forces that are eroding balance-sheet differences between thrifts and banks. The major balance-sheet difference that is fading most rapidly is the dominance of mortgages in thrift portfolios. Thrifts are becoming more like banks, and thus the thrift regulatory apparatus should be folded into the bank regulatory process.

Another reason why thrift and bank regulation should be interwoven is that the thrift industry has captured its regulatory process more thoroughly than any other regulated industry in the country. At the core of the capture is the historical predominance of thrift-industry executives in the Bank Board, the Federal Home Loan Bank system, and the formal and informal councils that advise the Bank Board and the Banks. In no other regulated industry have the levers of power been pulled as much by individuals who are in the regulated industry or have come from it and will return.

Moreover, unlike other depository and nondepository financial regulatory agencies, political appointees have held professional staff positions at the Bank Board in research, data collection, examination and supervision, and the general counsel's office. These appointees tend to be connected to the thrift industry. In subtle but profound ways, the process has skewed results to maintain the status quo and maximize the advantage to existing thrifts.

Ironically, the regulatory results are often harmful to thrifts. Throughout the 1980s, for example, the industry demanded and received regulatory forbearance, primarily in the form of lower net-worth requirements, accounting forgiveness, and forestalled closure of insolvent thrifts. Each of these acts provided short-run subsidies to thrifts—insolvent and solvent. A microcosm of this behavior exists today in Texas, one of the states hardest hit by thrift insolvencies—over 40 percent of income losses for the third quarter of 1987 were in thirty-nine Texas thrifts. Powerful thrift interests successfully lobbied Congress, particularly the Texas congressman who is Speaker of the House, to make regulatory forbearance part of the scaled-back FSLIC recapitalization plan described in Chapter 4. The result of the early 1980s forbearance, however, was an unintended exacerbation of thrift problems, as insolvent thrifts gambled for resurrection, fraud grew, and deflation further ravaged thrifts' portfolios. In the end, the prolonged forbearance has caused solvent thrifts to pay higher insurance premiums, and face higher deposit costs and the strongest thrifts to beat a retreat to the FDIC.

The U.S. League of Savings Institutions appeared to continue to argue for forbearance in its opposition to the FSLIC recapitalization plan. No independent analyst disputes that the cost of closing all of the institutions insolvent in early 1987 will be at least the $15 billion sought by the Bank Board and Treasury. The U.S. League has disputed it during the Congressional debate, however, contending that no more than $5 billion was needed. The real reason for this may be that the plan threatens the league in two ways. First, many of its members would be closed when the funds became available to the Bank Board. Second, the rest of its members' income would be used at least in part to pay for the closure. To avoid the second outcome, moreover, the largest and strongest of the U.S. League's members are trying to flee to the FDIC. As a result, the league is fighting for survival by attempting to lower what its members may have to contribute to the FSLIC's recapitalization. Since the Congressional debate, some leaders in the league have said that their opposition was based on their fear that the additional funds—though needed—would have been spent unwisely by the Bank Board.

Whenever the government regulates an economic activity, those who are regulated will seek to use the regulation for their benefit.

They will often succeed. But the thrift industry has often been a case of self-defeating excess. As Congress contemplates the reorganization of the regulation of insured depository institutions, it has the opportunity to strike an improved balance between the need for industry expertise in the regulatory process and the industry dominance of that process that has existed in the thrift industry.

ROLLBACK OF DEPOSIT INSURANCE AND THE ROLE OF THE FEDERAL RESERVE IN CLOSING INSOLVENT INSTITUTIONS

Phase IV of the framework for regulatory reform addresses the issue of how to provide the financial stability sought by deposit insurance with the least intervention by government in financial markets and the least potential cost to the taxpayer. As described earlier in more detail, the economic goal of deposit insurance is to forestall the externalities that can result from depositor runs. To understand the externalities, it is important to distinguish between solvent and insolvent institutions. Due to misinformation, runs can occur when all institutions are solvent, or runs against insolvent institutions can spread to solvent institutions. Regardless of whether an institution is solvent or insolvent, a run can force it to sell illiquid assets hurriedly below the value a more deliberate sale could bring. Such a fire sale can force a solvent institution into insolvency and can increase the degree of insolvency in an already insolvent institution.

In thinking about the future design of deposit insurance, a good place to start is with the role of the Federal Reserve. In the current system, the Federal Reserve is supposed to lend to solvent institutions when runs develop, based on collateral substantially exceeding the loan value, so that these institutions need not fear being driven into insolvency by a fire sale of illiquid assets. For depositors of solvent institutions, the Federal Reserve is an able protector. The depositors need to worry only if the Federal Reserve does not act when a run occurs on a solvent institution.

Generally, there are insolvent institutions in a crisis. In this situation, the insolvent institutions' shareholders, uninsured creditors and depositors, as well as the insurance corporations can lose money. One can ask, what would happen if there were no deposit insurance? As long as the Federal Reserve acted as it was designed to act, depositors in solvent institutions would be no worse off than otherwise: For them, deposit insurance is redundant. Shareholders and uninsured creditors and depositors of insolvent and solvent institutions would also be in the same condition as they would be otherwise. Previously insured depositors, however, would lose money.

This outcome is not necessarily undesirable from a societywide perspective. If insured depositors do not lose money, someone else does. The candidates for losses are the shareholders of solvent institutions that pay insurance premiums, and, if the losses are large enough—as they are in the current thrift crisis—the taxpayer. Customers of solvent institutions can also bear the burden if institutions shift the burden of premium payments by increasing prices or lowering services. If there were no deposit insurance and all depositors in insolvent institutions lost money based on their share of deposits, there would be no externality or greater social cost as long as solvent institutions were unscathed. Solvent institutions would continue to exist, and the stock of money, as well as other payment methods like wire transfers, would remain unchanged. Therefore, the intermediation process and payments mechanism would be unharmed. What would occur is a redistribution of the losses to formerly insured depositors from those who otherwise would have borne the loss—solvent institution shareholders and customers and taxpayers.

Deposit insurance could be eliminated without an increase in the instability of the financial system under circumstances that do not appear to be too formidable.[9] The Federal Reserve role would have to be specified by Congress in such a way that depositors were certain that solvent institutions were run proof. A method would need to be developed to resolve ambiguities in the definition of solvency so that institutions would never be in limbo about whether they were solvent. In order to ensure fair treatment of depositors of institutions closed by the Federal Reserve, the closure rule would have to be designed—as it should be today—to close the institutions before insolvency and to distribute funds to all creditors based on their *pro rata* claims. Moreover, the Federal Reserve has the financial resources to dispose of insolvent institutions without a fire sale of assets.

What would happen if an unforeseen event led to widespread insolvencies? The answer is the same as it would be today. In the thrift crisis, for example, Congress will reluctantly determine who will bear the losses, with the taxpayer ultimately liable for a share. The current thrift crisis is proof that in a crisis the deposit-insurance system breaks down, primarily because accumulated reserves cannot cover the unexpected losses. Reserves based on premium income and industry assessments could never be large enough to cover the magnitude of losses that could occur in thrift and bank industry crises. The fact that FSLIC reserves as a percentage of total thrift assets have only exceeded 2 percent twice since the FSLIC's creation in 1934 indicates that Congress never intended the FSLIC or the FDIC to handle large crises. Congress itself would intervene when accumulated losses exceeded the capability of the nontaxpayers to pay the costs.

As discussed in Chapter 2, the need for balance-sheet regulation developed with deposit insurance, which was created in the aftermath of the Great Depression, when the Federal Reserve failed to act as it was designed to act. If that defect were corrected, the need for deposit insurance would begin to evaporate. The system envisioned here has many benefits. Regulation of balance sheets by the government could be substantially reduced. Market discipline by depositors would increase. Problems created by state charters would abate. Moral hazard now exists because states can determine allowable activities and otherwise affect risk-taking, even though the states do not stand to bear the cost of their actions because of federal deposit insurance. With less need to regulate balance sheets, these problems would moderate. A role for private insurance could develop. The need to worry about the separation of depository institutions from activities like corporate security underwriting would also moderate. The result would be opportunities for depository institutions to diversify their portfolios and reduce risk.

Implementation of such a plan could be phased in with a gradual lowering of the deposit-insurance coverage limit along with a clarification of the Federal Reserve's role. The deregulation of balance sheets could also be phased in over time. The net effect would be less government involvement, no greater threat to financial stability, and a substantial reduction in the contingent liability of taxpayers for deposit-insurance losses.

Another purpose of deposit insurance has been to protect those who are both poor and financially naive by providing them with risk-free transaction and savings accounts. This objective could be achieved by lowering the current $100,000 limit to a much smaller amount and by insuring the individual rather than an individual account, which allows individuals to receive coverage beyond $100,000. The federal government directly, or indirectly through depository institutions, could also provide depositors with riskless transaction and savings accounts without deposit insurance, as it already does to purchasers of treasury securities. Other types of accounts backed by treasury securities could easily be developed.[10]

SUMMARY: INCREASINGLY BETTER INFORMATION SPELLS ACCELERATING VOLATILITY FOR DEPOSITORY INSTITUTIONS

Distilled to its essence, the reason that thrifts and banks exist is because of imperfect information between borrowers and lenders. If perfect information existed, borrowers and lenders would know about each other's financial characteristics and needs and interact directly. In such a world, intermediaries would be obsolete. Recently, significant improvements in information have occurred. The first computer was developed by the Pentagon only forty-one years ago, and nonmilitary use of computers developed relatively slowly until the 1970s. Since then the ability to collect and to analyze information has exploded and appears to be expanding at an accelerating rate.

Computers allowed the creation of financial instruments like mortgage-backed securities that would have been impossible without them. The new financial instruments reduce the uncertainty—imperfect information—traditionally associated with the assets that back securities. Nonfinancial firms have also benefited from the information explosion. Relatively large nonfinancial firms, for example, now issue commercial paper directly to the capital market. In doing so, they have to some extent supplanted the intermediaries to which previously they turned for loans. These new instruments are available in denominations that are accessible to individuals—as mentioned earlier, CMOs can be purchased in $25,000 denominations.

The implication for depository institutions and their regulation is profound. As information about existing thrift and bank products improves, others will provide the products. With mortgages, for example, financial subsidiaries of builders and real-estate firms are selling mortgages into securitized pools sold in the capital market. This is an example of how improved information distribution is beginning to erode the traditional staple of thrifts.

Nonbank lenders, commercial paper, high-yield ("junk") bonds, and subordinated debt are doing the same for commercial banks, as is the development of securities backed by commercial loans. A stunning example is the decline in U.S. banks' share of short- and intermediate-term credit to domestic nonfinancial corporations. Following a gradual decline from the mid-1950s through the late 1960s, it fell from approximately 85 percent in 1969 to just over 60 percent in 1985.[11] Rapidly developing information about the gamut of thrift and commercial bank assets—especially what is happening to mortgages—suggests that thrifts and banks will need to shift increasingly to new products. These new products will be those with more imperfect information, which in a world of rapidly improving information will still require intermediation between borrowers and lenders.

The erosion of traditional thrift and bank products implies reduced profit margins, and the need for new product development suggests greater risk. The thrifts' move into loans for the acquisition of real estate, for construction, for land development and the direct investment of real estate are examples. Each of these activities entails far greater effort to obtain accurate information than does residential housing finance. For commercial banks, the same is true of loans to developing countries relative to domestic commercial loans. By creating more competitors for thrift and bank products and services, better information has added to the economic volatility in thrift and bank markets. Beneath the surface of seemingly isolated, easily identified external causes of acute turmoil, systematically improving information is internally chipping away at all intermediaries.

As a result, the appropriate role for deposit insurance and regulation of depository intermediaries is radically different from what it was before 1980. From 1933 to 1980, the behavior of interest rates and other crucial economic phenomena were relatively stable for thrifts and banks. Information asymmetries only began to dissolve in the 1970s. The relative economic stability before 1980 and widespread information asymmetries made deposit insurance and balance-sheet regulation seem to work so smoothly. Now, economic volatility and widespread information distribution are facts of life, and exogenous and endogenous economic volatility for thrifts and banks are rendering deposit insurance, with its implicit taxpayer burden, and balance-sheet regulation increasingly untenable. Increasing disorder is the result.

Thus we come full circle from the aftermath of the Great Depression. A thrift and bank regulatory system based on the Federal Reserve lending to solvent banks appeared unworkable then because the Federal Reserve failed in a crucial test of the system. A paroxysm of legislative action created a new system based on deposit insurance that could work only as long as outside economic shocks were under control and information asymmetries persisted. Ironically, the Federal Reserve, by causing the interest-rate spiral of 1980, precipitated the shock that has undermined the deposit-insurance system. The circle should now be closed with the Federal Reserve reclaiming its central role as the provider of stability in financial markets and order in American banking.

NOTES

1. For a summary of mortgage holdings by type of institution annually from 1970 to 1985, with a breakdown of the components of the "other" column, see Federal National Mortgage Association, "A Statistical Summary of Housing and Mortgage Finance Activities" (Washington, D.C.: Federal National Mortgage Association, July 23, 1986), table 3, p. 3.

2. See Barry P. Bosworth, Andrew S. Carron, and Elizabeth H. Rhyne, *The Economics of Federal Credit Programs* (Washington, D.C.: The Brookings Institution, 1987), for a summary of the housing credit market. See also Kenneth T. Rosen, "Securitization and the Thrift Industry" (paper presented at the Twelfth Annual Conference of the Federal Home Loan Bank of San Francisco on Thrift Financial Performance and Capital Adequacy, December 11–12, 1986), for a summary of thrifts' involvement in the secondary mortgage market and a discussion of the market for mortgage-backed securities.

3. Bosworth, Carron, and Rhyne, *The Economics of Federal Credit Programs*, p. 72.

4. In *The Elements of Style* (New York: Macmillan Publishing Co., 1979), p. 54, William Strunk, Jr., and E. B. White write: "Many nouns have lately been pressed into service as verbs. Not all are bad, but all are suspect." Yes, but "securitize" is probably here to stay.

5. See First Boston Corporation, Fixed Income Research, "Mortgage-Related Securities," *CMO Quarterly* (May 1987): 19.

6. See Rosen, "Securitization and the Thrift Industry."

7. Bosworth, Carron, and Rhyne make this calculation in *The Economics of Federal Credit Programs*, p. 76.

8. Bosworth, Carron, and Rhyne, *The Economics of Federal Credit Programs*.

9. For precursors of this view, see John H. Kareken and Neil Wallace, "Deposit Insurance and Bank Regulation: A Partial Equilibrium Exposition," *Journal of Business* (July 1978): 413–452; John H. Kareken, "Deposit Insurance or Deregulation is the Cart, Not the Horse," *Quarterly Review* (Federal Reserve Bank of Minneapolis) (Spring 1983): 1–9; and *Idem.*, "The First Step in Bank Deregulation: What about the FDIC?" *American Economic Review* (May 1983): 198–203.

10. See, for example, Robert E. Litan, *What Should Banks Do?* (Washington, D.C.: The Brookings Institution, 1987).

11. *Ibid.*, p. 45.

APPENDICES

Appendix A.   Organizational Form and Charter-Type Data for FSLIC-Insured Institutions by State.[a]

State	All Institutions		Stock		Mutual		Federal		State	
	Number	Assets	Number	Assets	Number	Assets	Number	Assets	Number	Assets
AK	4	550,476	2	81,369	2	469,107	2	469,107	2	81,369
AL	37	8,541,870	9	4,512,447	28	4,029,423	35	8,271,364	2	270,506
AR	39	8,252,555	22	2,496,405	17	5,756,150	29	7,787,482	10	465,073
AZ	14	21,648,468	14	21,648,468	0	0	2	9,245,414	12	12,403,054
CA	216	310,455,472	189	294,593,436	27	15,862,036	66	178,886,360	150	131,569,112
CO	38	15,920,432	24	14,489,540	14	1,430,892	21	10,359,819	17	5,560,613
CT	31	11,252,915	12	8,344,075	19	2,908,840	19	10,065,649	12	1,187,266
DC	6	4,267,475	3	2,952,763	3	1,314,712	6	4,267,475	0	0
DE	4	353,336	1	218,556	3	134,780	1	218,556	3	134,780
FL	149	83,001,467	99	53,559,798	50	29,441,669	90	54,837,256	59	28,164,211
GA	67	16,174,395	23	8,052,849	44	8,121,546	67	16,174,395	0	0
GU	2	86,471	2	86,471	0	0	0	0	2	86,471
HI	6	3,668,295	2	527,111	4	3,141,184	3	2,858,942	3	809,353
IA	52	9,102,447	5	580,311	47	8,522,136	34	6,268,382	18	2,834,065
ID	9	1,529,889	3	312,847	6	1,217,042	9	1,529,889	0	0
IL	267	65,290,254	46	14,762,150	221	50,528,104	156	53,682,342	111	11,607,912
IN	115	12,744,508	11	2,690,046	104	10,054,462	90	11,557,708	25	1,186,800
KS	58	16,875,241	30	10,706,362	28	6,168,879	26	7,905,179	32	8,970,062
KY	67	7,205,216	2	500,863	65	6,704,353	63	7,119,627	4	85,589
LA	102	15,561,902	28	4,056,448	74	11,505,454	48	6,518,421	54	9,043,481
MA	33	7,003,652	6	3,442,891	27	3,590,761	26	6,271,561	7	762,091
MD	95	18,947,264	24	8,457,866	71	10,489,398	56	14,671,815	39	4,275,449
ME	15	1,219,055	3	751,087	12	467,968	11	1,135,275	4	83,780
MI	51	34,807,087	16	19,262,319	35	15,544,768	42	34,090,408	9	716,679
MN	37	16,069,503	6	6,692,925	31	9,376,578	37	16,069,503	0	0
MO	85	91,004,140	13	6,155,090	72	15,739,239	33	11,492,660	53	10,411,479

MS	45	4,811,282	27	2,413,797	18	2,397,485	32	3,435,212	13	1,376,070
MT	11	1,204,288	3	288,243	8	916,045	10	1,171,210	1	33,078
NC	139	19,337,597	36	5,864,328	103	13,473,269	69	12,501,130	70	6,836,467
ND	6	3,932,465	1	1,923,960	5	2,008,505	6	3,932,465	0	0
NE	23	9,091,188	6	4,627,670	17	4,463,518	18	8,823,960	5	267,228
NH	12	1,803,053	7	1,349,762	5	453,291	6	1,143,189	6	659,864
NJ	139	50,175,447	15	19,601,982	124	30,573,465	27	25,701,752	112	24,473,695
NM	25	5,873,098	22	5,732,710	3	140,388	22	5,525,329	3	347,769
NV	7	4,099,163	6	3,503,929	1	595,234	2	634,245	5	3,464,918
NY	86	48,329,933	9	12,579,375	77	35,750,558	70	47,311,619	16	1,018,314
OH	232	51,766,834	56	20,216,665	176	31,550,169	94	31,352,525	138	20,414,309
OK	53	10,100,625	33	7,622,164	20	2,478,461	41	9,059,050	12	1,041,575
OR	20	9,659,757	6	633,045	14	9,026,712	13	8,913,438	7	746,319
PA	169	38,112,413	15	11,154,404	154	26,958,009	69	23,344,159	100	14,768,254
PR	10	5,580,793	3	2,323,240	7	3,057,553	10	5,580,793	0	0
RI	3	3,592,252	1	3,512,277	2	79,975	1	3,512,277	2	79,975
SC	49	10,401,103	13	4,202,393	36	6,198,710	39	9,584,673	10	816,430
SD	12	1,386,701	3	58,572	9	1,328,129	8	1,221,883	4	164,818
TN	64	10,623,476	25	3,405,028	39	7,218,448	54	10,343,042	10	280,434
TX	281	97,345,175	224	83,604,173	57	13,741,002	66	14,672,950	215	82,672,225
UT	14	5,937,656	8	4,853,358	6	1,084,298	5	1,436,959	9	4,500,697
VA	66	22,939,381	44	18,409,425	22	4,529,956	35	16,428,762	31	6,510,619
VT	4	428,101	1	334,088	3	94,013	1	334,088	3	94,013
WA	43	17,116,336	20	10,633,323	23	6,483,013	27	14,998,145	16	2,118,191
WI	79	15,809,457	5	2,335,172	74	13,474,285	21	2,319,361	58	13,490,096
WV	18	2,212,434	2	700,893	16	1,411,541	18	2,112,434	0	0
WY	11	1,296,079	3	312,552	8	983,527	9	1,258,552	2	37,527
Total	3,220	1,165,319,880	1,189	722,341,751	2,031	442,978,129	1,744	748,397,800	1,476	416,922,080

a. In thousands of dollars as of December 1986.

Source: Author's calculations based on data from the Federal Home Loan Bank Board.

Appendix B. Concentration of Assets within the Savings and Loan Industry as of December 31, 1986.

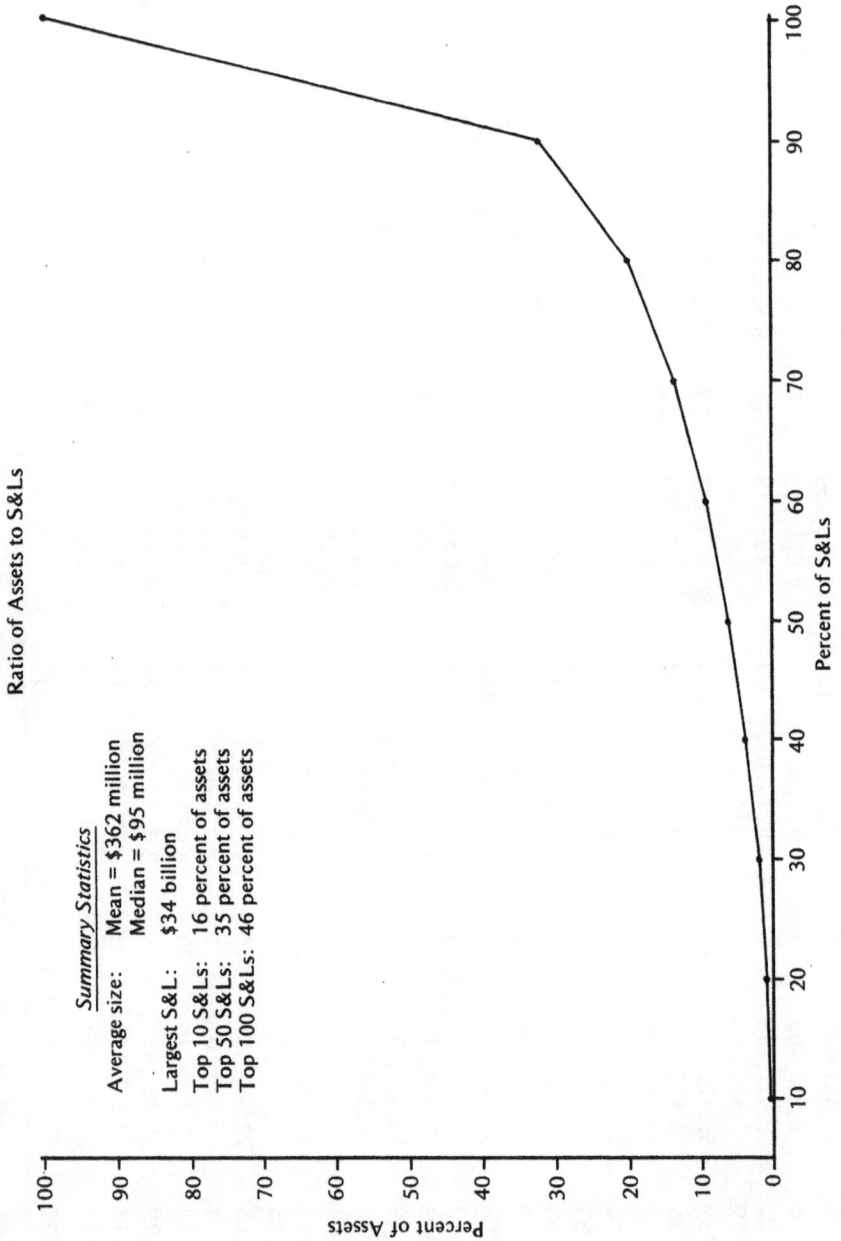

Ratio of Assets to S&Ls

Summary Statistics

Average size: Mean = $362 million
                 Median = $95 million

Largest S&L: $34 billion

Top 10 S&Ls: 16 percent of assets
Top 50 S&Ls: 35 percent of assets
Top 100 S&Ls: 46 percent of assets

Percent of Assets

Percent of S&Ls

Appendix C. GAAP Net Worth for FSLIC-Insured Institutions by State.[a]

State	All Institutions		GAAP NW < 0		0 ≤ GAAP NW < 3		3 ≤ GAAP NW < 6		GAAP NW ≥ 6	
	Number	Assets	Number	Assets	Number	Assets	Number	Assets	Number	Assets
AK	4	550,476	0	0	0	0	3	541,336	1	9,140
AL	37	8,541,870	5	1,571,558	7	581,835	13	4,943,088	12	1,445,389
AR	39	8,252,555	12	3,112,782	10	3,856,397	14	1,148,957	3	134,419
AZ	14	21,648,468	1	1,029,046	1	5,565,674	4	7,654,959	8	7,398,789
CA	216	310,455,472	32	14,786,516	26	71,918,396	71	176,573,918	87	47,176,642
CO	38	15,920,432	6	550,993	4	3,017,595	15	6,784,720	13	5,567,124
CT	31	11,252,915	1	152,774	4	794,565	15	7,383,817	11	2,921,759
DC	6	4,267,475	0	0	2	1,215,587	2	1,937,409	2	1,114,479
DE	4	353,336	0	0	2	265,740	2	87,596	0	0
FL	149	83,001,467	20	7,357,967	20	13,284,539	47	42,570,352	62	19,788,609
GA	67	16,174,395	8	928,126	16	4,995,989	18	4,354,458	25	5,895,822
GU	2	86,471	0	0	0	0	0	0	2	86,471
HI	6	3,668,295	0	0	3	2,443,462	1	503,551	2	721,282
IA	52	9,102,447	7	969,127	19	5,006,520	19	2,373,850	7	752,950
ID	9	1,529,889	3	616,668	1	185,014	3	449,915	2	278,292
IL	267	65,290,254	56	11,392,948	49	10,847,232	78	24,913,726	84	18,136,348
IN	115	12,744,508	14	1,761,966	12	1,282,548	32	4,432,328	57	5,267,666
KS	58	16,875,241	7	1,005,629	16	3,855,138	18	4,448,702	17	7,565,772
KY	67	7,205,216	4	385,804	10	1,923,945	25	2,262,442	28	2,633,025
LA	102	15,561,902	28	4,323,690	18	2,876,442	34	4,746,633	22	3,615,137
MA	33	7,033,652	1	156,498	1	683,569	7	1,172,712	24	5,020,873

(Appendix C. continued overleaf)

Appendix C. continued

State	All Institutions		GAAP NW < 0		0 ≤ GAAP NW < 3		3 ≤ GAAP NW < 6		GAAP NW ≥ 6	
	Number	Assets	Number	Assets	Number	Assets	Number	Assets	Number	Assets
MD	95	18,947,264	12	3,833,572	9	2,376,516	26	7,884,987	48	4,852,189
ME	15	1,219,055	0	0	0	0	5	252,140	10	966,915
MI	51	34,807,087	6	1,622,735	6	9,752,350	25	19,850,422	14	3,581,580
MH	37	16,069,503	8	4,281,239	9	3,868,051	11	7,280,042	9	640,171
MO	85	21,894,148	12	1,681,977	22	11,177,051	21	3,009,297	30	6,025,823
MS	45	4,811,282	7	1,022,736	10	659,759	16	1,765,413	12	1,363,374
MT	11	1,204,288	1	88,793	2	169,428	3	382,740	5	563,327
NC	139	19,337,597	5	1,824,833	11	3,072,052	50	6,451,879	73	7,988,833
ND	6	3,932,465	2	242,790	3	1,765,715	1	1,923,960	0	0
NE	23	9,091,188	8	1,334,345	5	2,632,683	6	4,940,705	4	183,455
NH	12	1,803,053	0	0	0	0	4	660,036	8	1,143,017
NJ	139	50,175,447	21	5,295,949	27	7,784,919	50	28,428,209	41	8,656,370
NM	25	5,873,098	3	786,976	5	3,629,129	7	756,011	10	700,982
NU	7	4,099,163	0	0	2	337,942	3	3,647,635	2	113,586
NY	86	48,329,933	6	2,396,517	20	18,741,346	25	17,805,372	35	9,386,698
OH	232	51,766,834	18	4,607,820	35	11,253,638	74	21,735,041	105	14,170,335
OK	53	10,100,625	16	3,262,587	10	1,475,201	16	3,229,660	11	2,133,177
OR	20	9,659,757	10	3,892,295	2	275,787	6	5,007,573	2	484,102
PA	169	38,112,413	4	2,852,281	12	1,457,282	75	25,500,053	78	8,302,797
PR	10	5,580,793	1	1,386,241	3	122,242	3	2,511,967	3	1,560,343
RI	3	3,592,252	0	0	1	23,615	1	56,360	1	3,512,277
SC	49	10,401,103	3	1,489,121	7	1,760,121	18	4,306,596	21	2,845,265
SD	12	1,386,701	1	108,441	2	401,376	6	701,836	3	175,048

TN	64	10,623,476	10	945,500	5	338,884	27	4,608,782	22	4,730,310
TX	281	97,345,175	81	28,616,443	61	25,774,102	75	31,644,169	64	11,310,461
UT	14	5,937,656	3	740,687	2	2,910,503	7	1,261,055	2	1,025,411
VA	66	22,939,381	7	1,547,989	5	1,760,453	28	9,016,346	26	10,614,593
VT	4	428,101	0	0	0	0	2	77,081	2	351,020
WA	43	17,116,336	5	610,251	6	2,057,674	15	7,757,960	17	6,690,451
WI	79	15,809,457	1	130,472	6	1,087,200	21	5,792,606	51	8,799,179
WV	18	2,112,434	2	177,676	1	62,044	5	905,726	10	966,988
WY	11	1,296,079	2	640,498	3	359,965	1	18,755	5	276,861
Total	3,220	1,165,319,880	460	125,522,856	513	251,687,215	1,054	528,464,883	1,193	259,644,926

a. Net worth in percent and assets in thousands of dollars as of December 1986.

Source: Author's calculations based on data from the Federal Home Loan Bank Board.

Appendix D. Net-Worth Requirement or Capital Requirement for Savings and Loan Associations as of February 1987.

Capital Requirement = Liability Component + Contingency Component – Maturity Matching Credit

I. Liability Component = base liabilities amount + increased liabilities amount

  • Base liabilities amount = base liabilities × liability factor

    • Base liabilities: The lesser of total liabilities on January 1, 1987 (adjusted for branch purchases and sales) or total liabilities at the end of the quarter for which regulatory capital is being computed.

    • Liability factor: Initially equal to the sum of an institution's base factor, growth factor and amortization factor (as defined by the capital regulation in effect prior to January 1, 1987), divided by total liabilities. This percentage rate increases, (until 6% is reached) each July and January by a fraction of the industry's average RDA for the preceding year.[a]

  • Increased liabilities amount = (total liabilities – base liabilities) × 6%.

II. Contingency Component = 2% of recourse liabilities
             +2% of standby letters of credit
             +20% of scheduled items
             +capital required for variable reserve elements

  • Variable reserve elements are direct investments, land loans, and nonresidential construction loans.[b]

  • Incremental capital required on variable reserve elements depends on an institution's level of capital and its portfolio concentration in the variable reserve element.

  • Define three groups of institutions

    • Group A: institutions not meeting their capital requirement net of variable reserve elements

    • Group B: institutions meeting their capital requirement net of variable reserve elements but whose capital is less than 3% of liabilities.[c]

    • Group C: institutions whose capital is greater than 6% of liabilities.[c]

% of Portfolio in Contingent Category	Incremental Capital on Direct Investments			Incremental Capital on Land Loans			Incremental Capital on Non-residential Construction Loans		
	Group A	Group B	Group C	Group A	Group B	Group C	Group A	Group B	Group C
Less than 10%	10%	5%	0%	4%	2%	0%	4%	2%	0%
Between 10% and 20%	10%	10%	5%	4%	4%	2%	4%	4%	2%
Greater than 20%	10%	10%	10%	4%	4%	4%	4%	4%	4%

III. Maturity Matching Credit

- Based on an institution's 1-year and 3-year cumulative hedged gap from 6 months prior.

- Credit equals 1% of liabilities for each gap less than 15% in absolute value.

- Credit equals $\{.02005 - [.067 \times (\text{the absolute value of the gap})]\} \times$ total liabilities for each gap between 15% and 25%.

- Credit equals 0 for each gap above 25% in absolute value.

a. The regulation ties the rate of increase in the liability factor to an institution's initial liability factor. The liability factor for an institution's initial liability factor. The liability factor for institutions with an initial liability factor of less than 3%—the lower group—increases annually by 90% of the greater of the industry's ROA or the institution's own ROA. The liability factor for institutions with an initial liability factor of 3%—the standard group—increases annually by 75% of the preceding year's ROA. The liability factor for institutions with an initial liability factor above 3%—the higher group—remains constant until the standard group catches up. It then increases along with the standard group.

b. Specific direct investments, land loans, or nonresidential construction loans made prior to June 30, 1986, and not subject to incremental capital requirements under the former regulation are not subject to incremental capital requirements under the new regulation. These assets do count toward portfolio concentration levels.

c. The actual criterion is 6% of liabilities or the fully phased-in capital requirement net of variable reserve elements, whichever is greater.

Source: Compiled by Donald Bisenius of the Federal Home Loan Bank Board.

Appendix E. Major Depository Financial Institution Legislation.

Date	Legislation	Key Provisions
September 17, 1787	U.S. Constitution	Granted the federal government the exclusive right to coin money and to regulate its value.
February 25, 1791	First Bank of the United States	Chartered the first federally chartered bank—for twenty years.
March 10, 1816	Second Bank of the United States	Chartered the second federally chartered bank—for twenty years.
February 25, 1863	National Currency Act	Provided for the federal chartering of national banks under the supervision of the Comptroller of the Currency.
June 3, 1864	National Currency Bank	Superseded the act of February 25, 1863. (National banks could not make real estate loans under this and the previous act.)
March 3, 1865	Act of 1865	Legislated state banks notes out of existence by imposing a tax of 10 percent (effective August 1, 1866) per annum on the circulating notes of state banks.
June 20, 1874	Act of 1874	Changed the name of the National Currency Act to the National Bank Act.
December 23, 1913	Federal Reserve Act	Provided for the establishment of the Federal Reserve System to furnish an "elastic currency" by advancing funds to illiquid but solvent member banks. Also increased supervision and regulation of banks. Gave national banks the power to make loans for real estate, but only with respect to farm land.
February 25, 1927	McFadden Act	Enlarged the power of national banks to make real estate loans and permitted national banks to branch within the state in which they are located to the same extent permitted state banks. Before this national banks had no power to branch.

July 22, 1932	Federal Home Loan Bank Act	Established twelve Federal Home Loan Banks under the supervision of the Federal Home Loan Bank Board to advance funds to savings and loan associations to promote home ownership.
May 27, 1933 and June 6, 1934	Securities Act and Securities and Exchange Act	Provided for the regulation of securities exchanges and brokers and dealers in securities to prevent manipulative and unfair practices in the securities markets. Established the Securities and Exchange Commission.
June 13, 1933	Home Owners' Loan Act	Created federal savings and loan associations and the Home Owners' Loan Corporation, which purchased deliquent home mortgages from financial institutions and refinanced the mortgages over longer terms and at lower interest rates.
June 16, 1933	Banking Act of 1933 (and Glass-Steagall Act)	Created the Federal Deposit Insurance Corporation (FDIC), prohibited the payment of interest on demand deposits, established Regulation Q, and forced a separation between banking and the securities business.
June 26, 1934	Federal Credit Union Act	Authorized federal credit unions in all states with an initial maximum maturity of loans of two years.
June 27, 1934	National Housing Act	Created the Federal Savings and Loan Insurance Corporation. Also authorized the FSLIC to regulate savings and loan holding companies.
August 23, 1935	Banking Act of 1935	Amended the Banking Act of 1933 and the Federal Reserve Act to restructure the Federal Open Market Committee and the Federal Reserve Board. Also permitted national banks to make five-year real estate loans.

(Appendix E. continued overleaf)

Appendix E. continued

Date	Legislation	Key Provisions
May 9, 1956	Bank Holding Company Act (and Douglas Amendment)	Prohibited interstate ownership of banks by companies owning more than one bank unless the law of the state of the bank to be acquired authorizes it and restricted the range of their permissible nonbanking activities to those approved by the Federal Reserve Board. Permitted the Federal Reserve Board to allow a bank holding company to engage directly, or acquire shares of, any company, the activities of which are found to be "closely related to banking as to be a proper incident thereto," and which if engaged in by a bank holding company will result in a net public benefit.
September 23, 1959	Spence Act	The original holding company legislation for savings and loan associations. Limited to FSLIC-insured institutions and to holding companies that controlled more than one insured association. Prohibited the control of more than one institution and an existing savings and loan holding company to acquire another association.
October 23, 1962	Bank Service Corporation Act	Authorized banks to invest in service corporations to provide clerical and related financial services to investing banks.
September 2, 1964	Savings and Loan Service Corporation Act	Authorized federal savings and loan associations to acquire and operate service corporations to engage (up to 1 percent of their assets) in businesses not otherwise considered permissible for a savings and loan institution to engage in directly, including stock brokerage, insurance brokerage and agency activities.
July 23, 1965	Coinage Act	Declared that all coins and currencies of the U.S., including Federal Reserve notes, are legal tender.
October 16, 1966	Financial Institutions Supervisory Act	Granted authority to the OCC, FRB, FDIC, and the FSLIC to issue cease-and-desist and suspension-and-removal orders that were effective immediately.

Date	Act	Description
February 14, 1968	Savings and Loan Holding Company Act	Defined a savings and loan holding company as any company that directly or indirectly controls an insured institution (FSLIC savings and loan or FDIC federal savings bank) or other savings and loan holding company. Prohibited a multiple savings and loan holding company controlling insured institutions in more than one state, except that under the Garn–St Germain Act of 1982 temporary authority was granted to the FSLIC to approve emergency acquisitions of insured institutions, including interstate and interindustry acquisition. Permitted unitary savings and loan holding companies (which meet the thriftness test of the IRS—60 percent of the assets in obligations of U.S. or state residential real estate loans, and urban-renewal loans—which was a part of the Garn–St Germain Act of 1982) to engage, through non-FSLIC insured subsidiaries, in any activity, even those unrelated to the savings and loan business (e.g., Sears, Roebuck, and Company). Multiple savings and loan holding companies may only engage in those activities approved by the FSLIC.
July 24, 1970	Emergency Home Finance Act	Established the Federal Home Loan Mortgage Corporation to strengthen the secondary market for conventional mortgages, as well as for federally insured or guaranteed mortgages, by purchasing residential mortgages from federally insured institutions.
October 19, 1970	Federal Credit Union Act	Established the National Credit Union Administration to charter federal credit unions and to provide federal insurance of credit-union member accounts.
December 31, 1970	One-Bank Holding Company Act	Subjected one-bank holding companies to the same regulations as multiple-bank holding companies and restricted the definition of a bank to those institutions that accept demand deposits *and* make commercial loans.

(Appendix E. continued overleaf)

Appendix E. continued

Date	Legislation	Key Provisions
November 10, 1978	Financial Institutions Regulatory and Interest Rate Control Act	Provided for FHLBB chartering of federal savings banks by permitting existing state chartered mutual savings banks to convert to federal charters.
September 17, 1978	International Banking Act	Made foreign banks and foreign holding companies with branches or agencies in the U.S. subject to portions of the Bank Holding Company Acts to place them on an equal footing with U.S. institutions.
March 31, 1980	Depository Institutions Deregulation and Monetary Control Act	Authorized NOW accounts for individuals and not-for-profit organizations at all federally insured depository institutions as of December 31, 1980, phased out Regulation Q over a six-year period ending on March 31, 1986, established mandatory reserve requirements set by the Federal Reserve Board for all depository institutions and permitted these institutions to utilize Federal Reserve services including discount and borrowing privileges, increased federal insurance of accounts from $40,000 to $100,000, permanently authorized automatic transfer services and remote service units, preempted state usury ceilings, and authorized federal savings and loan associations to issue credit cards, to act as trustees, to operate trust departments, to make loans on the basis of commercial real estate, to invest up to 20 percent of their assets in a combination of consumer loans, commercial paper, and corporate debt securities, and to invest up to 3 percent of assets in service corporations.
October 15, 1982	Garn–St Germain Depository Institutions Act	Expanded the authority of the FDIC and the FSLIC to provide direct aid to and facilitate mergers of insured depository institutions. Permitted for the first time interstate and interindustry acquisitions of troubled financial institutions. More specifically, authorized the FDIC and the FSLIC to increase or maintain capital of insured banks and savings and loan associations eligible for assistance through the purchase of capital instruments known as net-worth certificates.

Authorized commercial banks and thrifts to offer money-market deposit accounts and preempted state restrictions on the enforcement by lenders of due-on-sale clauses. Authorized the FHLBB to charter and regulate federal savings and loan associations and federal savings banks and granted them essentially similar powers. Allowed savings banks to be organized in either stock or mutual form. Permitted federal associations to make commercial, corporate, business, or agricultural loans, which after January 1984 could constitute up to 10 percent of an association's assets, invest as much as 30 percent of assets (up from 20 percent) in consumer loans, offer individual or corporate demand deposit accounts (although corporate checking accounts would be opened only by companies having other business with the association), increase from 20 to 40 percent the investment of assets in loans secured by nonresidential real estate, invest up to 10 percent of assets in personal property for rent or sale (thereby gaining access to the leasing business), make educational loans for any educational purpose (rather than just for college or vocational training), invest up to 100 percent of assets in state or local government obligations, and invest, for the first time in other savings and loan associations' time and savings deposits, and use such investments to help meet liquidity requirements. Abolished on all accounts on January 1, 1984, the slightly higher interest rate that savings and loan associations could pay relative to commercial banks.

August, 1987

Financial Institutions Competitive Equality Act

Permitted the FSLIC to issue $10.825 billion in bonds to close insolvent thrifts. Provided for forbearance for thrifts in economically depressed areas for three years. Forbade creation of new limited-service banks. Permitted nonthrifts to buy insolvent thrifts exceeding $500 million in assets. Prohibited banks from underwriting new securities or offering new real estate and insurance services until March 1, 1988.

REFERENCES

Associated Press Report of the testimony of Edwin J. Gray before the Senate
Banking Committee. Washington, D.C. (July 26, 1985).

Avery, Robert B., and Hanweck, Gerald A. "A Dynamic Analysis of Bank Failures." In *Proceedings of a Conference on Bank Structure and Competition*,
pp. 380–95. Chicago: Federal Reserve Bank of Chicago, 1984.

Avery, Robert B., Hanweck, Gerald A., and Kwast, Myron L., "An Analysis of
Risk-Based Deposit Insurance for Commercial Banks." In *Proceedings of a
Conference on Bank Structure and Competition*, pp. 217–50. Chicago: Fed-
eral Reserve Bank of Chicago, 1985.

Balderston, Frederick E. *Thrifts in Crisis: Structural Transformation of the Federal Savings and Loan Industry.* Cambridge, Mass.: Ballinger Publishing Co.,
1985.

Barth, James R., Bisenius, Donald J., Brumbaugh, R. Dan, Jr., and Sauerhaft,
Daniel, "The Thrift Industry is Rough Road Ahead." *Challenge: The Magazine of Economic Affairs* (September/October 1986): 38–43.

Barth, James R., Brumbaugh, R. Dan, Jr., and Saucrhaft, Daniel, "Failure Costs
of Government-Regulated Financial Firms: The Case of Thrift Institutions."
Research working paper no. 123, Federal Home Loan Bank Board, Office of
Policy and Economic Research, Washington, D.C., October 1986.

Barth, James R., Brumbaugh, R. Dan, Jr., Saucrhaft, Daniel, and Wang, George
H. K. "Insolvency and Risk-Taking in the Thrift Industry: Implications for
the Future." *Contemporary Policy Issues* (Fall 1985): 1–32.

_____ . "Thrift Institution Failures: Causes and Policy Issues." In *Proceedings of
a Conference on Bank Structure and Competition*, pp. 184–216. Chicago:
Federal Reserve Bank of Chicago, 1985.

_____. "Thrift Institution Failures: Estimating the Regulation's Closure Rule." Research working paper no. 125. Washington: Federal Home Loan Bank Board, Office of Policy and Economic Research, August 1986.

Barth, James R., Keleher, Robert E. "Financial Crises and the Role of Lender of Last Resort." *Economic Review* (Federal Reserve Banks of Atlanta) (January 1984).

Barth, James R., and Regalia, Martin A. "The Evolving Role of Regulation in the Savings and Loan Industry." In *The Financial Services Revolution: Policy Directions for the Future*, pp. 131-61. Edited by Catherine England and Thomas F. Huertas. Norwell, Massachusetts: Kluwer Academic Publishers, 1988.

Benston, George J. "Savings Banking and the Public Interest." *Journal of Money, Credit, and Banking*, Part 2 (February 1972).

_____. "The Regulation of Financial Services." In *Financial Services: The Changing Institutions and Government Policy*, pp. 28-63. Edited by George J. Benston, Englewood Cliffs, N.J.: Prentice-Hall, 1983.

_____. "Financial Disclosure and Bank Failure." *Economic Review* (Federal Reserve Bank of Atlanta) (March 1984): 5-12.

_____. *An Analysis of the Causes of Savings and Loan Association Failures.* Monograph Series in Finance and Economics, Monograph 1985-45. New York: Salomon Brothers Center for the Study of Financial Institutions, New York University, 1985.

_____, and Kaufman, George G. "Risks and Failures in Banking: Overview, History and Evaluation." In *Deregulating Financial Services*, pp. 49-77. Edited by George G. Kaufman and Roger C. Kormendi. Cambridge, Mass.: Ballinger Publishing Co., 1986.

_____, et al. *Perspectives on Safe and Sound Banking: Past, Present and Future.* Cambridge, Mass.: MIT Press, 1986.

_____. "Direct Investments and Losses to the FSLIC." Testimony before the Federal Home Loan Bank Board, February 13, 1987.

Bicrwag, G. O., and Kaufman, George G. "A Proposal for Federal Deposit Insurance with Risk Sensitive Premiums." *Bank Structure and Competition* (Federal Reserve Bank of Chicago) (1983): 223-42.

Bisenius, Donald J., Brumbaugh, R. Dan, and Rogers, Ronald C. "Insolvent Thrift Institutions, Agency Issues, and the Management Consignment Program." Presented at the Financial Management Association Meeting, October 1986.

Bloch, Ernest. "Two Decades of Evolution of Financial Institutions and Public Policy." *Journal of Money, Credit, and Banking* (May 1971): 555-70.

Bodfish, Morton. *History of Building and Loans in the United States.* Chicago: U.S. Building and Loan League, 1931.

_____. "The Depression Experience of Savings and Loan Associations in the United States." Address delivered in Salzberg, Austria, 1935.

_____ , and Theobald, A. D. *Savings and Loan Principles.* New York: Prentice-Hall, 1940.

Bosworth, Barry P., Carron, Andrew S., and Thyne, Elizabeth H. *The Economics of Federal Credit Programs.* Washington, D.C.: The Brookings Institution, 1987.

Bovenzi, John F., Marino, James A., and McFadden, Frank E. "Commercial Bank Failure Predictions Models." *Economic Review* (Federal Reserve Bank of Atlanta) (November 1983): 14-26.

Boyd, John H., and Graham, Stanley L. "Risk, Regulation, and Bank Holding Company Expension into Nonbanking." *Quarterly Review* (Federal Reserve Bank of Minneapolis) (Spring 1986): 2-17.

Brealey, Richard, and Myers, Stewart. *Principles of Corporate Finance.* New York: McGraw-Hill, 1984.

Brewer, Elijah, III, and Garcia, Gillian G. "A Logit Analysis of Insolvent S&L Recovery or Merger." Unpublished paper presented at American Economic Association meeting, December 1985.

Brickley, James A., and James, Christopher M. "Access to Deposit Insurance, Insolvency Rules, and the Stock Returns of Financial Institutions." *Journal of Financial Economics* (in press).

Brumbaugh, R. Dan, Jr., and Carron, Andrew S. "The Thrift-Industry Crisis: Causes and Solutions." *Brookings Papers on Economic Activity.* Washington, D.C.: The Brookings Institution, December 1987.

_____ , and Hemel, Eric I. "Federal Deposit Insurance as a Call Option: Implications for Depository Institutions." Research working paper no. 116. Washington, D.C.: Federal Home Loan Bank Board, Office of Policy and Economic Research, October 1984.

Bryant, John. "Bank Collapse and Depression." *Journal of Money, Credit, and Banking* (November 1981): 454-64.

Buser, Stephen A., Chen, Andrew H., and Kane, Edward J. "Federal Deposit Insurance, Regulatory Policy, and Optimal Bank Capital." *Journal of Finance* (March 1981): 51-60.

Carron, Andrew S. *The Plight of the Thrift Institutions.* Washington: The Brookings Institution, 1982.

_____ . *The Rescue of the Thrift Industry.* Washington: The Brookings Institution, 1983.

_____ . *Reforming the Bank Regulatory Structure.* Washington: The Brookings Institution, 1984.

Cassidy, Henry J. "An Approach for Determining the Capital Requirement for Savings and Loan Associations." Research working paper no. 97. Washington: Federal Home Loan Bank Board, Office of Policy and Economic Research, May 1980.

Clair, Robert T. "Deposit Insurance, Moral Hazard, and Credit Unions." *Economic Review* (Federal Reserve Bank of Dallas) (July 1984): 1-12.

Cluff, Laurence, Garcia, Gillian G., and Yeats, Kevin. "S&L Restructuring: 1977–1984." September 1985. (Mimeo.)

Committee on Government Operations. *Federal Regulation of Direct Investments by Savings and Loan Associations.* House report 99–358. Washington: U.S. Government Printing Office, November 5, 1985.

Croft, D. James. "Annual Report 1982." *Federal Home Loan Bank Board Journal* (April 1983).

Eisenbeis, Robert A. "Risk As a Criterion for Expanding Banking Activities." In *Deregulating Financial Services*, pp. 169–89. Edited by George G. Kaufman and Roger C. Kormendi. Cambridge, Mass.: Ballinger Publishing Co., 1986.

Ely, Bert. "Private Sector Depositor Protection Is Still a Viable Alternative to Federal Deposit Insurance." *Issues in Bank Regulation* (Winter 1986): 40–47.

England, Catherine. "Private Deposit Insurance: Stabilizing the Banking System." Cato policy analysis no. 54. Washington: Cato Institute, June 21, 1985.

_____. "Agency Problems and the Banking Firms: A Theory of Unregulated Banking." In *The Financial Services Revolution: Policy Directions for the Future*, pp. 317–43. Edited by Catherine England and Thomas F. Huertas. Norwell, Massachusetts: Kluwer Academic Publishers, 1988.

Ewalt, Josephine Hedges. *A Business Reborn: The Savings and Loan Story, 1930–1960.* Chicago: American Savings and Loan Institute Press, 1962.

Federal Deposit Insurance Corporation. "Deposit Insurance in a Changing Environment." Washington, D.C., April 15, 1983.

Federal Home Loan Bank Board. *Agenda for Reform, A Report to the Congress.* Washington, D.C.: Federal Home Loan Bank Board, March 1983.

Federal National Mortgage Association. "A Statistical Summary of Housing and Mortgage Finance Activities." Washington, D.C.: Federal National Mortgage Association, July 23, 1986.

First Boston Corporation, Fixed Income Research. "Mortgage-Related Security CMD Quarterly." New York, May 1987.

Flannery, Mark J. "Deposit Insurance Creates a Need for Bank Regulation." *Business Review* (Federal Reserve Bank of Philadelphia) (January/February 1982).

_____. "Recapitalizing the Savings and Loan Industry." Paper presented at the Eleventh Annual Conference of the Federal Home Loan Bank of San Francisco, December 1985.

_____, and Guttentag, Jack M. "Problem Banks: Examination, Identification and Supervision." In *State and Federal Regulation of Commercial Banks*, vol. 2, pp. 169–226. Edited by Leonard Lapidus. Washington: Federal Deposit Insurance Corporation, 1980.

_____, and Protopapadakis, Aris A. "Risk-Sensitive Deposit Insurance Premia: Some Practical Issues." *Business Review* (Federal Reserve Bank of Philadelphia (September/October 1984): 3–10.

Friedman, Milton, and Schwartz, Anna J. *A Monetary History of the United States, 1867–1960.* Princeton, N.J.: Princeton University Press, 1963.

Giles, Thomas G. Mayer, Thomas, and Ettin, Edward C. "Portfolio Regulations and Policies of Financial Intermediaries." In *Private Financial Institutions*, pp. 157–262. Edited by the Commission on Money and Credit. Englewood Cliffs, N.J.: Prentice-Hall, 1963.

Goldsmith, Raymond A. *Financial Intermediaries in the American Economy Since 1900.* Princeton, N.J.: Princeton University Press, 1958.

Gray, Edwin J. Excerpts of an address before the Nineth-Third Annual Convention of the United States League of Savings Institutions, Dallas, Texas, November 5, 1985.

Greenbaum, Stuart I. "Reform of the Thrift Industry." Banking Research Center working paper no. 123. Chicago: Banking Research Center, March 1985.

_____, and Haywood, C. F. "Secular Change in the Financial Services Industry," *Journal of Money, Credit, and Banking* (May 1971): 571–89.

Guttentag, Jack, and Herring, Richard. "The Insolvency of Financial Institutions: Assessment and Regulatory Deposition." In *Crises in the Economic and Financial Structure*, pp. 99–126. Edited by Paul Wachtel, Lexington, Mass.: D.C. Heath and Co., 1982.

_____. "Restructuring Depository Institutions." Paper presented at the Thirteenth Annual Conference of the Federal Home Loan Bank of San Francisco, December 10, 1987.

Hayerman, Deans, and Gajewski, Gregory. "Patterns of Financial Institution Failures: Some Thoughts on Policy Implications." *Banking and Economic Review* (FDIC) May/June 1987.

Harr, Luther, and Harris, W. Carlton, *Banking Theory and Practice*, 2d ed. New York: McGraw-Hill Book Co., 1936.

Hayek, F. A. *Denationalization of Money.* London: Institute of Economic Affairs, 1976.

Hess, Alan C. "Are Thrifts Worth Saving?" Unpublished paper presented at the Carnegie-Rochester Conference, Rochester, N.Y., April 1986.

Hjerpe, Edward A., III. "The Use of Futures and Options in the Thrift Industry." Washington, D.C.: Federal Home Loan Bank Board, October 1986. (Mimeo.)

Horvitz, Paul M. "Economies of Scale in Banking." In *Private Financial Institutions*, pp. 1–54. Edited by the Commission of Money and Credit, Englewood Cliffs, N.J.: Prentice-Hall, 1963.

_____. "Stimulating Bank Competition through Regulatory Action." *Journal of Finance* (March 1965).

_____. "A Reconsideration of the Role of Bank Examination." *Journal of Money, Credit, and Banking* (November 1980): 654–59.

_____. "The Case Against Risk-Related Deposit Insurance Premiums." *Housing Finance Review* (July 1983): 253–64.

_____. "Deposit Insurance after Deregulation: A Residual Role for Regulation." Paper presented at the Ninth Annual Conference of the Federal Home Loan Bank of San Francisco, December 1983.

_____. "More Is Better as Far as Capital Requirements Go." *American Banker* (April 24, 1986): 4–9.

_____, and Pettit, R. Richardson. "Short-Run Financial Solutions for Troubled Thrift Institutions." In *The Future of the Thrift Industry*, pp. 44–67. Conference series no. 24. Edited by the Federal Reserve Bank of Boston. Boston: Federal Reserve Bank of Boston, October 1981.

Huertas, Thomas F. "The Regulation of Financial Institutions: A Historical Perspective on Current Issues." In *Financial Services: The Changing Institutions and Government Policy*, pp. 1–27. Edited by George J. Benston. Englewood Cliffs, N.J.: Prentice-Hall, 1983.

Isaac, William M. "Risk-Based Insurance." Memorandum to the Chief Executive Officers of Insured Banks, September 20, 1985.

Jensen, M., and Meckling, W. "Theory of the Firm: Management Behavior, Agency Cost, and Ownership Structure." *Journal of Financial Economics* (October 1976): 305–360.

Kane, Edward J. "Accelerating Inflation, Technological Innovation, and the Decreasing Effectiveness of Banking Regulation." *Journal of Finance* (May 1981): 355–67.

_____. "S&Ls and Interest Rate Deregulation: The FSLIC as an In-Place Bailout Program." *Housing Finance Review* (July 1982): 219–43.

_____. "A Six-Point Program for Deposit Insurance Reform." *Housing Finance Review* (July 1983): 269–78.

_____. *The Gathering Crisis in Federal Deposit Insurance*. Cambridge, Mass.: MIT Press, 1985.

_____. "No Room for Weak Links in the Chain of Deposit-Insurance Reform." *Journal of Financial Studies Research* (March 1987).

Kareken, John H. "Deposit Insurance Reform or Deregulation is the Cart, Not the Horse." *Quarterly Review* (Federal Reserve Bank of Minneapolis) (Spring 1983a): 1–9.

_____. "The First Step in Bank Deregulation: What about the FDIC?" *American Economic Review* (May 1983): 198–203.

_____, and Wallace, Neil. "Deposit Insurance and Bank Regulation: A Partial Equilibrium Exposition." *Journal of Business* (July 1978): 413–52.

Kaufman, George G. "A Proposal for Eliminating Interest-Rate Ceilings on Thrift Institutions." *Journal of Money, Credit, and Banking* (August 1972): 735–43.

_____. "Implications of Large Bank Problems and Insolvencies for the Banking System and Economic Policy." *Issues in Bank Regulation* (Winter 1985): 35–42.

_____. "The Truth about Bank Runs." In *The Financial Services Revolution: Policy Directions for the Future*, pp. 9–40. Edited by Catherine England and

Thomas H. Huertas. Norwell, Massachusetts: Kluwer Academic Publishers, 1988.

Kendall, Leon. *The Savings and Loan Business.* Englewood Cliffs, N.J.: Prentice-Hall Publishers, 1962.

Kenneth Leventhal & Company. *Real Estate Newsline* 4, no. 3 (March 1987): 1, 6.

Keeton, William R. "Deposit Insurance and Deregulation of Deposit Rates." *Economic Review* (Federal Reserve Bank of Kansas City) (April 1984): 28–46.

Lintner, John. *Mutual Savings Banks in the Savings and Mortgage Markets.* Andover, Mass.: Andover Press, 1948.

Litan, Robert E. *What Should Banks Do?* Washington, D.C.: The Brookings Institution, 1987.

Locys, Jan G. "Deregulation: A New Future for Thrifts" *Business Review* (Federal Reserve Bank of Philadelphia (January/February, 1983): 15–26.

McCanan, David. "Failure of Bank Guaranty Plans." In *Federal Regulation of Banking,* pp. 161–71. Compiled by James Goodwin Hodgson. The Reference Shelf, vol. 8, no. 6. New York: H. W. Wilson Co., 1932.

McCulloch, J. Huston. "Interest Risk Sensitive Deposit Insurance Premia: Stable ACH Estimates." *Journal of Banking and Finance* (March 1985): 137–56.

Madala, G. S. "Some Problems in the Econometric Analysis of Thrift-Institution Failures." March 1986. (Mimeo.)

Maisel, Sherman J. "Risk and Capital Adequacy in Banks." In *The Regulation of Financial Institutions,* pp. 203–24. Conference series no. 21. Federal Reserve Bank of Boston, October 1979.

Marcus, Alan J., and Shaked, Israel. "The Valuation of FDIC Deposit Insurance Using Option-Pricing Estimates." *Journal of Money, Credit, and Banking* (November 1984): 446–60.

Marvell, Thomas. *The Federal Home Loan Banks Board.* New York: Praeger Publishers, 1969.

Mayer, Thomas. "The Roundtable." In *Interest Rate Deregulation and Monetary Policy: Proceedings of the Asilomar Conference, November 28–30, 1982,* pp. 118–26. San Francisco: Federal Reserve Bank of San Francisco, 1982.

Merrick, John J., Jr. and Saunders, Anthony. "Bank Regulation and Monetary Policy." *Journal of Money, Credit, and Banking,* Part 2 (November 1985): 691–717.

Merton, Robert C. "An Analytic Derivation of the Cost of Deposit Insurance and Loan Guarantees: An Application of Modern Option Pricing Theory." *Journal of Banking and Finance* (June 1977): 3–11.

_____ . "Discussion." In *The Regulation of Financial Institutions,* pp. 256–63. Conference series no. 21. Edited by the Federal Reserve Bank of Boston. Boston: Federal Reserve Bank of Boston, October 1979.

Mingo, John J. "Short-Run Structural Solutions to the Problems of Thrift Institutions." In *The Future of the Thrift Industry,* pp. 81–106. Conference series no. 24. Edited by the Federal Reserve Bank of Boston. Boston: Federal Reserve Bank of Boston, October 1981.

Modigliani, F., and Miller, H. M. "The Cost of Capital, Corporate Finance, and the Theory of Investment." *American Economic Review* (June 1958): 261–97.

_____. "Corporate Income Taxes and the Cost of Capital: A Correction." *American Economic Review* (June 1963): 433–443.

Peltzman, Sam. "Entry into Commercial Banking." *Journal of Law and Economics* (October 1965).

Pettway, Richard H., and Sinkey, Joseph F., Jr. "Establishing On-Site Bank Examination Priorities: An Early-Warning System Using Accounting and Market Information." *Journal of Finance* (March 1980): 137–50.

Posner, Richard. "Theories of Economic Regulation." *Bell Journal of Management Science* (Autumn 1974): 336.

Pratt, Richard T. "Annual Report 1982." *Federal Home Loan Bank Board Journal* (April 1983).

Pyle, David H. "Pricing Deposit Insurance: The Effects of Mismeasurement." Unpublished paper presented to seminar at Federal Reserve Bank of San Francisco and to finance seminar at University of California at Berkeley, October 1983.

_____. "Comment on Bank Regulation and Monetary Policy." *Journal of Money, Credit, and Banking*, Part 2 (November 1985): 722–24.

Quinn, Jane Bryant. "Staying Ahead: Keeping a Close Eye on Your Savings and Loan." *San Francisco Chronicle*, April 17, 1987, p. 38.

Rolnick, Arthur, J. "Bank Regulation: Strengthening Friedman's Case for Reform." *Quarterly Review* (Federal Reserve Bank of Minneapolis) (Summer 1977): 11–14.

_____, and Weber, Warren E. "Banking Instability and Regulation in U.S. Free Banking Era." *Quarterly Review* (Summer 1985).

Rosen, Kenneth T. "Securitization and the Thrift Industry." Paper presented at the Twelfth Annual Conference of the Federal Home Loan Bank of San Francisco on Thrift Financial Performance and Capital Adequacy, December 11–12, 1986.

Rosenblum, Harvey, Siegal, Diane, and Pavel, Christine. "Banks and Nonbanks: A Run for the Money." *Economic Perspective* (Federal Reserve Bank of Chicago) (May/June 1983): 3–12.

Scott, Kenneth E., and Mayer, Thomas. "Risk and Regulation in Banking: Some Proposals for Federal Deposit Insurance Reform." *Stanford Law Review* (May 1971): 537–82.

Short, Eugenie D., and O'Driscoll, Gerald P. "Deregulation and Deposit Insurance." *Economic Review* (Federal Reserve Bank of Dallas) (September 1983): 11–22.

Sinkey, Joseph F. "Identifying 'Problem' Banks: How Do the Banking Authorities Measure a Bank's Risk Exposure?" *Journal of Money, Credit, and Banking* (May 1978): 184–93.

Stigler, George J. "The Theory of Economic Regularion." *Bell Journal of Economics and Management Science* (Spring 1971): 3.

_____ . *The Citizen and the State: Essays on Regulation.* Chicago: Chicago University Press, 1975.

Strunk, William, Jr., and White, E. B. *The Elements of Style.* New York: Macmillan Publishing Co., 1979.

U.S. Department of Commerce, Bureau of the Census. *Historical Statistics of the United States: Colonial Times to 1970*, Part 2. Washington, D.C.: U.S. Government Printing Office.

Upham, Cyril B., and Lamke, Edwin. *Closed and Distressed Banks.* Washington: The Brookings Institution, 1934.

U.S. General Accounting Office. "Thrift Industry: Net Worth and Income Certificates." Washington, D.C., June 1986.

_____ . "Thrift Industry Problems: Potential Demands on the FSLIC Insurance Fund." Washington, D.C., February 1986.

Vartanian, Thomas P. "Regulatory Restructuring of Financial Institutions and the Rebirth of the Thrift Industry." *Legal Bulletin* (January 1983): 1–22.

Wall, Larry D. "The Future of Deposit Insurance: An Analysis of the Insuring Agencies' Proposals." *Economic Review* (Federal Reserve Bank of Atlanta) 69 (March 1984): 26–39.

_____ . "Regulation of Banks 'Equity Capital." *Economic Review* (Federal Reserve Bank of Atlanta) (November 1985): 4–18.

Wallace, Neil. "Panel Discussion." In *Interest Rate Deregulation and Monetary Policy: Proceedings of the Asilomar Conference, November 28–30, 1982*, pp. 221–29. San Francisco: Federal Reserve Bank of San Francisco, 1982.

Walter, James E. "The Financial Soundness of Savings and Loan Associations," pp. 183–281. In *Study of the Savings and Loan Industry.* Directed by Irwin Friend. Washington: Federal Home Loan Bank Board, July 1969.

Westerfield, Ray B. "Defects in American Banking." In *Federal Regulation of Banking*, pp. 49–62. Compiled by James Goodwin Hodgson. The Reference Shelf, vol. 8, no. 6. New York: H. W. Wilson Co., 1932.

Yang, John. *Wall Street Journal*, June 15, 1987, p. 5.

Wilcox, James A., ed. *Current Readings on Money, Banking, and Financial Markets.* Boston: Little Brown & Company, March 1987.

INDEX